MORAL DEVELOPMENT AND SOCIALIZATION

MORAL DEVELOPMENT AND SOCIALIZATION

Myra Windmiller
University of California, Berkeley

Nadine Lambert
University of California, Berkeley

Elliot Turiel
University of California, Santa Cruz

ALLYN AND BACON, INC.
Boston London Sydney Toronto

Production Editors: Nancy Doherty, Ann T. Kilbride
Manufacturing Buyer: Karen Mason

Library of Congress Cataloging in Publication Data
Main entry under title:

Moral development and socialization.
  Includes index.
  1. Moral development. 2. Socialization.
3. Moral education. 4. Values. I. Windmiller,
Myra. II. Lambert, Nadine M. III. Turiel, Elliot.
BF723.M54M68   155.4'18   79-22099
ISBN 0-205-06844-8

Printed in the United States of America.

Contents

7 MORAL DEVELOPMENT AND THE CONCEPT OF
VALUES   201

John Paul McKinney

8 CAN VALUES BE TAUGHT?   219

Edmund V. Sullivan

9 EPILOGUE   245

Nadine M. Lambert

Preface

This book is the result of a symposium held by the school psychology program at the University of California at Berkeley in 1971. As part of the graduate training program, a conference weekend is held each spring to consider current academic issues that have meaning for the school psychology professional. The 1971 colloquium was planned around the different theoretical bases for moral development, with the expectation that the contradictory points of view would provoke interest in further study and research on moral development.

There was an immediate response to the presentation on the social learning theory of moral behavior by Joan Sieber, to the psychoanalytic explanation for moral development by Rudolf Ekstein, and to the structural-developmental view by Elliot Turiel. The forum produced intense student interest and commitment, which resulted in many review papers and four doctoral dissertations over the next five years.

The paper on social learning theory originally presented by Joan Sieber is reprinted here in updated and revised form, and the psychoanalytic or Freudian view is presented by Terrence Tice. The presentation of the structural-developmental perspective has been broadened and is represented in the chapters by William Damon, Golda Rothman, and Elliot Turiel. Other chapters have been added because their topics were not originally represented at the conference. Consequently, this book includes a chapter on values by John McKinney, and a chapter on the teaching of values in the schools by Edmund Sullivan.

In addition to presenting the three theoretical orientations, this book deals with fundamental issues and problems in moral development and socialization. The relationship between moral judgment and moral conduct, how to define what is moral and what is nonmoral, whether values can be taught, and the role of parental socialization are the areas in which the contradictions among the social learning, psychoanalytic, and structuralist perspectives are most apparent.

We think that this book will serve classes in developmental psychology and education to inform undergraduates, as well as graduate students, teachers, and other school professionals, as to a basic knowledge of each theory, some analysis and empirical findings from research on the theories, and some synthesis when it is applicable. The basic fundamentals of each perspective are presented, recognizing that there are adherents of each theoretical position who do not agree entirely with all aspects of a particular theory as presented. Not all structuralists, for example, agree on the function of role-taking or on the cognitive prerequisites for moral stages of development. Nor do all social learning theorists see eye-to-eye on the use of induction or the role of the media in influencing moral behavior. Each contributor is presenting his or her own perception of a perspective or an issue, as he or she sees it.

Finally, a word needs to be said about the applicability of moral development to social life. Is it enough simply to study moral development, do empirical research, and present the issues? Some people would say yes. But because there is always a concern about morality and socialization practices, there is a seeking after solutions to apply to current problems in our society, whether they be in schools, families, or political life. Where there appears to be applicability, the writer has stated it in a concluding section of the chapter. Where the applicability is not readily apparent, the writer has said that is the case. In one instance, the entire chapter is applied: "Can Values Be Taught?" by Ed Sullivan. In other instances, the *implications* of the perspective are significant, and it is not appropriate to talk about application. The "Epilogue" attempts to synthesize the implications for the classroom teacher.

No claim is made that the material presented here is unbiased. More space is devoted to the structural-developmental view because that is where much of the current empirical research is being done. The student is encouraged to investigate and to challenge the assumptions of *each* of the perspectives and identify the weaknesses, as well as the strengths, that reside in all of them.

List of Contributors

William Damon is a developmental psychologist who teaches in the Psychology Department at Clark University in Massachusetts.

Nadine M. Lambert is Professor of Education and Director of the School Psychology Program at the University of California, Berkeley.

John Paul McKinney is a Professor in the Department of Psychology and in the Department of Pediatrics and Human Development, Michigan State University, East Lansing.

Golda R. Rothman is Assistant Professor in the Developmental Psychology Program at Teachers' College, Columbia University, New York.

Joan E. Sieber is Professor of Psychology at California State University, Hayward, and Senior Research Scholar at the Kennedy Institute of Ethics, Georgetown University, Washington, D.C.

Edmund V. Sullivan is Joint Professor of Applied Psychology and of History and Philosophy in Education at the Ontario Institute for Studies in Education, Toronto, Ontario, Canada.

Terrence N. Tice, a philosopher, is Professor of Education, University of Michigan, Ann Arbor, and an advanced candidate at the Michigan Psychoanalytic Institute.

Elliot Turiel is Professor of Psychology at the University of California, Santa Cruz, and Research Fellow at the Institute of Human Development, University of California, Berkeley.

Myra Windmiller is Coordinator of the School Psychology Program and Lecturer in Education at the University of California, Berkeley.

1

Introduction

MYRA WINDMILLER

This book will: (1) examine three current theories of moral development, (2) look at several issues that emerge from the contradictions among the theories, (3) contrast moral development with the study of values, and (4) look at the question of whether or not morality or values can be taught.

This introductory chapter is divided into two parts and is designed to serve two functions. Part I is a general guide to the book and introduces the perspectives on moral development and socialization that are reviewed and elaborated in the succeeding chapters by proponents of the respective positions. Part II provides an example of the commonalities and differences among the theoretical positions by discussing the ways each theory deals with the role of parents in the child's moral development. Parental influence was selected because this question is one of general concern and because parents are considered by many to be the dominant force in the socialization of the child.

PART I
A GUIDE TO MORAL DEVELOPMENT
AND SOCIALIZATION

I have made an effort in this introductory chapter to describe very complex ideas in an uncomplicated way for a person new to the study of moral development. Morality as a concept is an abstraction. Theoretical models, however, can help make an abstract concept more concrete. Models represent logical propositions, in that they organize and elaborate philosophical and psychological concepts, allowing the learner to compare, contrast, and evaluate. Each of the three models of moral development presented here—the cognitive-developmental or structuralist model, the social learning model, and the Freudian or psychoanalytic model—offers a conceptualization of what morality is, as well as its origin, consistency, and representation in the individual. Each theory has recognizable antecedents, but all are presented from a contemporary perspective. Extensive reviews of these theoretical positions are to be found in Hoffman (1970), Kohlberg (1964), and Maccoby (1968).

The Structural Developmental View

The structuralist view dominates this book. That it does is a reflection of the influence of developmental psychology on American academic psychology over the last twenty years. The structuralist position grows out of the philosophy of Immanuel Kant, in which a person is a "self-organizing being" (Langer, 1969) in that one develops largely by one's own actions. This means that the human being has certain innate capacities which (1) influence the kinds of interactive experiences that one will have and which (2) determine the reciprocal effects of these experiences upon oneself and one's future development. In effect, the individual "structures" his or her own development while at the same time being shaped by previously acquired structures.

The most eminent spokesman for the structuralist position is Jean Piaget (1970). His early work on intellectual development (1923/1926, 1924/1926) was soon extended to investigations of moral development (1932/1965) in young children and adolescents. While Piaget greatly extended his early work on the development of logical-mathematical reasoning (Piaget & Inhelder, 1955/1958) and concepts about the physical world (1936/1954), he never followed up on his early work on morality. (Piaget's ideas on moral development are discussed in Part II of this chapter and in Chapter 2 by Damon and Chapter 3 by Turiel). Piaget's work, a stage theory of moral development, has, however, been elaborated by Lawrence Kohlberg (1958).

Kohlberg studied 10- to 16-year-old boys and proposed that their moral development could be characterized as a progression through a sequence of discrete stages. These stages were derived from interview responses to a series of moral dilemmas. (*See* Chapter 8 for a review of these stages.) The responses to the dilemmas were not analyzed on the basis of whether they were correct or incorrect, but instead were categorized on the basis of the type of reasoning that went into the solutions of the dilemmas. Thus, the structuralist view offers insights into the way moral judgments and reasoning take place, as opposed to the occurrence of moral or immoral behavior. It is concerned with *how* people make decisions rather than with the actions based upon those decisions. Kohlberg has followed his original sample for some years and this now constitutes a longitudinal study, meaning that he has been able to observe change in moral development over time within the same individuals.

Kohlberg claims that cognitive development establishes the broad limits of the individual's progress through moral stages. As cognitive structures become more complex, a corresponding complexity of moral reasoning is possible, although not guaranteed. As the individual moves through moral levels, ever more sophisticated forms of moral reasoning are apparent.

For Kohlberg and other structuralists (Damon, 1977; Turiel, 1975), morality is defined as justice. Justice is viewed as a universal concern. Moral development, therefore, is not relative or unique to a particular culture, but endemic to all cultures. This point of view, therefore, rejects the notion that moral development is the internalization of cultural norms about what is right or wrong.

William Damon has extended the empirical data on moral development from a structural-developmental point of view into investigations of the origin of concepts of *justice* in preschool children. In Chapter 2 he reports on these investigations while identifying the underlying assumptions of the structuralist position and the early work of Piaget and Kohlberg. Related to the child's acquisition of concepts of justice is his or her understanding of what constitutes *authority*. Damon takes us through the child's most primitive reaction to authority before age four to his or her recognition of legitimate authority by age ten. Also in Chapter 2, Damon addresses two issues which arise from a consideration of moral development from the structuralist point of view: (1) the *consistency* of moral behavior, and (2) whether a *stage ordering* of moral development from low to high constitutes a kind of elitism, as has been sometimes charged. In discussing the latter, he draws upon the work of structuralists in other disciplines, such as Claude Levi-Strauss in anthropology.

The generative aspects of the structural-developmental approach are evident not only in Damon's work on justice and authority, but also in Turiel's investigations of *social convention* as a separate structure from that of morality. Scholars who have been reluctant to accept the concept of universality in moral development will now find a logical explanation for certain social behaviors that are not culture-free. Sexual mores, manners, forms of address, and some social attitudes can be viewed as independent of moral development, which is defined solely as justice and fairness. Both Damon and Turiel are attempting to demonstrate that social development is multi-faceted and that moral development is but one dimension of that development. There is no *one* structure, therefore, but many structures that determine development. Within the parameters of the structuralist approach, then, there is room for several investigators, who, while adhering to the general structural-developmental position, may depart from each other on specific theoretical points.

The Social Learning View

Social learning has its antecedents in the empiricism of John Locke and in the American behaviorism of John Watson. According to this view, the human being is a clean slate on which society writes the experience for the individual. The family, the social class, the institutions, and the culture into which one is born determine to a great extent the life of the individual.

Joan Sieber, in Chapter 5, explains how traditional learning theory has been tempered by developmental theory to become "social learning theory." Moral learning is socially learned behavior. It is initiated through direct teaching and modeling and imitation, and it's maintained by positive reinforcement. The person eventually internalizes these behaviors and they become part of him or her.

This is the view that holds parents most accountable for early moral teaching through child-rearing practices and modeling behavior. This is also the approach that is found in the Education Code of the State of California (SECTION 13556.5, 1973) for the "instruction of pupils in morals, manners and citizenship. . . ." The assumption is that morality can be taught didactically through a standard curriculum. Teachers are advised to "teach them [students] to avoid idleness, profanity, and false-hood, and to instruct them in manners and morals and the principles of a free government." This approach to instruction is consistent with the view that the school is an agent of the culture and part of the teaching function is the transmission of cultural values. The socialization of the child, then, is a positive and legitimate function for the school to undertake.

An early European proponent of the view that the school is society's agent was the sociologist, Emile Durkheim (1925/1961). Durkheim wrote that the task of moral education and the duty of the school was to teach the values of society. He felt that the social unit of the family was not consti-tuted to be the agent to impart what was important to the culture. He saw the family as too small and too personal to reflect the whole of the social system. He noted that "morality begins where and when social life begins . . . " and " . . . school has, above all, the function of linking the child to this society." He saw the teacher "as society's agent, the critical link in cultural transmission. It is his task to create a social, a moral being" (1925/1961, p. 71). Durkheim believed that society was the source of all moral authority. In fact, he said "when our conscience speaks, it is society speaking within us" (p. 90). Durkheim was, thus, among the first modern theorists to suggest that parents should voluntarily relinquish their tradi-tional function of attempting to teach morality and give it over to the schools. Social learning theorists place much more emphasis on the role of parents than did Durkheim, but the social learning model is consistent with his argument that the school is an arm of society to transmit moral and cul-tural rules.

The question of internalization of cultural norms as values clearly separates the social learning theorists and the Freudians (whose point of view will be discussed next) from the structuralists on social development and socialization. The role that cultural norms play in the three theories is clear in the definitions given by each to moral values or moral behavior. Maccoby, in writing about social learning theory, says that "moral behavior is behavior a group defines as good or right and for which the social group administers social sanctions." She says that "moral values are beliefs, again shared in a social group about what is good or right" (1968, p. 229). Here the society says what is right and the child learns it, like a rule. For the Freudians, or psychoanalytic theorists, what is moral is that which is socially sanctioned and that which the individual internalizes through identification with his or her parents.

Piaget and the structuralists are also concerned about rules, but they are not necessarily socially sanctioned rules. "All morality consists in a system of rules, and the essence of all morality is to be sought for in the respect which the individual acquires for these rules" (Piaget, 1932/1965, p. 13). Piaget feels that the rules are generated by the child from his or her understanding of the social situation. He hypothesizes that the system of rule generation is universal and that the child's understanding of these rules shifts in stages depending on his or her cognitive understanding. This is also true of Kohlberg (1971) and other structuralists, since morality implies a universal concern for justice and fairness.

The Psychoanalytic View

The psychoanalytic view of moral development is like the psychoanalytic view of human beings: they are driven by irrational impulses which must be controlled through social prohibitions. It is a view which says that agents of social control must intervene at a very early age to introduce necessary restraint and conforming behavior.

The Freudian or psychoanalytic perspective of moral development is infrequently presented, although there is, as Tice points out in Chapter 6, a body of literature and a band of theorists who have kept the psychoanalytic point of view current and who continue to revise and publish reformulations of Freud's theory. Freud's views on the status of women, which later theorists have expanded on, is a case in point. The difficulty in presenting the psychoanalytic approach to moral development is that it requires a thorough understanding of Freudian theory before the Freudian view of moral development can be appreciated. Tice has provided that background for us and has "interwoven the development of morality through the threads of the theory itself."

Tice's presentation of the psychoanalytic point of view is fresh and novel. He has formulated the stages and turning points in moral development as seen through Freudian eyes, and he has successfully shown how the work of other theorists as divergent as Piaget and Erikson complement the psychoanalytic perspective. Most of all he shows that many of us may hold a rather simplistic view of what the psychoanalytic belief incorporates. He details, for example, how adolescence is still a formative period in moral development. The structuralists have always said this, but many have assumed that in Freudian thought the formation of the superego through the resolution of the Oedipal complex at about age 6 ended any further development. Chapter 6 also clearly shows that social learning theorists and Freudians share the view that the essential mechanism by which values are acquired is identification with parental views and the internalization of cultural norms.

Aside from its intrinsic interest as a theory of moral development, the psychoanalytic perspective is significant for two reasons: (1) It is the only theory of moral development tied to a theory of personality development wherein the forces operating to form the personality of the individual also form the mechanism of moral restraint by which the personality is partially maintained. (2) Its antecedents, somewhat metaphorically, are found in our Biblical traditions. The precedents of original sin, concurrent guilt, and eventual absolution have a powerful appeal. For centuries morality has been tied with duty to God and the concern with values dominated by the Church. Thus, superego as conscience has functioned to help us maintain discipline and propriety in order to avoid both guilt and retribution.

Issues that Emerge from a Consideration of the Theories

This book considers several important issues that result from the differences among the three perspectives. The first is the relationship between moral judgment and moral behavior; the second is the significance of parental role in the acquisition of a value system.

The relationship between moral judgment and moral behavior. This is one of the issues which clearly separates the social learning position from that of the structuralists. The empirical research in social learning theory has dealt almost exclusively with moral behavior; that of the structuralists has dealt primarily with moral reasoning or judgments. Social learning theory does not recognize strong affiliation between moral judgment and behavior, while structuralists say that moral judgment is predictive of moral behavior under certain conditions. Golda Rothman, in Chapter 4, indicates that moral judgment and behavior are related, as the literature demonstrates, but that it is complicated.

Most of the research that has proposed to find a concrete relationship between moral judgment and behavior has been done by structuralists using Kohlberg's moral dilemmas or variations of value dilemmas. Studies that will allow prediction of action from reasoning are hard to design, although occasionally they can be done retrospectively as in the cases of the Free Speech Movement at Berkeley (Haan, Smith, & Block, 1968) and the Milgram (1963) obedience to authority experiment at Yale. Here the behavior occurred first and the participants were subsequently interviewed to determine their moral stage and reasoning. In other instances the behavior and the judgment measures are obtained during the same experimental period (Rothman, 1976; Turiel and Rothman, 1972; DeMersseman, 1976).

Kohlberg has consistently maintained that thought and action cannot be separated. He cites the fact that there are "moderate correlations between level of moral judgment and behavioral measures of resistance to various types of adult and peer pressure to change or violate moral beliefs" (1963, p. 324). Kohlberg and Kramer (1969) have reported, however, that there is greater consistency between judgment and behavior in adulthood than earlier. Much more recently, Kohlberg has noted:

> To act in a morally high way requires a high stage of moral reasoning. One cannot follow moral principles (Stage 5 and 6) if one does not understand or believe in them. One can, however, reason in terms of such principles and not live up to them. A variety of factors determine whether a particular person will live up to his stage of moral reasoning in a particular situation, though moral stage is a good predictor of action in various experimental and naturalistic settings. (1976, p. 32).

Turiel who has been particularly concerned to demonstrate the relationship between structure and content, and judgment and behavior, says:

> Reasoning is related to action. The two are interrelated in the sense that the way an individual reasons relates to how he acts and the way he acts relates to how he reasons—theoretically a developmental stage reflects these two components and their interrelationships. (1973, p. 750).

The Rothman study (1976) demonstrates that it is the moral stage level and specific task *interaction* which determines the correlation between moral reasoning and moral behavior.

Maccoby (1968), on the other hand, says that neither moral judgment, moral knowledge, nor moral behavior can be predicted one from the other. Social learning theorists cite evidence to show that the effectiveness of behavior modification and social reinforcement on an individual's behavior does not depend on that person's prior moral judgments. It seems reasonable that immediate behavior change is not necessarily indicative of moral reasoning. The question becomes one of knowing whether the elicited behavior will persist or transfer to new situations in the absence of concurrent moral reasoning.

Kohlberg and Turiel (1971) cite a number of studies on children's cheating that blend the moral action and behavior inquiry. They state that at the higher levels of moral reasoning there is a relationship between non-cheating behavior and moral development. In other words, it is easier to predict who will *not* cheat, than it is to predict who will cheat.

I leave it to Rothman to provide the additional data to clarify these discrepancies.

Parental role.   A general concern for society has always been how to raise children so that they become moral adults. In fact, some think that parents are the most important influence in providing moral education. Prior to the structuralists, no one raised the question that parents might not be of such great importance. The issues then are how and the degree to which parental influence is manifested. What or who are the forces, other than parents, who contribute to the moral education of the child? Each theory provides a different answer to these questions and we will take them up in some detail in Part II of this chapter. Part II provides a case study in theoretical contrasts. By examining an issue from each of the three perspectives we are able to grasp similarities and differences on several dimensions. In examining the role of parents, we will look at child-rearing practices, the role of discipline, rewards and punishment, opportunities for social interaction, and parental morality itself.

Moral Development and the Study of Values

The study of values has a different body of literature, a distinct history, and a separate set of empirical data from that of the three perspectives of moral development presented here. The work on different aspects of value by Rokeach (1968), Kelman (1974), and McKinney (1971, 1975), for example, proceeds from very different assumptions than do investigations of moral development. According to the structural approach, the basic unit of analysis is moral judgment. The term *moral value* is used to refer to a particular moral judgment or often it is used interchangeably with the term *moral judgment*. In social learning or psychoanalytic theory, the word *value* is used interchangeably with internalized standards or norms of behavior. McKinney uses the term to refer to ideals used in making choices. The term has traditionally meant basic attitudes and core beliefs.

The Allport, Vernon, and Lindzey Study of Values (1931) published an early tool to evaluate value orientations that are associated with attitudes, motives, and interests. The self-reporting inventory has been used primarily to help students determine occupational interest areas and value orientation in six areas: theoretical, economic, aesthetic, social, political, and religious. Items on the inventory ask the student, for example, which article in a newspaper would he or she be more apt to read: "Protestant

Leaders to Consult on Reconciliation" or "Great Improvements in Market Conditions." Or the student is asked to rank in order of preference how a man who works in a business all week can best spend his Sunday: "A) Trying to educate himself by reading serious books, B) trying to win at golf or racing, C) going to an orchestral concert, or D) hearing a really good sermon." Scores on the inventory are then grouped to show priorities of interest or to show which one of the interest areas listed is compatible with the basic ideals of the person.

More recently, Values Clarification (Simon, Howe, & Kirschenbaum, 1972) has caught on in schools as a way to help children become aware of values and the process of valuing. Teachers use exercises from a prepared text to acquaint the student with value themes and the necessity of making choices. An example of the values clarification approach is presented by Kohlberg and Turiel (1971, p. 419) when they quote a curriculum unit on decision-making that is presented to the student. The question, "Why don't we all make the same decisions?" is first asked of the student. The answers are given as:

1. We don't all make the same decisions because our values are different.
2. Our values tend to originate outside ourselves.
3. Our values are different because each of us has been influenced by different important others.
4. Our values are different because each of us has been influenced by a different environment.

Notice that their recurring theme is "everyone has one's own values." Another theme is that values are relative since they are culturally determined. Within this framework all values are equally acceptable; it is the process of arriving at the value decision that is the focus of the unit.

But are all values equally acceptable? The structuralists would not agree that they are. Note the difference in approach to moral education by structuralists in response to the four answers (Kohlberg and Turiel, 1971, p. 430):

1. We often make different decisions and yet have the same basic moral values.
2. Our values tend to originate inside ourselves as we process our social experience.
3. In every culture and subculture of the world the same basic moral values are found, and the same steps toward moral maturity are found. While social environments directly produce different specific beliefs . . . they do not engender different basic moral principles. . . .
4. Insofar as basic values are different, then it is largely because we are at different levels of moral maturity in thinking about basic moral and social issues and concepts. Exposure to others more mature than ourselves helps stimulate maturity in our own value processes.

It seems that point by point the structuralists and the values clarification proponents differ in their approach to moral education. The structuralists use discussion for confrontation of ideas, for exposure to alternative points of view, all in the interest of inducing cognitive conflict to move youngsters to a higher level of development. The values clarification proponents are interested, quite legitimately, in getting children to use a method for learning to make choices. Once the method is learned, teachers can use this skill in teaching specific content.

There is, however, no contradiction between social learning theory and values clarification curricula. Social learning theorists, because they see morality as being taught through modeling and imitation, agree that exposure to more mature others helps stimulate maturity in our own value processes. They think values are relative and a reflection of the particular culture in which they are found. In fact, part of the responsibility of parents and teachers is transmitting cultural values. They do not agree with the structuralists that values come from inside, but rather they maintain values originate from outside. Once internalized, however, the values are a part of the individual. Social learning theorists would not necessarily see the *process* of learning to value as significant, so much as the manifestation of specific values. This is because the behavior that follows from holding certain values is considered to be preeminent.

The differing assumptions about value study and moral development become significant in the classroom in a moral education program when the teacher has specific objectives. If the aim were to stimulate moral development, the teacher would proceed very differently than if the desired outcome were value choice. Both may be reasonable objectives, but the means to them should not be thought of simply as alternative approaches. In other words, the exercises designed for a values clarification model are not consistent with a model that presumes children progress through the same stages toward moral maturity regardless of the culture or subculture in which they live.

The John Paul McKinney chapter (*see* Chapter 7) helps clarify the distinction between moral development and the study of values, as well as the distinctions among differing value connotations. He also presents some empirical data which argue for a behaviorist approach to child-rearing in order to foster prosocial behavior.

Moral Education: Can Values Be Taught?

It is a useful exercise to try to reflect on how one first became aware of value issues and one's moral education. For me it was when I first became interested in politics as a late adolescent and began to argue about the basic goodness or badness of men and women and whether or not it was possible to create a just society. I think that the process of continual argument and struggle with fellow students began to clarify for me what my basic moral assumptions were. I am sure that the process of moral education started much earlier, but it was only in adolescence that I became cognizant of a personal value system. Those of us who are interested in improving public school education are also interested in the questions of moral education. The problem becomes one of determining what *kind* of moral education, however, and whether or not it is feasible to introduce "moral" education into a school curriculum. This is not a new question. It is one with which John Dewey and others have struggled.

Dewey had very definite ideas about the purpose of education in the moral development of the child. His ideas departed from the traditional Puritan ethic where children were instilled with wisdom and advice. He did not see the school's role as one of transmitter of the culture. He felt:

> The ethical responsibility of the school on the social side must be interested in the broadest and freest spirit; it is equivalent to that training of the child which will give him possession of himself that he may take charge of himself; not only adapt himself to the changes that are going on, but have the power to shape and direct them. (1909/1959, p. 11).

While Dewey saw education as important in determining the citizen's participation in the society, he did not see it as giving moral instruction. He said flatly, "Apart from participating in social life, the school has no moral end nor aim" (1909/1959, p.11). He noted:

> . . . the general principle that when a study is taught as a mode of understanding social life it has positive ethical import. What the normal child continuously needs is not so much isolated moral lessons upon the importance of truthfulness and honesty, or the beneficent results that follow from a particular act of patriotism, as the formation of habits of social imagination and conception. (1909/1959, p. 40).

In other words, Dewey argued that education does not teach specific content so much as the framework for the processing and evaluation of content. This view is still being argued for where development is seen as the "aim of education" (Kohlberg & Mayer, 1972). Dewey can be viewed in the tradition that has contributed to the structuralist position on moral education.

Today it is the structuralists who are talking about moral education programs. Kohlberg has initiated some in schools and some in prisons, as have others. Rest (1974) has reviewed many of these programs, including those associated with values clarification. The structuralists base their programs on discussion groups, using moral issues as the curriculum for debate. There is an underlying assumption that disequilibrium must be created for structural change to a higher level of reasoning to occur. These programs focus on moral reasoning, not behavior, although structuralists would claim that moral behavior follows from moral reasoning at higher levels. The effectiveness of moral education programs depends on cognitive conflict and disequilibrium as the mechanism by which growth and development take place. Edmund Sullivan discusses the generation of disequilibrium by these means in Chapter 8.

If we are to believe Sullivan, there is an institutional force, with an apparent existence of its own, that projects certain kinds of values into education. The values that pervade the institutions·are indicative of the effort to teach conformity to social norms. Sometimes this projection of values is explicit, as in the State of California Education mandate:

> Each teacher shall endeavor to impress upon the minds of the pupils the principles of morality, truth, justice, patriotism, and a true comprehension of the rights, duties, and dignity of American citizenship including kindness toward domestic pets and humane treatment of living creatures, to teach them to avoid idleness, profanity, and falsehood, and to instruct them in manner and morals and principles of a free government. (SECTION 13556.5, State of California, Education Code).

Most of the time, however, this projection of values is subtle but implicit in the way curriculum is introduced, in the content of the curriculum, and in the general aim of education to indoctrinate. The dilemma for the believer in genuine moral education is whether one attempts to alter the character of the institution or whether one is satisfied to try discrete, neatly packaged programs that stimulate discussion and promote some growth in moral judgments, but leave untouched the basic question of the purpose of education and the function of teachers.

Epilogue

Nadine Lambert's approach to some of these questions in the Epilogue (*see* Chapter 9) is an integrative one as she addresses the role of the public school teacher in the classroom and the ways in which knowledge of theoretical approaches to moral development affect the application of that knowledge. She also demonstrates that the teacher confronts genuine moral dilemmas in the classroom while simultaneously attempting to confront children with the complexity of other moral issues!

The Epilogue is an effort to synthesize the three perspectives by applying them to different situations. Part II of this chapter now attempts to analyze how the three perspectives differ or compare in one situation, that of parenting.

PART II
THE ROLE OF PARENTS IN MORAL
DEVELOPMENT AND SOCIALIZATION

The conceptions of parental role in moral development are diverse, and the research is contradictory. Parents or parent surrogates are more important in some theories than in others, and the ways in which parents demonstrate influence are given very different emphases. Parents are very important in psychoanalytic thought and their importance is critical to an explanation of Freudian theory. Parental role is important, although less so, in social learning theory. But it is relegated to relatively minor significance in a structural view of moral development. Kohlberg sees parents simply as one additional element in the child's interaction with the environment that determines his or her general development.

Most parents feel, however, that they are charged with the responsibility for determining the moral thought and behavior of their children. Some feel a social obligation to instill the values that they deem necessary for the child to function in society. "Train up a child in the way he should go: and when he is old he will not depart from it" (Proverbs 22:6). The child must succeed, otherwise they have failed as parents. If the parents are religious, they might think of sharing their training responsibility with the Church, the traditional custodian of moral values, but generally not with the school, and not with the child's peer group.

But is it parents who are accountable to the rest of us for the way the child adopts his or her moral views? How realistic is it to expect parents to teach moral values? A comparison of parent role as conceptualized in the three theoretical positions on moral development may help provide an answer to that inquiry.

Parental Role in Structural-
Developmental Theory

Structuralists have not paid as much attention to parent role as have the Freudians or the social learning theorists. The reason for this is inherent in the different theoretical positions. Early internalization, characteristic of the social learning and Freudian views, presupposes identification with parents or parent surrogates. The structuralist view as articulated by Piaget and Kohlberg is somewhat different.

Piaget's ideas. Piaget (1932/1965) is concerned primarily with the stages of cognitive development through which a child progresses. Fundamental to his conception of the child's growth and development is the notion that the child is an active participant in constructing his or her own world. The child is not a passive object; he or she actively interacts with the environment to produce his or her intellectual and mental structures. That includes the structures of moral development. Piaget holds that parental authority early in a child's life is a critical factor in the child's moral development, and that moral views are "interiorized" and later become the source of a child's "autonomous" functioning.

The roles for parents in the child's moral development can be divided into two categories: one where the child assigns authority to the parent, and the other where the parent provides continuing guidance during childhood until this role is weakened by peers. According to Piaget, it is the peers who ultimately bring the child's development to a higher level.

Piaget says that parents initially place certain constraints or rules on the child which the child then extends to other situations and circumstances. The child's respect for these "laws" is forged by his or her respect for the parents and his or her awe of them as adults. Indeed, the child sees them as figures of authority simply because they are older, and larger. It does not occur to the child to question their wisdom or to suspect that rules might be arbitrary or capable of change. Operating simultaneously is the child's egocentrism which prevents him or her from seeing alternative points of view. Piaget says (1932/1965, p. 93) that egocentrism is the inability to distinguish between the self and the social environment. This inability ties the child to the thought and will of others, especially parents. And parents act so as to delay the demise of egocentrism, both intellectual and moral, because they continue to impose rules and to promote obedience to their authority (p. 190). It is only later, with the end of egocentrism, that the child begins to perceive that he or she may have options for beliefs, including the belief in an alternative rule system.

Piaget's stages of cognitive development are based on the assumption that certain cognitive structures develop with age through interaction with the environment. The ability to decenter is one of these. The young infant, the child at the sensorimotor period, the child at the preoperational level, all are bound by their unique perceptions of the world. They are unable to coordinate more than one dimension perceptually, and they cannot conceptualize alternative cognitive views that are distinctly different from their own. It is only with the advent of the stage of concrete operations that they become decentered—their views are no longer absolute. At this point they can entertain the possibility that others may perceive and think differently from the way they do. This happens in part because of growing peer influence. When the child begins to enlarge his or her social circle to peers, he or she is given the opportunity to confront and be challenged, and the process of decentering is accelerated.

By the age of eleven to thirteen (Piaget, 1932/1965, p. 103) the child begins to free himself or herself from parental constraints through the creation of disequilibrium. This disequilibrium is generated by peer confrontations and interactions. According to Piaget's theory, disequilibrium is the mechanism by which reorganization of thought and structure comes about. The individual naturally seeks equilibrium as a self-regulating mechanism (Piaget, 1973, p. 147). When equilibrium is upset through the introduction of inconsistencies and challenges to existing thought, a reorganization of structures can take place to accommodate to the new content. Turiel (1974) suggests that disequilibrium leads to a compensatory activity resulting in transition to a more advanced structure or to a new stage. Thus the child, in interaction with peers, forms the capacity to cooperate and gradually adopt an "autonomous" point of view, and to make decisions in accord with the new ability to appreciate the "reciprocity" of human relationships. This means that as the child becomes more developed socially, peer interaction assumes a primary influence and parental influence correspondingly declines. The child comes to form relationships based on mutual respect rather than on parental authority. Piaget says that one makes autonomous decisions about morality only after one understands the reciprocity of human relationships. One is no longer obeying a parental injunction or rule simply because it is a rule, but because one understands and appreciates "the desire to treat others as he himself wishes to be treated" (1932/1965, p. 196).

It is this reciprocity of thought and newfound equality with peers that hastens the end of subordination to adult authority. Cooperation with equals leads to the decline of egocentrism and, reciprocally, as egocentrism declines, greater cooperation ensues, leading gradually but steadily toward autonomy of thought. The increased ability of the child to take another's point of view exposes him or her to confrontations and alternative perspectives that disturb previously held beliefs. These challenges result in a new accommodation and a new equilibrium at a higher moral level: "Heteronomy steps aside to make way for a consciousness of good. . . . Obedience withdraws in favor of the idea of justice. . ." (p. 404). The child has reached a level of moral autonomy.

Piaget formulated his moral stage theory, in part, from the responses of children to a series of stories in which some sort of accident or transgression took place (*see* Chapter 2). The young child saw the magnitude of the error as proportional to the amount of damage done and not related to the intentions of the character in the story who committed the error. Later in the child's development, intentions became significant. The rapidity with which the child came to view intentions as important varied with parental guidance. Intentionality as a concept is inevitable for the child, but the time of its appearance, whether late or early, can be determined by the parents and their behavior and modified by the influence of peers.

While peers are the primary facilitators of the child's moral development, Piaget believes that parental behavior can accelerate or deter the child's moral development. Child-rearing practices that employ consistency of punishment and that incorporate discussion or reasoning between the parent and child in the face of competing demands are important.

Piaget sees moral development progressing like other aspects of structural development—through the creation of disequilibrium accompanied by continual accommodation to, and assimilation of, the environment. The crucial thing to be emphasized is that the child's cognitive ability at any given stage in life is operating to determine his or her moral level and the way he or she goes about making moral judgments.

Piaget (1932/1965, p. 190) on occasion chastises parents for their inconsistencies and their inability to see clearly the effects of their own behavior on their children. He points out, for example, that a parent often perpetuates egocentrism in the child. This is done by arbitrarily making general dictums without explaining why certain activities may be necessary on certain occasions, and not on others, or by failing to present multiple options for analysis by the child.

Piaget has reported often on his own three children, and indeed, he formulated much of his theory by observing them during infancy and early childhood. He recalls his own child-rearing practices with respect to moral development when he cites (1932/1965, p. 178) the fact that as parents he and his wife always told the children the reasons they were expected to do or not to do something. (Note the parallel here with the *induction* [see page 23 for a discussion of this concept] of social learning theory.) They did not punish the children for what might be regarded as wrong doing. And yet, he tells of incidents in which Jacqueline, before the age of three, actually felt guilt, or at least acted upset, upon accidentally breaking something. This was despite assurances that it had not been her fault. Piaget expresses surprise that even with the most enlightened child-rearing practices, children initially have a sense of duty and allegiance to authority that resists deliberate efforts to diminish such a sense of obligation. It is only with progress toward decentering that the child begins to temper obedience to authority with obligation to conscience. Piaget acknowledges the term *conscience* as representing the "interiorization" of rules. The parent can hasten this process of tempering obedience by early and continuous introduction of *intention* as a topic for discussion. The parent can delay the process by insisting that the child blindly follow rules and subordinate his or her will to that of the parent. Piaget (1932/1965, p. 193) sadly comments that children reared in the latter fashion frequently grow up unable to make wise choices. Often they perpetuate this same pattern of behavior in child-rearing practices with their own children.

A word needs to be said about Piaget's work on how children develop the concept of justice. He believes that only later with the development of autonomous reasoning about morality is justice as an idea likely to be understood. It is well to remember that justice is an advanced concept, an abstract notion, and children are unlikely to grasp it before a certain level of development. Kohlberg (1971) places justice at the core of his system; for Turiel (1969), the concept of what is moral *is* justice at several levels, the highest of which is a concern with equity. Piaget notes that parents have very little to do with the child's notions about justice once he or she reaches a cooperative, autonomous level of moral reasoning. At this level, it is peers who are of greater significance.

> The conclusion which we shall finally reach is that the sense of justice, though naturally capable of being reinforced by the precepts and the practical example of the adult, is largely independent of these influences, and requires nothing more for its development than the mutual respect and solidarity which holds among children themselves. It is often at the expense of the adult and not because of him that the notions of just and unjust find their way into the youthful mind. (Piaget, 1932/1965, p. 198).

Piaget does say, however, that the sense of justice and equality develops much earlier in homes where children imitate parents who set good examples, rather than in homes where parents exercise constant supervision and freely use punishment as a preferred method of discipline. More specifically, he (1932/1965, p. 276) says that in homes where heavy punishment predominates and rules are stringent, the children continue to believe in the effectiveness of punishment, or retributive justice, much longer than children who move toward more advanced stages of distributive justice. Retributive justice implies expiation of a wrong, of the punishment fitting the severity of the crime, while distributive justice is defined by acts of equality. For example, parents who bestow affection and material rewards on all their children equally, without favoring one over another, are operating under principles of distributive justice.

Overall, Piaget devotes much more time to detailing the negative impact of parents on a child's moral development than he does to the positive contributions they might make. He appears to chide parents from time to time for not providing experiences that would guide a child in one direction rather than another. He speaks of the inadequacy of adult justice and its impact on the child:

> When, as is almost bound to happen, a child is submitted to unjust treatment by his parents or his teachers, he will be less inclined to believe in a universal and automatic justice. (1932/1965, p. 262).

But then he goes on to say that the child continues to move on in his development, and that he survives his recognition of imperfections in adult justice. For Piaget most children are extremely resilient and, given a minimum of environmental support and interaction, will manage to grow, develop, and emerge as healthy, wise, and moral individuals.

Kohlberg's ideas.   Lawrence Kohlberg (1958) reformulated Piaget's stages of moral development, and while he has a similar structuralist theoretical orientation, he places even less emphasis on parental role. In fact, Kohlberg has stated categorically that "family participation is not unique or critically necessary for moral development. . ." (1969, p. 399). Compared to the very direct role that Freud and the social learning theorists assign to parents and the early significance that Piaget places on their role as authorities, this is quite a different view.

If the theorists were placed on a continuum of belief in parental impact on moral development, Freud would be near one end, the social learning theorists would be very close to him, Piaget would be somewhere in the middle, and Kohlberg would appear at the other end. In fact, Kohlberg (1969) goes so far as to say children are no more like their parents in level of moral development than they are like a random selection of adults of the same socioeconomic level. In opposition to the social learning theory which postulates that values are acquired through modeling and imitation, Kohlberg argues that children are at different stages of development from their parents. If they were modeling after their parents, they would be found at their parents' levels of moral reasoning—even in early childhood. In Kohlberg's system of levels and stages, children show growth and development over a number of years before reaching an adult level of moral development which is most often Level II, and less frequently, Level III. (For a description of Kohlberg's Stages, see page 224.)

Empirical support for the view that parents' level of moral development is not necessarily predictive of that of their children is found in a study by Haan, Langer, and Kohlberg (1976). They compared the responses of a group of 382 parents and children on a series of moral dilemmas. They found that husbands' and wives' stages of moral development were related, while those of siblings were not. They discovered positive correlations between the moral development of the parents and their sons under 21 years of age, but none with sons over 21 or with daughters of any age. They concluded that while moral reasoning of younger sons is significantly related to that of parents, it does not last. They also noted that ". . . parents' moral level is not a critical, enabling condition of offspring achieving principled Stages 5 and 6 moral reasoning" (p. 1206). They based this conclusion on their finding that 30 percent of the over-21-year-olds had reached a higher level of moral reasoning than their parents.

In Kohlberg's system, parents can be of some consequence, but their effect is indirect. They can facilitate the child's interaction with his or her total environment. They provide "opportunities for role-taking," the mechanism by which, according to Kohlberg, the child develops moral reasoning. This is the way acceleration through the stages may be enhanced. In Kohlberg's scheme, "moral development is a role-taking process" (1971, p. 195). What, then, is role-taking in Kohlberg's view? How does it become the vehicle of change for the moral development of the child? And how do parents facilitate or hinder its impact?

Stated simply, role-taking is the ability to adopt a perspective different from one's own; that is, to take the point of view of someone else. It is related to decentering, Piaget's concept of what happens to a child's perceptual ability when he or she is no longer egocentric.

Kohlberg (1969) has elaborated on what he means by role-taking opportunities. He equates ability to communicate and to engage in reciprocal interactions with role-taking. This interaction serves as a sort of looking glass in which one sees one's self and obtains an assessment of one's own behavior. It is a process similar to that described by Mead (1934) for the formation of a self-concept in which one derives self-image from the reactions of those around him or her as if he or she were looking in a mirror. In role-taking, one is able to weigh one's conduct or ideas from the perception of others. This phenomenon is related to both communication skills and to empathy. According to Kohlberg, these reciprocal interactions may take many forms, and it is just these varied, but predictable, forms of reciprocity that function as the bases of his moral stages of development.

> The most primitive form of reciprocity is that based on power and punishment, i.e., the reciprocity of obedience and freedom from punishment. Next (Stage 2) comes literal exchange. Then comes a recognition (Stage 3) that familial and other positive social relations are systems of reciprocity based upon gratitude and the reciprocal maintenance of expectations by two social partners. At Stage 4, this develops into a notion of social order in which expectations are earned by work and conformity, and in which one must keep one's word and one's bargain. At Stage 5, the notion of social order becomes a notion of flexible social contract or agreement between free and equal individuals, still a form of reciprocity (and equality). At Stage 6 . . . the social order is derived from principles of justice which it serves. Principles of justice or moral principles are themselves essentially principles of role-taking. . . . At the principled level, then, obligation is to the principles of justice lying behind the social order rather than to the order itself, and these principles are principles of universalized reciprocity or role-taking. (1969, p. 398).

While Kohlberg says that parents provide opportunities for role-taking, he also points out that they are not the only ones to provide these opportunities. Peers, the community, and other adults also provide opportunities for social interaction even if the parent fails. Potential failures, then, due to parental inadequacy would not necessarily diminish moral reasoning ability. This is a hopeful view for the child, for unless he or she is kept in extreme isolation, the environment will provide some degree of contact with others and he or she will progress through moral stages.

In addition to cognitive role-taking, there is a phenomenon that may be called *social role-taking* (Selman & Damon, 1975). Social role-taking focuses on the interpersonal realm. It is the ability to process information from someone else, match it against one's own interpretation, and then adjust one's own position on the basis of new information. In other words, it is being able to respond to social stimuli in the environment in an interactive way. The child actively responds, attends to feedback, and sees himself or herself as part of a larger social context. While developing socially, or becoming socialized, the child realizes what is expected behavior. Parents are the main avenues to social interaction for the child. Initially they provide interaction; later they give the child access to others, whether peers or adults, with whom he or she can interrelate.

There have been a number of empirical studies on role-taking and its relationship to cognitive decentering (Flavell, Botkin, Fry, Wright, & Jarvis, 1968), to communication skills (Rubin, 1972; Rubin & Schneider, 1973), and to moral development (Selman, 1971; Keasey, 1971). Selman found that role-taking ability was significantly related to level of moral reasoning, while Keasey found that social participation and popularity were positively related to moral development. Selman and Damon (1975), as well as others (Flavell et al., 1968), have proposed a stage theory of role-taking ability. Selman and Damon presume role-taking ability level to be "necessary but not sufficient" in determining stages of moral development. They note that role-taking or "social perspective" ability can be defined by hierarchical stages, can be demonstrated empirically, and can be related to other concepts like that of justice.

Other investigators, like Hoffman (1975) and Turiel (1979), have reported role-taking ability at much earlier ages than those defined by Selman and Damon. Hoffman says that "certain forms of role-taking in familiar and highly motivating natural settings may precede the more complex forms investigated in the laboratory by several years" (1975, p. 141). Turiel contends that research findings do not support the proposition that role-taking defines a structural or developmental dimension. He does not accept a stage theory of role-taking ability or the idea that role-taking ability is related to moral stages. What he does say (1979) is role-taking is better explained as a *method* for gathering information about the social environment which should be separated from a conceptual task. Therefore, children may take roles at almost any age, but the complexity of the task must not be beyond the child's conceptual level. While Kohlberg thinks that role-taking is the way moral development proceeds, Turiel (1974) thinks that stage transition to higher moral levels is motivated by disequilibrium. This disequilibrium is induced by inconsistencies in content that cannot be addressed by existing structures. Turiel's view is compatible with that of Piaget (1932/1965) who has used equilibration theory to explain progress of cognitive and moral development.

Kohlberg (1976, p. 50) has reported on one study that bears on moral development and what he calls role-taking opportunities provided by parents. Holstein (1968) investigated the moral judgment level of a group of upper middle-class parents in order to determine their influence, if any, on the moral reasoning of their children. She found that parents at

Kohlberg's higher or principled stages provided many more opportunities for children to discuss moral dilemmas and to engage in communication about issues involving moral decisions. Consistent with these findings were those demonstrating that the children who contributed to these discussions tended to move rapidly to higher moral stages, while children who did not engage in such discussions remained longer at lower stages. Kohlberg argues that these parents are providing their children significantly greater time for role-taking exercises and are, thus, aiding them to accelerate their level of moral development. It is possible to argue that these are not instances of role-taking, but of children listening to moral arguments emanating from stages higher than their own and that this facilitates the children's movement to higher stages, as in the stage transition research of Rest, Turiel, and Kohlberg (1969). Therefore, this is rather an example of cognitive conflict (Turiel, 1969, 1974) where the child must formulate his or her thinking at a higher level as a result of the disequilibrium created at his or her current level by the arguments discussed.

To summarize, Kohlberg does not think that any one individual, group, or institution has special importance in providing for the moral development of the child. He sees many individuals, groups, and institutions interacting in the child's environment to stimulate moral development through role-taking. He adheres to "the general belief that the more the social stimulation, the faster the rate of moral development" (1969, p. 402).

This view provides the basis for Kohlberg's thesis that moral development is universal. While different cultures have different child-rearing practices, different customs, laws, and regulations, the fact that role-taking opportunities exist to some degree in all cultures suggests that the stages of development are universal and are not unique to one particular culture (1971). According to Kohlberg, the child's role in acquiring moral values is active, and regardless of attempts at inculcation by parents, church, school, or peers, there is no such thing as the passive acceptance of moral teachings. This is in opposition to what the social learning theorists and the psychoanalytic theorists hypothesize.

The Social Learning View of Parental Role

The social learning theory approach to socialization is that cultural norms, including beliefs about what is right or wrong, are internalized in the child at a very early age and become the basis of his or her moral system. If one accepts this assumption about the inculcation of morality, then the social learning view of the parents' role is very persuasive. Indeed, this is probably the most popular public view as to how beliefs governing moral behavior are acquired.

There are no one or two major theorists, analogous to Piaget and Kohlberg, who have conceptualized the social learning position on moral development. Rather, there are several investigators who are associated with various aspects of moral behavior from the social learning point of view. Social learning theory has an inventory of empirical research which deals primarily with specific responses to stimulus situations in the laboratory: with modeling and imitation (Bandura & McDonald, 1963), with resistance to temptation (Grinder, 1962), with punishment effect (Parke, 1969), and with altruism (Aronfreed, 1970). Another body of information comes from studies of child-rearing practices, based on retrospective parent interviews (Sears, Maccoby, & Levin, 1957; Hoffman, 1963).

In social learning theory, there is the presumption that morals are first acquired from one's parents through modeling and imitation. These are then gradually internalized in early childhood, probably between the ages of five and eight. Reinforcement, whether positive or negative, and punishment help determine which of the learned moral behaviors will be internalized. If the child considers violating a parental prohibition, he or she will experience feelings of guilt. The anxiety that accompanies the guilt, or the anticipation that guilt will follow from a violation, deters the child, and later the adult, from committing an act contrary to that sanctioned by the parent, and later, by society.

Much of the social learning literature reporting parental influence on moral understanding emphasizes three categories of parental contribution to their children's moral learning: (1) the direct modeling role filled by the parent, (2) the administration of simple rewards and punishments and the effect of discipline on children's behavior, and (3) the general impact of child-rearing practices on moral behavior. While all these behavior patterns are related and proceed simultaneously, it is useful to examine them independently.

Modeling. In the case of direct modeling, the child observes the behavior of the parent over time and imitates what he or she sees. The phenomenon is gradual, and according to Bandura, "the extent to which the resultant observational learning is activated into overt performance is governed by a variety of incentive variables and self-regulatory processes" (1969, p. 278). With sufficient reinforcement, the child continues to behave like the parent, and later, these values become internalized and are said to be his or hers. The child no longer needs the parent as a direct model because the behavior emanates from within.

Bandura (1969) also notes that parents are not the sole models for the child. Other adults, peers, and "symbolic" models are also imitated. Bandura further suggests that "modeling outcomes are significantly affected by dissimilarities in the response patterns displayed by different adults . . . , by inconsistencies in the same model over time, and by discrepancies between the standards of behavior that a person models and those that he imposes upon others . . ." (1969, p. 278). In other words, the influence on the child does not derive simply from a one-to-one unidimensional imitation, but rather from a combination of factors so that the child's total resulting behavior is uniquely his or her own. While modeling and imitation appear to be simple and straightforward, the total process is extremely complex. It is known, for example, that peer group influence at adolescence assumes a much greater role than in childhood.

Discipline. According to the social learning theory of behavior, reinforcement/punishment is a primary explanation of how all learning is maintained. This includes the learning of moral behavior. Discipline is one facet of reinforcement and punishment. Becker (1964) has noted that parents who behave aggressively toward their children cause their children to be aggressive. Similarly, Kohlberg says there is "evidence that punitive aggression by the parent leads to aggression by the child, but there is no evidence that it leads to moral learning" (1963, p. 303). Excessive physical punishment, rather than producing docility in the child, increases the probability that the child will respond with hostility. Physical punishment seems to be counter-productive in preparing a child for moral understanding. Burton (1976) reports that physical punishment often induces so much anxiety that a child is unable to differentiate an unacceptable act from an acceptable one.

According to Parke (1970), whether or not punishment is effective may depend on a number of other variables that coincide with the punishing. He says that timing, consistency, and intensity of punishment, as well as the prior relationship between the punisher and receiver of the punishment, are important. He also says that reasoning coupled with punishment is more effective than punishment used alone. Prior relationship and reasoning recur as themes in much that is written today in social learning theory about moral behavior and whether or not discipline is effective in producing results desired by parents.

The prior relationship that has existed between the parent and the child can sometimes determine whether or not discipline is effective. The most effective relationship depends on established patterns of nurturance and caring, with the character of the parents' child-rearing seen as a very consistent force.

Reasoning introduces cognitive content as to why it is important to do or not to do something. In this reasoning process, called *induction* (Aronfreed, 1976; Hoffman, 1970; Saltzstein, 1976), the focus is on the consequence of the behavior to the child and to others. In other words, the parent explains to the child why the behavior is inappropriate. This is not regarded as discipline, however. On the contrary, it is an alternative to discipline, or it can be used in conjunction with discipline.

This explanation parallels those offered by Piaget and Kohlberg in a developmental view. Piaget would say that the discussion involved in induction is apt to create disequilibrium, thus forcing a child to a more sophisticated level of development. Kohlberg would say that the child's movement to a higher stage is facilitated by the cognitive conflict generated by the parent's arguments.

Child-rearing. *Child rearing practices* is a term which denotes a careful, well-thought-out approach to bringing up a child. But we know that most parents do not have a well-thought-out approach. Child-rearing is generally haphazard and expedient, rather than a highly controlled system of child management (Bell, 1968). There are, however, consistent patterns or characteristics that can define styles of bringing up children. Parents who obtain compliance from children by both controlling material resources and using physical force or the threat of force are called "power-assertive" by Hoffman (1970). He suggests that this kind of child-rearing prevents the child from using his or her internal controls to master his or her own behavior. On the other hand, parents who are not power-assertive have access to more varied strategies for effecting compliance with their wishes; one of these is "love-withdrawal." Using this technique, the parent and child discuss the consequences of possible misbehavior and the child is made to assume some responsibility for his or her own acts. Other investigators argue that nurturance, or love and warmth, is one of the most significant variables in the parent's approach to the child and in the child's response to parental controls. Child-rearing, according to Sears, Maccoby, and Levin (1957), determines how the child's "conscience" develops as a product of the internalization of parental values. Those parents who are "love-oriented" (as opposed to those oriented to the "use of power") are more successful because their children internalize parental values earlier and begin to exert their own controls on their behavior.

Maccoby (1968) tells us that the social learning view of moral development can only explain a child's development to the equivalent of Kohlberg's Stage 4, or Conventional level. Social learning theory cannot explain, then, how particular individuals behave in situations where there are no socially sanctioned alternatives. It seems reasonable to suggest that rewards and punishments may operate to produce behaviors other than those acquired during the internalization period.

And how do social learning theorists explain failures to acquire a "conscience"? Either effective internalization could not have taken place under the usual conditions of reinforcement theory, or the child internalized the features of a "bad" model. If the parent is not a positive model, then the child could be expected to imitate and internalize negative qualities. If Bandura is correct in saying that other influences attenuate the parent modeling role, then that too can explain why some children incorporate undesirable behaviors.

To sum up, parental role, as projected in social learning theory, is the central feature in the moral development of the child. The socialization process ensures that the child, through identification, adopts the parents' moral standards as his or her own (Hoffman, 1963). The parent is crucial in modeling, in teaching what is moral, and in directly inculcating the values of the culture. He or she does this through a system of reinforcement resulting in the gradual internalization of those values by the child. It is this view of morality that holds the parent most accountable, because it is the one that depends most heavily on the environment to explain behavior. The early formative years are seen as critical because it is then that parents are likely to be the most salient in the child's life.

The Psychoanalytic View of Parental Role

In Freudian theory (Freud 1950a, 1950b, 1957), the parents are given the responsibility for the origin of moral thought and the acquisition of moral values. Freud created the term *superego* which has been absorbed into the language as a synonym for *conscience*. Many people have adopted the word *superego* without accepting the whole of Freud's theory of moral development, or without necessarily being aware of what it represents as a construct. Freud used the term to refer to that portion of the personality that functions as an agent of restraint, that keeps the individual from committing wrongful acts, and that instructs the individual in what is right and wrong. The superego is born out of the resolution of the Oedipal complex, and its unique characteristics come from one's parents.

Thus, in psychoanalytic thought, the resolution of the Oedipal complex plays an important role in the moral development of the child. From ages three to five, during the phallic period in Freud's stages of psychosexual development, the child, if male, develops feelings of erotic love for his mother and comes to regard the father as a rival and a threat. As these feelings develop, the child simultaneously wishes to please the parents and adopt their ideas and preferences. He seeks to avoid their displeasure and to enjoy their love and approval.

Gradually, as the child develops, he no longer sees the mother as a love object but turns his sexual desires into a harmless affectionate relationship. At the same time he resolves his relationship with his father by identifying with him as a model. It is the fear of castration at the hands of his father that causes the child to give up his desire to assume his father's role and possess his mother.* The trauma of this process precipitates the birth of the superego from the ego, the important organizer of the self. As in an algebraic equation, the superego, then, is to the ego, as the parents were to the child.

According to Freud (1946), the superego is the direct representation of the value system of the parents—a kind of transubstantiation of parental morality. The child absorbs their standards of conduct and their beliefs, and imitates their actions. He or she may do this out of love, out of a feel-

---

*While there is a counterpart to the Oedipal concept in the female, the internalization of parental values is not quite the same. The female never feels the Oedipal complex as strongly as the male, and it is "later gradually abandoned." On the assumption that they feel castrated already, women, according to Freud, have lost what in men is a powerful motive to form a superego.

ing that they are wise, or out of a fear of losing their love. It is this identification with parental views that is internalized. In the process of internalizing
the values of his or her parents, their prohibitions now become the child's.
As identification with the parents is solidified, "the authority of the father or
the parents is introjected into the ego and there forms the kernal of the
superego" (1946, p. 273).

During the next developmental period, the latency period which
occurs from about age six to age eleven, the superego of the child is further
consolidated. The basic formation, however, has already taken place during the earlier phallic period. As Tice elaborates in Chapter 6, there are
qualitative changes in the child's value system during adolescence and into
adulthood. Freud recognized that at later periods in one's life, teachers,
authority figures, and heroes may serve as models because they are associated with early memories of parents. They are models because they augment the already internalized parental view. Since the superego is thought
to be purely internal and to operate unconsciously, the means by which
change can come about is not simple. Thus, parental influence remains for
a lifetime, even though the individual may later make modifications in
standards and values through subsequent identifications.

Ekstein (1964) has elaborated on the way Freudian thought has been
refined to a working model by many psychiatrists working with child and
adolescent patients. Ekstein's views incorporate many of the psychosocial
ideas of Erik Erikson as they apply to the child's acquisition of a value system. Ekstein (1964) stresses Erikson's life stage of Trust-Mistrust, that
stage in which the child, dependent on others for all care, derives a sense
of trust from the mother through love, food, attention, and care. Erikson
says this is the basis of the child's sense of identity "which will later combine
a sense of being 'all right,' of being oneself, and of becoming what other
people trust one will become" (1950, p. 249).

Ekstein (1964) goes on to say that the child then learns to trust not
only others but himself or herself. The child learns to control impulses and
acquires inner discipline. He or she sees the resolution of earlier trust-mistrust conflicts in that societal rules are now accepted. And, according to
Erikson, by the time the child goes to school he or she has acquired a
knowledge of society's rules. Teachers then form a link between the family
and society.

Ekstein sums up the psychoanalytic view by saying "the origin of all
values, moral and otherwise, rests in the early child-parent situation." He
thinks the "transmitting mechanism is the child's identification with the
adult generation," implying that other adults as well as parents have impact on the child (1964, p. 526).

The Freudian approach is less lengthy than the others to discuss, not
because it is less complicated as a theory (indeed, it is probably more complex and has more hypothetical constructs), but because it has no body of
empirical research to refer to. Social learning theory, on the other hand,

has a substantial amount, as has structural-developmental theory. The psychoanalytic perspective does not readily lend itself to an experimental approach. Its theoretical reformulations must come, then, from others, such as Erikson, who share the same methodological tradition.

Similarities and Differences among the Three Perspectives

As theoretical systems, the social learning and psychoanalytic approaches are in direct opposition, and yet there are certain discrete similarities in their approach to morality. The social learning and psychoanalytic approaches have more in common with each other than either has with the structuralist point of view. Both the social learning and the psychoanalytic views focus on behavior, as opposed to moral judgments. Both assume that the child's basic moral system is formed between the ages of five to eight, rather than showing extended growth and development over time. Both say that early child-rearing practices are critical, as opposed to the structuralist view that they are largely inconsequential. Both social learning and psychoanalytic theory hold that anticipated feelings of guilt act as a deterrent to committing acts of misbehavior. And most importantly, they agree that parental and societal norms are internalized and become the child's own moral base.

The social learning and the Freudian approaches differ in basic theoretical assumptions however, as a review of the Sieber and Tice chapters will document. Social learning theory, for example, has no counterpart of the Oedipal complex, nor the superego as a construct. Modeling and imitation is much more important in social learning theory than in the psychoanalytic, although observation of parental behavior and parental ideas is taken into account in the Freudian approach. Rewards and punishment are an important consideration in the social learning perspective, while they are not of immediate import in the psychoanalytic view.

Turning to a different comparison, as Sieber's chapter demonstrates, social learning theory has begun to incorporate aspects of structuralist-developmental theory within it. Social learning as an approach to morality advocates the use of reason and discussion with children, called *induction*, as being instrumental in facilitating appropriate moral behavior. The structuralists have a counterpart in the use of discussion to promote cognitive conflict or disequilibrium to facilitate higher level moral reasoning.

Social learning differs from the structuralist view, however, in that it has no analogue to Kohlberg's role-taking explanation for movement through stages, although social learning theorists might subsume it under modeling and imitation. It is certain, however, that these approaches disagree on the ways in which parents are important in the moral development of the child.

CONCLUSIONS AND APPLICATION

I have attempted to synthesize the roles that parents play in each of the theories of moral development as one of the issues that emerges when comparing the three perspectives. Other issues, such as the relationship between moral behavior and moral reasoning, the nature of moral education, and how the concept of valuing is acquired, are subsequent chapters in this book. Here are the main points to be made from this introductory chapter.

At the beginning of this chapter, the question of accountability was raised and whether or not parents are responsible to the rest of us for the way the child ultimately acquires a moral code. In social learning and psychoanalytic theory, the parents are always the ones who are held accountable. It is they who provide the models, administer the rewards and punishments, and inculcate through direct teaching what a child needs to know to function in a moral way. If the child fails to internalize the proper values, it is the parents' deficiency and it is the parents who have failed.

On the other hand, evidence suggests that there is change in moral development over time. We know that peer influence becomes more important during early adolescence, and we know that moral changes occur into adulthood. The structuralist view is one that can best account for change over time.

Parents are important, both directly and indirectly, in the social development of the child. Even if they do not necessarily provide the *content* of the child's value system, they do provide opportunities for structural development from which content emanates. Thus, developmentalists cannot dismiss the role of parents. Even if one accepts Kohlberg's dictum that they have "no more impact than any adult of the same socioeconomic level," it must be acknowledged that they are the child's initial avenue to the experiences in the environment which promote the child's development. Parents or parent surrogates wield enormous power, especially in the preschool years, in determining what precise interactions the child will engage in, whether with them or with others. They control the situations in which the child learns how to function and develop as a social being.

Thus, parents are important, but so are others. Peers, other significant adults, and institutions like the school provide the interactions and the arena in which the child "can actively construct his world." Moreover, at different developmental levels, the child's opportunities for moral development come from multiple and varying sources.

If one accepts Piaget's equilibration theory, then the multiple and varying sources are precisely the stimuli needed to move the individual toward more integrated levels of development. The more varied the sources, the greater the probability that disequilibrium will be produced. As structures become more elaborated to achieve a new equilibrium, development is enhanced. This developmental structure can be conceptualized as a series of concentric circles on a seashell, incorporating and integrating all previous development within it, adding more convolutions as necessary. This process of moving from equilibrium to disequilibrium to equilibrium offers a plausible explanation for dynamic change.

As a theoretical model, the structuralist position is dynamic rather than static. Of the three perspectives, it is the one which continues to be reformulated and to offer challenge for empirical research. On the one hand, Kohlberg has reformulated Piaget's stages, while on the other hand, other structural theorists have presented formulations different from those of Kohlberg. This is reflected in the next chapter by Damon and elsewhere (Damon, 1975, 1977) on the acquisition of stages of justice, and in Turiel's work on social convention (1975, 1978) as a structure separate from that of moral development. Kohlberg (1976) himself is now moving to include a "social perspective" within his three moral levels.

The reader may be disappointed that there is no precise formula for child-rearing practices that follows directly from this account. Each of the theories, however, places some emphasis on early communication and social experience. If Turiel is correct in saying that "values and concepts are not learned but represent the transformations of structures of interaction with social experiences" (1975, p. 13), then social experience is the primary avenue to acquisition of value concepts. It seems a truism to say that parents can foster these social experiences, but as we learn more about social cognition, hopefully we can more precisely specify the different types of social experiences that contribute to moral development.

REFERENCES

Allport, G. W., Vernon, P. E., & Lindzey, G. *A study of values.* Boston: Houghton Mifflin Company, 1931.

Aronfreed, J. The socialization of altruistic and sympathetic behavior: Some theoretical and experimental analyses. In J. Macauley & L. Berkowitz (Eds.), *Altruism and helping behavior.* New York: Academic Press, Inc. 1970.

Aronfreed, J. Moral development from the standpoint of a general psychological theory. In T. Lickona (Ed.), *Moral development and behavior.* New York: Holt, Rinehart and Winston, 1976.

Bandura, A. Social learning of moral judgments. *Journal of Personality & Social Psychology,* 1969, *2,* 275-279.

Bandura, A., & McDonald, F. J. Influence of social reinforcement and the behavior of models in shaping children's moral judgments. *Journal of Abnormal and Social Psychology,* 1963, *67,* 274-281.

Becker, W. Consequences of different kinds of parental discipline. In M. L. Hoffman & L. Hoffman (Eds.), *Review of child development research.* New York: Russell Sage Foundation, 1964.

Bell, R. Q. A reinterpretation of the direction of effects in studies of socialization. *Psychological Review*, 1968, *75*, 81-95.

Burton, R. Honesty and dishonesty. In T. Lickona (Ed.), *Moral development and behavior.* New York: Holt, Rinehart and Winston, 1976.

California State Department of Education. *Moral and civic education and teaching about religion.* Sacramento, Calif.: California State Board of Education, 1973.

Damon, W. Early conceptions of positive justice as related to the development of logical operations. *Child Development*, 1975, *46*, 301-312.

Damon, W. *The social world of the child.* San Francisco: Jossey-Bass, Inc., Publishers, 1977.

DeMersseman, S. *A developmental investigation of children's moral reasoning and behavior in hypothetical and practical situations.* Unpublished doctoral dissertation, University of California, Berkeley, 1976.

Dewey, J. *Moral principles in education.* New York: Greenwood Press Inc., 1959. (First published, 1909.)

Durkheim, E. *Moral education.* New York: The Free Press, 1961. (First published, 1925.)

Ekstein, R. Origin of values in children. *Educational Leadership*, 1964, *21*, 8, p. 523-526.

Erikson, E. *Childhood and society.* New York: W. W. Norton & Company, Inc., 1950.

Flavell, J. H., Botkin, P., Fry, C., Wright, J., & Jarvis, P. *The development of role-taking and communication skills in children.* New York: John Wiley & Sons, Inc., 1968.

Freud, S. *Collected papers* (Vol. II). London: Hogarth Press, 1946.

Freud, S. *Collected papers* (Vol. V). London: Hogarth Press, 1950.(a)

Freud, S. *Totem and taboo.* New York: W. W. Norton & Company, Inc., 1950.(b)

Freud, S. *Civilization and its discontents.* London: Hogarth Press, 1957.

Grinder, R. Parental childrearing practices, conscience, and resistance to temptation of sixth grade children. *Child Development*, 1962, *33*, 803-820.

Haan, N., Langer, J., & Kohlberg, L. Family patterns of moral reasoning. *Child Development*, 1976, *47*, 1204-1206.

Haan, N., Smith, B., & Block, J. Moral reasoning of young adults: Political-social behavior, family background, and personality correlates. *Journal of Personality and Social Psychology*, 1968, *10*, 183-201.

Hoffman, M. L. Childrearing practices and moral development: Generalizations from empirical research. *Child Development*, 1963, *34*, 295-318.

Hoffman M. L. Moral development. In P. H. Mussen (Ed.), *Carmichael's manual of child psychology* (Vol. II). New York: John Wiley & Sons, Inc., 1970.

Hoffman, M. L. The development of altruistic motivation. In D. J. DePalma & J. Foley (Eds.), *Moral development: Current theory and research.* Hillsdale, N.J.: Lawrence Erlbaum Associates, 1975.

Holstein, C. B. *Parental determinants of the development of moral judgment.* Unpublished doctoral dissertation, University of California, Berkeley, 1968.

Keasey, C. B. Social participation as a factor in the moral development of preadolescents. *Developmental Psychology*, 1971, *5*, 216-220.

Kelman, H. Attitudes are alive and well and gainfully employed in the sphere of action. *American Psychologist*, 1974, *29*, 310-324.

Kohlberg, L. *The development of modes of moral thinking and choice in the years ten to sixteen.* Unpublished doctoral dissertation, University of Chicago, 1958.

Kohlberg, L. Moral development and identification. In H. Stevenson (Ed.), *Child psychology* (62nd yearbook of the National Society for the Study of Education). Chicago: University of Chicago Press, 1963.

Kohlberg, L. Development of moral character and moral ideology. In M. L. Hoffman & L. Hoffman (Eds.), *Review of child development research.* New York: Russell Sage Foundation, 1964.

Kohlberg L. Stage and sequence: The cognitive-developmental approach to socialization. In D. Goslin (Ed.), *Handbook of socialization theory and research.* Chicago: Rand McNally & Company, 1969.

Kohlberg, L. From is to ought: how to commit the naturalistic fallacy and get away with it in the study of moral development. In T. Mischel (Ed.), *Cognitive development and epistemology.* New York: Academic Press, 1971.

Kohlberg, L. Moral stages and moralization. In T. Lickona (Ed.), *Moral development and behavior.* New York: Holt, Rinehart and Winston, 1976.

Kohlberg, L., & Kramer, R. B. Continuities and discontinuities in childhood and adult moral development. *Human Development*, 1969, *12*, 93-120.

Kohlberg, L., & Mayer, R. Development as the aim of education. *Harvard Educational Review*, 1972, *42*, 449-496.

Kohlberg, L., & Turiel, E. Moral development and moral education. In G. Lesser (Ed.), *Psychology and educational practice.* Chicago: Scott, Foresman & Company, 1971.

Langer, J. *Theories of development.* New York: Holt, Rinehart and Winston, 1969.

Maccoby, E. The development of moral values and behavior in childhood. In J. A. Clausen (Ed.), *Socialization and society.* Boston: Little, Brown & Company, 1968.

McKinney, J. P. The development of values—prescriptive or proscriptive? *Human Development*, 1971, *14*, 71-80.

McKinney, J. P. The development of values: A perceptual interpretation. *Journal of Personality and Social Psychology*, 1975, *31*, 801-807.

Mead, G. H. *Mind, self and society.* Chicago: University of Chicago Press, 1934.

Milgram, S. Behavioral study of obedience. *Journal of Abnormal & Social Psychology*, 1963, *67*, 371-378.

Parke, R. Effectiveness of punishment as an interaction of intensity, timing, agent nurturance, and cognitive structuring. *Child Development*, 1969, *40*, 213-235.

Parke, R. The role of punishment in the socialization process. In R. A. Hoppe, G. A. Milton, & E. C. Simmel (Eds.), *Early experiences and the processes of socialization.* New York: Academic Press, 1970.

Piaget, J. *The language and thought of the child.* London: Routledge & Kegan Paul Ltd., 1926. (First published, 1923.)

Piaget, J. *Judgment and reasoning in the child.* New York: Harcourt, Brace & World, 1926. (First published, 1924.)

Piaget, J. *The construction of reality in the child.* New York: Basic Books, Inc., Publishers, 1954. (First published, 1936.)

Piaget, J. *The moral judgment of the child.* New York: The Free Press, 1965. (First published, 1932.)

Piaget, J. Piaget's theory. In P. H. Mussen (Ed.), *Carmichael's manual of child psychology.* New York: John Wiley & Sons, Inc., 1970.

Piaget, J. *The child and reality.* New York: Grossman Publishers, 1973.

Piaget, J., & Inhelder, B. *The growth of logical thinking from childhood to adolescence.* New York: Basic Books, Inc., Publishers, 1958. (First published, 1955.)

Rest, J. Developmental psychology and value education. *Review of Educational Research,* 1974, *44,* 241-259.

Rest, J., Turiel, E., & Kohlberg, L. Level of moral development as a determinant of preference and comprehension of moral judgments made by others. *Journal of Personality, 1969, 37,* 225-252.

Rokeach, M. *Beliefs, attitudes, and values.* San Francisco: Jossey-Bass, Inc., Publishers, 1968.

Rothman, G. The influence of reasoning on behavioral choices at different stages of moral development. *Child Development,* 1972, *43,* 741-756.

Rothman, G. R. The influence of moral reasoning on behavioral choices. *Child Development,* 1976, 47, 397-406.

Rubin, K. H. Relationship between egocentric communication and popularity among peers. *Developmental Psychology,* 1972, 7, 364.

Rubin, K. H., & Schneider, F. The relationship between moral judgment, egocentrism, and altruistic behavior. *Child Development,* 1973, *44,* 661-665.

Saltzstein, H. Social influence and moral development: A perspective on the role of parents and peers. In T. Lickona (Ed.), *Moral development and behavior.* New York: Holt, Rinehart and Winston, 1976.

Sears, R. R., Maccoby, E. E., & Levin, H. *Patterns of child rearing.* Evanston, Ill.: Row, Peterson, 1957.

Selman, R. L. The relation of role-taking to the development of moral judgment in children. *Child Development,* 1971, *42,* 79-91.

Selman, R., & Damon, W. The necessity (but insufficiency) of social perspective taking for conceptions of justice at three early levels. In D. J. DePalma & J. M. Foley (Eds.), *Moral development: Current theory and research.* Hillsdale, N.J.: Lawrence Erlbaum Associates, 1975.

Simon, S. B., Howe, L. W., & Kirschenbaum, H. *Values clarification.* New York: Hart Publishing Co., Inc., 1972.

Turiel, E. Developmental processes in the child's moral thinking. In P. Mussen, J. Langer, & M. Covington (Eds.), *Trends and issues in developmental psychology.* New York: Holt, Rinehart and Winston, 1969.

Turiel, E. Stage transition in moral development. In R. Travers (Ed.), *Second handbook of research on teaching.* Chicago: Rand McNally & Company, 1973.

Turiel, E. Conflict and transition in adolescent moral development. *Child Development*, 1974, *45*, 14-29.

Turiel, E. The development of social concepts: Mores, customs, and conventions. In D. DePalma & J. Foley (Eds.), *Moral development: Current theory and research.* Hillsdale, N.J.: Lawrence Erlbaum Associates, 1975.

Turiel, E. The development of concepts of social structure. In J. Glick & A. Clarke-Stewart (Eds.), *The development of social understanding.* New York: Gardner Press, 1978.

Turiel, E. Distinct conceptual and developmental domains: Social convention and morality. In C. B. Keasey (Ed.), *Nebraska symposium on motivation. 1977.* Lincoln, Nebraska: University of Nebraska Press, 1979.

Turiel E., & Rothman, G. The influence of reasoning on behavioral choices at different stages of moral development. *Child Development*, 1972, *43*, 741-756.

2

Structural-Developmental Theory and the Study of Moral Development

WILLIAM DAMON

Ever since Diogenes roamed the streets in search of an honest man, and even long before that ancient time, philosophers have argued about the moral side of human nature. Over the centuries certain basic questions have intrigued and puzzled moral philosophers, and have engendered an extraordinary amount of speculation. Is human nature predisposed toward good or toward evil? How does a person acquire a sense of morality? Can it be said that some persons are consistently moral whereas others are not? Is it ever right to say that one individual's sense of morality is superior to that of others; or that the predominant moral codes of a particular society are better than those of another society?

In comparatively recent times (within the last fifty years or so), psychologists have entered this debate and have attempted to resolve empirically many of the age-old issues in moral philosophy. Some of the largest problems, over course, have remained untouched. Except through blind faith or speculation, the inherent goodness or badness of human nature may never be determined. But psychologists have made important progress toward resolving at least three of the most fundamental problems relating to human morality: the problem of how morality is acquired in the course of human development; the problem of moral consistency within individuals; and the problem of how (and whether) it is appropriate to order different types of human morality on a scale ranging from primitive to advanced.

Although inroads into each of these three problems have been made by psychologists from various theoretical orientations, one particularly fruitful and coherent approach to the study of these classic issues has been the work of the structural-developmentalists. Since the early writings of

James Mark Baldwin, Jean Piaget, and Lawrence Kohlberg, through the contemporary research of their many followers, the structural-developmental approach to moral development has formed a genuine tradition in which progress has been made through systematic theoretical revisions of prior insights and achievements. In this chapter I shall describe the past and current contributions of structural-developmental psychology to our understanding of the three basic problems in human morality: moral acquisition, moral consistency, and the ordering of individual moral behavior. But first, I shall briefly mention some underlying assumptions that distinguish the structural-developmental approach from other viewpoints in the psychological literature.

All developmental psychologists are interested in "changes in the individual's behavior as he grows older" (Wohlwill, 1973, p. ix). But all changes with age are not equally informative to those interested in an individual's developmental progress. Many new types of behavior may come and go from one week to the next without any long-lasting implications for the way a person thinks and acts in this world. A child may pick up any assortment of facts and information from elders or friends; or he or she may learn to imitate father one day and the school teacher the next, all without great consequence for the child's intellectual or social maturity. Structural-developmental psychologists have focused on certain aspects of behavior as bearing special significance for an individual's development. These significant aspects of behavior are those that reveal the organization, or structure, of an individual's behavioral tendencies. The key assumption behind the structural-developmental approach is that development is a process of reorganizing, or restructuring, one's pattern of behavior. A corollary assumption is that only those behavioral changes that result from such major developmental reorganizations are of permanent significance for an individual's mode of relating to the world. Blurton-Jones has put it most succinctly, "The developmental question is, 'What are the changes in the organization of behavior as the individual grows?' " (1972, p. 8).

The emphasis on organization of behavior has enabled structural-developmentalists to discover coherence in individual behavior where others have seen only a shambles of unrelated acts, abilities, and knowledge. The structuralists have always argued against the associationist position (for years dominant in American psychology) that a person acquires new behavior bit by bit, according to whatever random order the environment happens to present new information. Opposing this passive and atomistic view of learning, the structural-developmentalists have maintained that a person actively wrests new information from the environment; and that the type of new information gained is very much a function of the person's current knowledge and abilities. In short, it is a function of the person's mode of structuring the world. New behavior, therefore, is seen to derive systematically from interactions between the environment and a person's ongoing means of organizing the environment, rather than from environmental inputs alone. Ultimately, the acquisition of important new behaviors will lead to changes in the person's means of organizing the world, and hence to development. Both the acquisition of new behavior and the subsequent developmental reorganizations are seen as systematic and predictable, being linked to a person's previous state of progress rather than to mere chance occurrences in his or her world experience.

In the study of moral development, the structuralist/associationist debate has led to some particularly extreme positions. For example, one associationist assertion (Berkowitz, 1964) was that moral values are learned one by one, in the order in which they are introduced to the child by his or her environment. Kohlberg (1969), in response, labeled this the "bag-of-virtues" approach which mistakenly assumes that a child gradually collects discrete moral virtues and accumulates them for future use. Kohlberg's own work is certainly the most extreme manifestation of structuralist assumptions in moral psychology. In his strongest statements (Kohlberg, 1971), Kohlberg claims that individuals organize their entire social world through one or more of the six basic "justice structures" that comprise his six-stage moral judgment model. He argues that justice is the essential factor in human social life, and consequently, that human knowledge about social relations and social institutions is organized primarily around conceptions of justice. A reorganization in a person's conception of justice (in other words, a progressive movement along Kohlberg's moral judgment stage sequence) has, in Kohlberg's view, the broadest possible implications for an individual's social behavior.

Even persons sympathetic to structural-development theory have often felt that Kohlberg's approach is too ambitious and too global. Turiel (1975), for example, has written that structuralism does not necessarily imply that one unitary structure governs all thinking. He quotes from Piaget: "I must emphasize that these [structural] systems are merely partial systems with respect to the whole organism or mind. The concept of structure does not imply just any kind of totality and does not mean that everything is attached to everything else" (Piaget, 1967, p. 143). For example, Turiel has suggested that sexual and romantic relations between individuals are better understood with reference to notions like attraction and intimacy than to notions like justice and morality. Elsewhere in this book, Turiel carefully distinguishes social-conventional concerns from moral concerns. He does not claim that the two types of concern are totally unrelated or independent, but rather that each is unique in some way, and that neither is reducible to the other. Developmentally, we might expect each to follow its own course as the child grows (although the development of each may still have some mutual influence on the other). In this chapter we shall encounter other instances of distinct, yet developmentally related, structures within the general realm of morality. The interpretation of structuralism presented in this chapter is therefore a moderate one, considering partial rather than global systems of behavioral organization and attempting to convey the uniqueness as well as the relatedness of the many different aspects of an individual's moral development.

HOW MORALITY IS ACQUIRED

Most adults tend quite naturally to think of children as minor reflections of themselves. Accordingly, a common view of moral development holds that children acquire moral values either by observing adults or by being instructed in moral virtue at the hands of adults. Moral development, according to this view, is a process of replicating the codes and standards of adult society in the behavior of the developing child. The more a child is instructed in moral virtue, the better his or her moral behavior will be, at least in the sense that this behavior should increasingly conform to the prevailing moral norms of adult society.

For decades, structural-developmentalists have attacked this common view of moral development; and yet, until less than fifteen years ago, this adult-centered and mechanistic position dominated American psychology. Perhaps the most telling criticism of this common view is that it cannot explain novelty in moral judgment. Yet moral novelty is by no means rare: it is manifest in the often bizarre beliefs of young children as well as in the visionary statements of prophets, saints, and all other individuals whose moral judgment seems actually superior to the society that raised them. In fact, to a close observer, moral conformity seems neither typical of development nor ideal as an endpoint to development. Rather, it is one of many types of behavioral patterns that a moral development model must seek to explain. To predicate an entire theory on the assumption that moral conformity characterizes moral development in general is clearly a mistake.

Opposing this common view of moral acquisition, structural-developmentalists have tried in their work to capture both the creativity of an individual's moral development and the uniqueness of the individual's moral knowledge during each of several distinct developmental periods. The basic notion is that a person works out his or her own sense of morality through actively structuring and restructuring his or her social experience. The key underlying assumption is that the person's own behavioral representation of moral rules and values is uniquely organized at each developmental level. Progress consists of a series of reorganizations, each of which radically changes the nature of the individual's moral knowledge. These developmental reorganizations occur in an *invariant sequence*— that is, in the same order for all children—because each mode of moral organization is necessary for the emergence of its successor. In structural-developmental language, modes of organization with these properties have traditionally been called *stages*.

One early, and still influential, moral-developmental stage system was proposed by Piaget in his classic study of children's rule-following behavior (Piaget, 1932). Piaget treats morality as a respect for social rules, and his moral judgment model describes four stages in the development of a child's respect for social rules. Piaget also places special emphasis on the implications of his moral-rule stages for the child's emerging sense of justice. The major part of Piaget's investigation focused on children's play in the context of a common Geneva street game of marbles. In this study, Piaget observed children's rule-following behavior and interviewed them about the origins, meaning, and importance of game rules. In further extensions of his investigation, Piaget interviewed children directly about their conceptions of justice, introducing the "moral story" technique as a means of evoking from children their judgments of right and wrong. Many of Piaget's moral stories embodied problems in retributive justice—that is, in culpability and punishment. For example, one famous story asked children to decide who did worse, a child who broke one cup while trying to snitch some jam while his mother was away, or a child who accidently broke fifteen cups while coming in to dinner when called by his mother. Other of Piaget's moral stories embodied problems in distributive justice. For example, one such story asked children whether or not it was fair for a father to give all the chores to one son who does them gracefully rather than to share them between that son and another who grumbles whenever given a chore. Piaget administered these stories according to his "méthode clinique," which called for children not only to make moral decisions, but also to justify them with reasons.

The first and last stages in Piaget's four-stage moral judgment model received only perfunctory attention in Piaget's writings. It was the child's transition from stage two to stage three that was the heart of Piaget's moral judgment book. Nevertheless, Piaget's brief descriptions of the first and last stages were suggestive from a developmental point of view, and they prepared the ground for work that was to come later.

The first of Piaget's stages* is more a stage of play than one of true morality. Toward the end of infancy (at approximately two years of age), the child engages in a great deal of "symbolic play," during which he or she ceaselessly invents private rituals and games of make-believe. The child pretends to drive cars; to be animals, clocks, and buildings; to clean the house; and so on. Piaget's first rule-following stage corresponds to this

---

*In other writings, Piaget (1951) traced the genesis of rule-following in individuals even further back than this stage to the infant's playful (nonhungry) sucking. The rationale for these genetic speculations is such primitive playful activity is the earliest manifestation of repetition and regularity in childhood behavior. From such regularity derives later symbolic rituals, games with rules, and eventually respect for moral codes and laws. It must be emphasized, however, that Piaget does not go so far as to call playful repetitions and rituals *early morality*. To serve a social-regulating function (as does real morality), rules must have both social and obligatory characteristics, and infant activities like playful sucking are nonsocial and nonobligatory.

period of symbolic play in the life of a young child. The child will play at a common game (like marbles), but in an idiosyncratic rather than a collective way. The child will invent his or her own rules, will change these rules at will, and in general will assimilate the game to his or her own private rituals and symbolic fantasies. Although the game will have certain regularities (which form the precursors to later social rule-following), the game is strictly private and individual, without any possibility of either cooperation or competition between the child and another. During this early stage, the child does not distinguish the regularities in his or her individual rituals from real moral rules (for example, don't lie). It is not until the child conceives of obligation that he or she separates moral rules from other kinds of behavioral regularity; and, writes Piaget, "The feeling of obligation only appears when the child accepts a command emanating from someone whom he respects" (Piaget, 1932, p. 53).

The second and third stages of Piaget's moral judgment model portray the development of two kinds of interpersonal respect that can engender moral obligation: unilateral respect and mutual respect. Unilateral respect emerges in the second stage of Piaget's system. During this second stage (beginning at about age five), the child regards rules as external to one's self and one's conscience, and as "handed down from above" by adults or even by supernatural figures. Accordingly, the child regards rules as permanent and sacred, not as subject to modification for any reason. Because the child at this second stage confuses morality with adult constraint, Piaget describes this mode of moral judgment as a "heteronomous" respect for the commands of a superior. Such heteronomy leads to unique features of childhood thought, such as "moral realism". In one manifestation of moral realism ("objective responsibility"), the letter of law is valued rather than the human need for the law; and the consequences of an act are valued more than the intention behind the act. Breaking fifteen cups by accident is considered worse than breaking one during an act of willful disobedience. In another manifestation of moral realism ("immanent justice"), punishment is seen to inevitably follow an act of wrong doing, even if it takes an unusual act of God or nature. For example, a child might say that, after telling a lie, it is likely that one may be hit with a falling branch. Such judgment, according to Piaget, reveals the child's confusion between moral and physical laws. The child assumes that, like the law of gravity, moral laws are predetermined and permanent aspects of the world we live in.

When, at about age eight, the child establishes a mutual respect for peers, he or she begins to see rules as cooperative regulatory agreements useful to all. Heteronomous morality begins to decline, and an "autonomous" morality emerges. During this third stage of Piaget's system, the child regards rules as man-made and changeable agreements between equals, rather than as unalterable commands handed down from adults. Social reciprocity develops, and cooperation with peers, rather than adult constraint, becomes the child's reason for obeying moral rules. As noted earlier, Piaget also makes brief mention of a stage-four-conception of rules; this emerges at about age eleven. During this period, the child demonstrates certain second-order reasoning abilities, such as the ability to construct new rules to cope with all possible situations. This stage is associated with an "ideological" mode of moral reasoning. The child's moral thought can now operate on a plane of complex political and social issues, rather than simply with individual persons and interpersonal relationships.

Although greatly influenced by Piaget's theory, Kohlberg (1963) is critical of the content of Piaget's moral stage system. First, Kohlberg believes Piaget's stages to be inadequately formulated. According to Kohlberg, Piaget wrongly describes the child's progression from heteronomous to autonomous morality as a result of the child's responsiveness to peer, rather than adult, expectations. Kohlberg's position is there is nothing more mature about heeding peers rather than heeding adults. In addition, Kohlberg believes that there are several stages of autonomous morality, some continuing well into adulthood. In building on Piaget's insights, Kohlberg's main contribution has been to describe these later stages of moral development. Kohlberg has also been willing to make stronger statements about the stage-like nature of his moral judgment sequence than has Piaget. Kohlberg clearly states that his stage model should be considered an invariant sequence of moral structures, each of which organizes vast sections of an individual's social experience. Piaget, on the other hand, is not quite willing to call heteronomous and autonomous morality true stages of development. Piaget is concerned that, in the children he observed, autonomous morality did not seem to replace heteronomous morality in any clear-cut or definitive fashion. Rather, the two existed side by side even in some young children; and the proportion of the children's autonomous moral behavior seemed to increase only gradually while the proportion of their heteronomous behavior decreased. Thus Piaget's stage model does not seem to quite match structural-developmental criteria for an invariant sequence of structured wholes. Kohlberg's claim is that his own sequence is an improvement over Piaget's, precisely because it does.

In his own investigations of moral development, Kohlberg has embodied the traditional issues of moral philosophy (such as the issues of responsibility, value of life, rules and norms, property) in a series of moral story-dilemmas. These story-dilemmas pose issues in a way that is understandable to fairly young children (down to age ten or so), and yet also challenges the most sophisticated adult. For example, in Kohlberg's famous Heinz dilemma, the problem is whether or not a man should steal a cancer-curing drug to save his wife's life, assuming that the man can get the drug no other way. Other dilemmas present moral crises experienced by soldiers challenged in combat, doctors asked to perform euthanasia for suffering patients, air raid personnel sent on duty during an enemy attack, and so on. These dilemmas, of course, are considerably more dramatic and adult-oriented than those created by Piaget. In fact, one major difference between Kohlberg's approach and Piaget's approach is Kohlberg's methodology relies heavily on issues normally faced only in adulthood, whereas Piaget investigated such mundane and childish concerns as the rules of a marble game. We might accordingly expect Kohlberg's view of adolescent and adult moral development to be sharper than is his view of childhood moral development, and vice versa for Piaget.

With a new methodology and a lifespan perspective on development, Kohlberg revised and expanded Piaget's original moral judgment stage system, postulating a six-stage sequence of moral development that spans the years from late childhood through adulthood. Kohlberg's Stage 1 is very similar in content to Piaget's heteronomous morality. Kohlberg describes Stage 1 as a "punishment and obedience orientation":

> The physical consequences of action determine its goodness or badness regardless of the human meaning or value of these consequences. Avoidance of punishment and unquestioning deference to power are valued in their own right . . . (Kohlberg, 1963, p. 34).

Age norms presented by Kohlberg have shown the most frequent occurrence of Stage 1 morality in our culture to be among ten year olds. However, since ten was the youngest age in Kohlberg's sample, it may be assumed that Stage 1 is also to be found in children somewhat younger.

Stage 2 in Kohlberg's system shows the first workings of moral reciprocity. The individual conceives of justice as the equal exchange of favors (for example, "You scratch my back, I'll scratch yours") or of blows (for example, An eye for an eye, a tooth for a tooth). Stages 3 and 4 are the "conventional" moral judgment stages, the normal adult modes that operate to maintain the family and the social order. The Stage 3 individual understands and upholds the principle of the golden rule, valuing such acts as generosity for the needy and forgiveness for wrongdoing. Justice at Stage 3 means doing good within the context of interpersonal relationships. Stage 4 extends the concept of justice to include the entire social order. Justice at Stage 4, thus, becomes establishing good citizenship, working hard, and maintaining the law of the land.

Stages 5 and 6 are the "principled" stages of moral judgment. The principled moral thinker at Stage 5 can contemplate such meta-ethical issues as "Why one should be moral." He or she conceives of moral responsibility as binding upon all those who would claim the rights of society. This, then, is a "social contract" conception of morality. At the highest level in Kohlberg's system, Stage 6, the individual can freely take the role of all parties in a moral conflict. He or she arrives at a just solution that may, in certain instances, transcend obedience to society's codes. But such solutions always respect the universal rights of others. A just solution at Stage 6 "is a solution acceptable to all parties . . . assuming none of them knew which role they would occupy in the situation" (Kohlberg, 1971,

p. 213). Although there is, at Stage 6, a fundamental respect for the human social order, laws may occasionally be ignored in instances where great injustice would result from blind obedience. Principles such as the equal right of all to human life are supreme, and law is seen as an imperfect means to such ends, rather than as a moral end in itself.

The great advances made by the work of Piaget and Kohlberg have enabled us to recognize the uniqueness of each period of moral development. No longer must we assume that the moral judgments made by children and adolescents are simply imperfect versions of adult moral values. Rather than a view of individuals attempting to copy the standards of their elders, we have from the work of Piaget and Kohlberg rich descriptions of moral stages which are to some extent independent of adult values, and which are self-constructed by children and adolescents as they grow and experience society. Although some philosophers and psychologists expounded this "structural-development" position long before Piaget and Kohlberg, it is only in the work of the latter two that we find convincing descriptions of the stages and sequence of individual moral growth.

Nevertheless, it would be a mistake to assume that the descriptions of moral stages provided by either Piaget or Kohlberg are perfectly wrought at this point. As noted earlier, there are incompatibilities between the two models themselves. One problem that I suggested earlier was the weakness of Piaget's system for describing adolescents or adults; another was the weakness of Kohlberg's system for describing young children. Other problems have been raised by psychologists working with developmental models of moral judgment. Hoffman (1970) has reviewed several studies that cast doubt on the universal nature of Piaget's sequence. Hogan (1970) and Gibbs (1977) have questioned whether Kohlberg's Stages 5 and 6 meet structural-developmental criteria for real stages. These and other critiques of existing stage models serve the useful function of helping us to revise and improve these models. The ultimate hope is to establish better and better descriptions of moral development. At the present time, the most extensive work in this direction has been that of Turiel (1975) and myself (Damon, 1977). Turiel's efforts, described in Chapter 3 of this volume, have been directed at distinguishing moral from social-conventional aspects of development. Both of these have been confused in the models of Piaget and Kohlberg. My own efforts have been directed at reformulating our view of early social and moral development (between the ages of four and ten). I find neither Piaget's nor Kohlberg's descriptions of development during this period adequate; and, like Turiel, I believe that distinctly different aspects of social development have been confused in both preceding models.

Two social-moral concerns of young children have been of particular interest to me: (1) concerns of positive justice—including problems like why, how, and under what conditions one should share with others, how one ought to distribute property and rewards fairly, and how one should treat friends; and (2) concerns of authority—including problems like what legitimizes authority, whom one should obey (and under what conditions), and why one should obey another in the first place. I have assumed that these two concerns are central in the lives of young children, and that each has its own, unique developmental path. The first, positive justice, is mainly a moral concern, since it represents the issue of justice in the child's early social life. The second, authority, is mainly a pragmatic concern, since the crux of the authority relation is deciding how (and whether) obedience best serves the needs of the self. Beyond enlightened self-interest, there is no social or moral basis for subservience to another (although there may occasionally be justice problems that arise in an authority relation, for example, when the rights of an employee may conflict with unreasonable demands made by an employer). In recent work (Damon, 1977), I have charted the course of the positive justice conception and the authority conception throughout their separate developments during childhood. As will be described later in the chapter, I have had the opportunity to study the development of each in both real-life and in hypothetical contexts. Here I shall briefly describe the general stages through which the child's early knowledge of each concept develops.

A sample hypothetical dilemma used to derive a child's opinions about positive justice is a story about a classroom of children who spent one day in school making crayon drawings. Some children worked well, some did not; some were lazy, others were diligent; some were poor; some were boys, and some were girls; and so on. The class sold the drawings at a school bazaar. How should the money be fairly distributed? For the authority concept, one story depicts a mother demanding that her child clean his room before going out; another depicts a team captain telling a player what position to play. In each case the child is asked what gives the authority figure the right to make commands. (Is it his/her size, strength, wisdom, good will, niceness, or what?) The child is also asked why the authority figure should be listened to at all. Furthermore, what happens when the authority figure goes beyond normal bounds (as in the case of the mother, in a bad mood, keeping her child inside even after he has cleaned his room, or of the team captain telling the player to run down to the store to buy him a Coke).

The development of the positive justice concept is marked by a sequence of unfolding mental confusions, each of which is less basic than the preceding one. At the earliest level, found primarily in children four and younger, fairness is confused with the child's own desires. For example, a child might say that it is fair that he should get more ice cream than his sister because he likes ice cream and wants more. A bit more advanced than this is the justifying of such egocentric desires with reference to some quasi-objective criterion. For example, a child might say that he should get what he wants because he's the fastest runner in his house, or because he's a boy, etc., even if such criteria may be illogical, untrue, or irrelevant to the reward under consideration. At the next level, fairness is confused with strict equality in actions: it is fair that everyone get the same treatment, regardless of special considerations like merit or need. Next comes a confusion of fairness with deserving: those who worked hardest, were smartest, acted best, etc., should be rewarded because they deserve it. Children are normally at this point in middle childhood, in the early elementary school years. Among children a bit older, fairness is confused with compromise, special attention being paid to those with special needs. The child might say that everyone with a claim should get some justly determined proportion of the resources in question, but perhaps poor people who have less to begin with should receive more to make up the difference. Finally, in the age range that I have studied (up to ten years), the oldest children confuse fairness with a situational kind of ethic. All potential justice claims—equality, need, deserving, compromise—are considered, but the one that is selected is chosen with a view to the specific function of the reward in the specific situation under question. Often these children sound like utilitarians. For example, a child might argue that people who work the hardest and do the best jobs should be rewarded most, because that way everyone will be encouraged to do better next time, and then the entire class will earn more money.Or another child at this same level might argue that all should be rewarded equally, because this is by nature a cooperative situation and all other considerations would violate the implicit agreement of all present. Although positive justice development beyond age ten still has a long way to go in constructing principles that will apply more adequately to complex social problems, even in this short, early age span young children's conceptions are constantly changing in a regular, predictable pattern of growth.

The early development of the authority concept is no less dramatic. In some ways the changes coincide with parallel changes in other social-moral concepts like positive justice; in other ways the authority changes are unique to themselves. Throughout the entire period from age four through ten, a "punishment and obedience" orientation can be seen. This orientation, which has been described by Kohlberg, is itself radically reformulated between the beginning and end of this period.

In brief, the earliest levels of the authority conception altogether deny the existence of external authority, at least insofar as it conflicts with the wishes of the subject. One obeys because one wants to; a command conflicting with one's desires is unimaginable. Parents are obeyed because they tell you to do what you want to do; commands that go against one's desires do not have to be listened to. This level is quite primitive and is normally no longer dominant even at age four. At the next level the reality of punishment is grasped. Obedience is seen in pragmatic terms: one obeys because one must if bad things (like punishment) are to be avoided.

Parents and other authority figures are there to tell you what to do and that is enough reason to listen to them. The next level infuses authority figures with certain attributes legitimizing their commands. At this point attributes of authority are usually ones of physical power, such as size or strength, although a sense of omniscience is often present as well. One obeys the mother, the team captain, etc., because he or she is bigger and stronger, and because he or she will inevitably find out if one disobeys. There is no such thing as "getting away with it," and hence, the inevitable association of wrongdoing and punishment as described by Piaget and Kohlberg. Toward the end of this period, authority becomes legitimized by psychological rather than physical attributes, and the attributes invoked are less extreme. One obeys one's parents because they know best and are usually wiser than a child, or because they have had more training, experience, etc. Therefore, it is in one's best interest to listen. Nevertheless, one also realizes that authorities can be wrong or unfair and that it's possible they won't catch you if you disobey. Thus, for the first time, obedience becomes a matter of choice, based on voluntarism. Finally, the most advanced children in this four-to-ten age-group begin seeing authority as a consensual and reversible relation shared for the mutual benefit of the governor and the governed. One obeys one's mother because she takes care of you, cares about what's best for you, and tells you what to do for your own good. If, in a given situation, you might know more than she, then she should listen to you. Likewise, one obeys rules because the city cared enough about you to protect you with the rules. In some other situation you might yourself be in the position of making a rule, and you would expect others to follow. The role of leaders is therefore seen as temporary and situationally determined. Again, although to some extent still simplistic and socially naive, children's conceptions of authority have come a long way by age ten.

CONSISTENCY

One of the most important questions in psychology is: How much consistency can we expect to find in a person's behavior? Any psychological explanation of moral behavior or moral development certainly must address this problem. Is it possible to make general statements about a person's mode of responding to a variety of moral situations, or does an individual's behavior fluctuate from context to context? For example, may we ever say that one person is generally more trustworthy, honest, or responsible than another? Or that some people usually operate in a relatively mature or sophisticated way when faced with moral concerns, whereas others usually act in a primitive and confused manner? Such issues are at the heart of any attempt to understand individual moral behavior and moral development.

They are central to moral-developmental theory as well as to educational practice, for they concern the very nature of the moral side to the human self. A part of the moral consistency problem is examined in Chapter 4 of this book where Golda Rothman discusses the relationship between an individual's moral judgment and his or her moral conduct. Here we shall look at the broader issue of individual consistency across different moral contexts. Why this is a broader issue will be a subject of discussion later in this section.

Psychologists in the structural-developmental tradition have a great stake in maintaining that an individual's behavior has some consistency across different situations. Most structuralists have gone to great length to describe developmental stages of morality, such stages representing general *modes* of responding to moral problems. As noted earlier, the postulating of such modes assumes that there is some structure or pattern in an individual's moral behavior. Although a diversity of behaviors may be representative of each particular moral mode, the assumption is that there is an underlying organization that gives this diversity a basic coherence. Thus, even though any structuralist would admit that most persons operate at more than one moral mode, it is clearly essential to the structuralist claim that there is some relatedness or consistency in at least great segments of the person's moral behavior. Otherwise, if there is nothing but situational flux in an individual's morality, there is absolutely no point in bothering to describe basic modes of morality. Nothing of interest (at least as far as human behavior is concerned) would derive from such modes, since they would provide us with no expectations regarding how a person would act from one instance to the next.

It should also be reemphasized that, in the structural-developmental tradition, the basic modes of moral behavior are always considered to be stages or levels, ranging from primitive to advanced. This means it is assumed that even young children at the earliest stages demonstrate some pattern or organization in their moral behavior. Therefore, the structuralist claim of consistency, or relative wholeness, extends not only to sophisticated adults (from whom we might well expect some carefully reflected cohesiveness) but to immature and impulsive children as well.

The original and still classic empirical study of consistency in children's moral behavior (Hartshorne & May, 1928-1930) did not yield results boding well for structuralists' claims. In Hartshorne and May's elaborate series of investigations, intercorrelations between children's moral behavior in a variety of settings were generally low, nonexistent, or insignificant. Included in Hartshorne and May's extensive studies were tests of children's "moral knowledge" (for example, their familiarity with the Ten Commandments); tests of children's moral conduct (for example, their propensities to cheat on tasks requiring them to list names of countries without copying from peers, or to place pencil marks within circles without opening their eyes); and external indexes, such as teacher ratings of children's moral behavior. Hartshorne and May were very much predisposed toward looking for general moral traits like honesty that would mark certain children's behavioral tendencies. But they failed to establish empirically the existence of such traits despite years of correlational studies with thousands of subjects. To explain their large-scale failure to establish empirical relations between different aspects of children's moral behavior, Hartshorne and May proposed the notion of "specificity." Virtues like honesty or dishonesty, they wrote, should *not* be viewed as unified character traits, but as specific behaviors that conform to certain situations in life. If an individual demonstrates consistent behavior from one situation to another, this is only because the two situations happen to have similar features. Consistency, they decided, may be found across certain life situations, but not in individuals.

With the advantage of forty-five years of further theory and research on children's moral development, we may speculate on other possible explanations of Hartshorne and May's striking findings. Three possible interpretations are prominent and and worth pursuing. The first of these is: Hartshorne and May's methodology missed whatever consistency does exist in the moral behavior of individuals. This criticism has been made from at least two different points of view in developmental psychology. Kohlberg (1969) has argued that Hartshorne and May's tests of moral knowledge were not aimed at children's reasoning about moral issues, but rather at their familiarity with moral "facts" (such as the Ten Commandments, the Boy Scout code, and so on). As such, Hartshorne and May's tests were insensitive to the basic structure of their subjects' moral judgment. Likewise, their tests of moral behavior (cheating, lying, and so on) were trivial and did not tap children's true moral concerns. Since the measures themselves were invalid, correlations between them (or the lack of correlation) demonstrates nothing. From a different perspective, Burton (1963) asserted that there was some fundamental consistency in Hartshorne and May's own data that was overlooked by the original investigators. Using more sophisticated factor-analytic techniques, Burton pulled out some basic components that accounted for considerable variance in Hartshorne and May's scores. Burton concluded that even in Hartshorne and May's original data there was some support for a generality dimension underlying honesty across different contexts. In addition to these basic methodological problems (that is, the inadequate instruments and data analyses in Hartshorne and May's original investigation), there are always a host of other measurement factors that may mask individual consistency across moral tasks. But measurement is a technological problem which, we may be sure, will eventually be resolved (by just such improvements as suggested by Kohlberg and Burton). The more basic question is whether or not, given a perfect methodology, moral consistency is there to be found.

This brings us to the second of the three possible interpretations of Hartshorne and May's findings. Let's assume that there was some validity to Hartshorne and May's investigation, despite its methodological flaws. It is indeed possible that the very nature of moral behavior in childhood is fragmented. Perhaps there is actually very little moral consistency early in development. According to this possibility, a well-reasoned, unitary quality in an individual's moral performance across a diversity of situations comes only with maturity. Since Hartshorne and May's work was mainly with children and young adolescents, it is not surprising that they failed to find many significant intercorrelations between their moral tasks. This second possibility has also been suggested by Burton (1963), who found that, among Hartshorne and May's original subjects, consistency in performance across moral tasks increased with age. In addition, findings reported by Turiel and Rothman (1972) and Saltzstein, Diamond, and Belenky (1972) support this possibility. Turiel and Rothman found greater consistency in higher-stage subjects than in lower-stage subjects between verbalized reasoning about an issue and actual behavior related to that issue. This and related studies are described in greater detail in Chapter 4. Saltzstein, et al. also found greater consistency in higher-stage subjects than in lower-stage subjects; in the Saltzstein et al. study, subjects' responses to a social-influence type of situation were compared with their reasoning about group versus individual rights. Beyond such empirical evidence, Piaget (1932) and Kohlberg and Kramer (1969) have theorized that, relative to advanced moral behavior, the primitive morality of childhood is fragmented and inconsistent.

Of course, if one is a good structuralist, there are always ways to find uniformities even across behavior that appears fragmented. For example, one might say that young children's behavior is "consistently primitive" even though there are no actual commonalities between various aspects of the behavior other than certain specifically defined confusions or inabilities, i.e., "primitivisms." This was precisely Piaget's approach when he tried to explain an apparent contradiction or "paradox" in the moral behavior of young children with regard to social rules. Piaget noticed that the same young children who claimed that rules were sacred and immutable were also the ones who in practice frequently broke the rules, or who at best obeyed them only irregularly. Although this appears to be an inconsistency, Piaget wrote that "this paradox is general in child behavior and constitutes . . . the most significant feature of behavior belonging to the egocentric stage" (Piaget, 1932, p. 61). According to Piaget, both parts of the paradox—a belief in the sacredness of rules and irregular rule-following—are really two aspects of the same moral structure: the primitive and egocentric mode of heteronomous morality. Further, Piaget treats the paradox itself as an index of childhood egocentrism. We shall soon discuss this and other features of Piaget's moral judgment system in greater detail. But, for the present, it is interesting to note how Piaget found structural unity in the apparent inconsistency of children's behavior. This is not a one-to-one type of unity that proclaims that all of a child's moral behavior will be identical in all contexts. Rather, it asserts only that we may find similar organizational features in seemingly diverse types of behavior. The strengths and limitations of this approach to the problem of moral consistency will be considered shortly.

The third possibility I have referred to is the most obvious one: Hartshorne and May were essentially right; there is not much consistency in the moral behavior of anyone, child or adult, beyond that which is determined by certain confining situations. Although I do not agree with this possibility other than in an extremely modified form, I think that its implications are worth elaborating. They help us think clearly about the general issue of moral consistency and fragmentation.

First of all, if we expect that an individual's behavior will fluctuate across different situations, we might examine a bit more closely this notion of "different situations." What are some differences between contexts that might potentially elicit differences in a person's moral behavior? One contextual distinction that concerns psychologists, educators, and all those who use Kohlberg-type moral judgment interviews to assess an individual's state of moral development is the potential difference between hypothetical moral dilemmas and real-life moral problems. Although Kohlberg type moral dilemmas have been used increasingly to assess individuals' moral development, we cannot assume that a person's responses to such dilemmas will be consistent with his or her real-life moral behavior. As Roger Brown has noted, "the connection between story problem morality and conduct is still . . . mostly unknown" (Brown & Herrnstein, 1975, p. 356). As noted earlier, this "connection" may in part be treated as the relation between moral judgment and moral conduct. Chapter 4 is devoted to exactly this problem. But a broader and more general treatment of this problem considers judgment and conduct, thought and action, all to be part of the same behavioral system. Judgment and conduct may both be considered to be inseparable components of a person's moral knowledge; and this knowledge may be expressed in a variety of different contexts, among them the context of the hypothetical story-dilemma and the context of a real-life moral problem. The type of knowledge tapped in a hypothetical-story context is theoretical, reflective knowledge; the type tapped in a real-life context is a practical, active type of knowledge. This is a very inclusive way of dealing with the problem of moral consistency between what a person says and what the person actually does, since it considers all aspects of the person's moral thought, reasoning, judgment, action, and conduct, and focuses only on general behavior patterns (behavioral tendencies and their modes of organization). The question then becomes whether hypothetical contexts elicit different behavioral patterns than do real-life ones.

When an individual's moral behavior is considered in this very inclusive way, there is reason to expect less than perfect consistency between organization of an individual's moral behavior in the two types of contexts. First, common sense tells us that a person's real-life knowledge does not always "live up to" his or her theoretical knowledge, particularly in real-life situations that invoke the person's self-interest. A child, for example, may have a sophisticated theoretical understanding of right and wrong, but in an immediate peer-group situation may not fully employ this knowledge. In certain instances, therefore, we should see a child's real-life performance lagging behind his or her hypothetical performance on imaginary story-dilemmas. But, to further complicate the matter, there is reason to expect exactly the opposite tendency in other instances. Piaget (1932) has suggested that, in the course of development, active knowledge is often at the forefront of the theoretical. Piaget's assertion is that knowledge is first worked out on the plane of practical activity, and only later becomes reflective, theoretical, and hypothetical. According to this view, we should often find a child's moral behavior to be at higher level in a real-life situation than in a hypothetical context. In his own moral judgment book, Piaget cited examples of children in real-life circumstances showing an understanding of moral intentionality (i.e., the notion that good intentions may excuse acts with bad consequences) long before they were able to show a similar understanding about his hypothetical moral dilemmas (Piaget, 1932). It seems clear, therefore, that the differences between real-life and hypothetical moral situations may well lead to a variety of contextual differences in an individual's moral behavior.

In addition to this important distinction between real-life and hypothetical moral contexts, there is also a distinction to be made between different types of social problems that may present an individual with a moral choice. For example, a child may express one type of judgment about sharing a toy with a friend and another about sharing a toy with a sibling. Or the child may feel differently about sharing food than about sharing a toy. There are virtually limitless parameters that might vary from moral problem to moral problem, and it is possible that any of these parameters might affect an individual's moral behavior. Unfortunately, data that might shed light on this problem have not been reported. For example, it would be interesting to know how the different dilemmas in the Kohlberg-moral-judgment-interview change or do not change a subject's moral judgment score. Kohlberg, however, has never reported empirical relations between his separate dilemmas. The closest we come to such data in Kohlberg's studies is his finding that, on the average, individuals perform at their major stage 45 percent of the time throughout their entire interview (Kohlberg 1963). This statistic tells us something about how much consistency to expect from a person in general during a hypothetical interview, but it is too global to inform us of the exact differences between different parts of the interview that may lead to particularly striking contextual inconsistencies.

Finally, in addition to the distinctions already noted, further distinctions must be made between the various issues or concerns that psychologists often group under the single title—*morality*. Kohlberg's moral judgment system, for example, includes issues of law, responsibility, life, authority, contract, conscience, honesty, religion—and this is not even a complete list. Turiel, in Chapter 3, argues forcefully that, at the very least, those issues which pertain to moral concerns (that is, concerns relating to justice) should be distinguished from those issues pertaining to conventional concerns (that is, those issues relating to the expectation of others in society). Nucci and Turiel (1978) have gathered some data which demonstrate that children do indeed behave differently in moral situations than in social-conventional situations. My own view is that all of Kohlberg's moral issues are potentially distinct. I see no reason to assume a priori that these separate concerns are subparts of a coherent, unified "moral" system; and Kohlberg has never adequately demonstrated empirical relations between them (Kurtines & Greif, 1974). Why should we assume that, for example, a child's conception of honesty will have anything in common with his or her conception of life?

Now it does not take much of a mathematician to realize that, if one multiplies all the distinctions I have made, one will come up with an infinite number of situational combinations that could potentially affect an individual's moral behavior. Clearly no two life situations are ever identical, particularly if one considers all the variables previously mentioned—the hypothetical versus the real-life nature of a situation, the specific parameters of the moral problem during a particular occurrence, and the variety of moral issues that may concern an individual in a social situation. If we then take Hartshorne and May seriously and accept that consistencies within an individual's moral behavior are mainly a function of similarities in life situations we should rarely expect to find consistent moral behavior within individuals, whether they be children or adults. Other than in random or chance occurrences, we should generally expect to find nothing more than flux and fragmentation in human moral performance.

But even common sense tells us that this is too strong a statement. We know that some people can be "depended upon" to act in generally moral fashion, whereas others may not. In fact, as Hoffman has quite reasonably argued: "It seems clear (from a number of studies) that both specificity and generality can be found in moral behavior as in any other trait. Individuals do vary between their general predispositions towards honesty and dishonesty but their actual behavior in moral conflict situations is not an all-or-none matter" (1970, p. 344). Accepting, therefore, the assertion that there is *both* consistency and fragmentation in individual moral performance, we must then go one step further and propose principles that inform us of when to expect consistency and when to expect fragmentation. I think that, with the help of our earlier discussion and a few further bits of data, we may now move in this direction.

In a series of recent studies (Damon, 1977), I have had the opportunity to compare children's moral behavior in real-life *versus* hypothetical contexts, and also to compare children's development across a number of distinct social and moral issues, such as authority, justice, rules, manners and sex-role conventions. Although these studies had many purposes, one focus was the problem of moral consistency during childhood (ages four through twelve). I shall briefly summarize a few findings from these studies, and then end this section with some general conclusions concerning moral consistency throughout development.

The first pair of studies I shall summarize compared children's hypothetical behavior with their behavior in real-life moral situations. In Study I, 144 boys and girls between the ages of 4 and 10 were presented with distributive justice problems in both hypothetical and real-life contexts. Briefly the children's task in both contexts was to decide how to distribute rewards among a group of boys and girls (including themselves) who had done some good work. The level of the children's moral reasoning in both contexts was analyzed and some predictions about how the children would actually distribute rewards in the real-life context were made, based on the different reasoning levels. As we might well expect, results indicated some consistency between children's moral behavior in the two contexts as well as some inconsistency. First, it was found that children's moral reasoning in a real-life distributive justice situation develops through stages, in an age-related manner, similar to the stages that characterize the development of children's hypothetical moral reasoning. But individual children's real-life reasoning did not correlate strongly with their hypothetical reasoning ($r = .26$). Furthermore, there was a distinct tendency for children's real-life reasoning to lag behind their hypothetical reasoning. It was also found that certain general tendencies in children's real-life conduct (i.e., their actual distributions of rewards) could be predicted from their hypothetical moral behavior. For example, children at the lower reasoning levels tended to reward themselves more than did more advanced reasoners; whereas children at the more advanced levels showed greater preference to those who demonstrated meritorious behavior, or to those who demonstrated special needs. But in many cases, specific predictions were not confirmed. One factor that seemed to lead to inconsistency between children's hypothetical behavior and their real-life behavior was the general tendency of many subjects at all levels to find a way to favor themselves. Although, as noted above, this tendency was significantly strongest among the most primitive children, it was still present even at the highest childhood moral levels.

Study 2 also compared children's hypothetical behavior with their real-life behavior, but this time the comparison was in relation to a problem of peer authority. Subjects were 64 boys and girls between the ages of 4 and

10. Specifically, the problem for the experimental groups of children was to choose a basketball team captain from amongst themselves, and then decide either to obey, disobey, or remove their captain in the course of an actual game. In this situation, an almost surprising degree of consistency between all aspects of the children's behavior in the two contexts was found. First, there was a strong correlation between the children's hypothetical and real-life authority reasoning. This had not been the case in the real-life distributive justice study. Second, there was no developmental lag between hypothetical and real-life authority reasoning—again in contrast to the distributive justice situation. Finally, on all measures of the children's conduct in the real-life situation, there was consistency between reasoning and behavioral choice. This included measures of the children's obedience, their propensities to pick themselves or others as captain, and so on.

My own explanation for the differing sets of results in the two studies is that children's self-interest plays a different role in relation to justice problems than in relation to peer authority problems. Unlike justice, authority is largely a pragmatic conception to begin with, reflecting a concern with how one's self-interest is best served through a relation with authority. Justice, on the other hand, is a means of resolving conflicts between individuals. Fair resolution of conflicts often demands the denial of the self's needs and desires, rather than the furthering of them. Self-interest, therefore, is less an intrinsic part of justice than authority, and plays more of an opposing role. It is the opposition between self-interest and justice that accounts for the lag between children's real-life hypothetical justice behavior, as well as for the inconsistencies between their justice reasoning and their distribution conduct.

One message derived from the differing sets of results in the two studies is that there is indeed a difference between children's behavior as related to different social issues. It does not seem that the moral domain is a unitary one, at least during childhood.

The last set of findings I shall mention here comes from a cross-sectional study of 40 boys and girls between the ages of 4 and 9. The children were presented with a range of hypothetical social and moral dilemmas, including stories concerning justice, peer authority, parental authority, and social conventions (rules, manners, and sex-role conventions). Rank-order correlations between all tasks were significant, but some were markedly (and significantly) higher than others. For example, the relation between peer and parental authority was particularly close, and the relation between justice and parental authority was particularly low. This should surprise no one, since it is clear that peer and parental authority share a great number of common concerns, unlike justice and parental authority. But what is interesting is that the empirical relations actually seem to follow our intuitions about conceptual affiliations between the concepts. And here, once again, is evidence that the social-moral realm is less than unitary. As for consistency, as I said earlier, I see no reason to expect that a child's conception of authority will be similar in important ways to his or her conception of justice.

Three Conclusions about Moral Consistency

As noted, it is less revealing at this point to say that there is both consistency and fragmentation in an individual's moral knowledge than to offer principles that explain the occurrence of each. I shall suggest three such principles here. The first is a structural principle, the second a developmental principle, and the third a functional principle.

Structural principle. If *consistent* moral behavior is taken to mean behavior that derives from the same underlying organization of beliefs and ideas, rather than to mean behavior that is identical act for act, we may find inherent consistency in behaviors that appear to be quite different, or even contradictory. This *structural* principle was at the heart of Piaget's approach when he decided that a child's belief in the immutability of rules and the same child's irregular rule-following were really two sides of the same coin, namely egocentric (or heteronomous) morality. Such an approach focuses on the structure, and ultimately on the developmental status, of a person's behavior, rather than on the person's specific choices, decisions, or acts. Because of this, behaviors that appear inconsistent and even incompatible may have something in common in an organizational sense. Consider the following argument, which I presented in an earlier work (Damon, 1977) to illustrate the distinction between organization and belief in children's social knowledge:

> The following quotes are taken from moral judgment interviews with young children:
>
> A. The teacher should give more ice cream to the girls, because she likes them better. The boys aren't as nice; they just make noise and fight all the time.
> B. You shouldn't let a girl be President. Girls are too stupid, and they're not strong enough to make real decisions.
> A. You always have to do what your mother says, because if you don't she'll find out about it and make you wish you did.
> B. If you don't follow the Ten Commandments God will punish you for your sins.
>
> Aside from certain incidental distinctions, each of the statements quoted above is structurally similar to the statement that it is paired with. That is, each of the pairs above represents a particular organization of an aspect of social reality, and this organization is similar for each of the two statements within a pair. There are, however, some surface differences between each of the paired statements. For example, the statements within the first pair dis-

cuss different issues and arrive at differing conclusions. In the first statement, the allocation of ice cream is discussed, and the conclusion is that girls are more deserving; whereas in the second case, the choice of a leader is discussed, and the conclusion, contrary to the first statement, is that girls are not at all deserving. Nevertheless, these contrasting statements are organized by an identical social principle. This principle may be simply stated as an allocation of reward, or other preference, according to personal characteristics attributed to sex. Obviously, such a principle may be used to support either sex, and to allocate a variety of different rewards or preferences. Similarly, the statements in the second pairing above are united by their adherence to the common principle that obedience to authority is based on fear of retribution to an omniscient authority figure. Whether the authority figure is God, mother, or anyone else makes no difference to the functioning of the organizing principle.

Just as different-sounding statements may contain identical structural features, so too may similar-sounding moral views be structured by very different organizing principles. Consider the following pairs, again quoted from actual interviews with four young children:

A. They should split the money up evenly, because it's not fair if someone gets more than anyone else. That just leads to a lot of fussing and fighting, and everyone getting mad.
B. Everyone should get the same amount. Everyone worked real hard to earn the money, so they all deserve to get it. If someone gets less, he'll just say, "Well, I worked as hard as everyone else, so I should get the same." and he could get pretty upset.
A. He [the team player] has to do what the captain says, 'cause he's the captain now and all the kids have to do what the captain tells them to. They probably picked him because he knows who should go where and stuff. If they don't like what he says, if he keeps making mistakes and stuff, they should pick someone else, but right now if they want to be on the team they have to listen to him.
B. Whatever the captain says, he [the player] should do. They pick the best hitter, the best player and everything, to be captain. If you're a good player you'll always be the captain, if you're better than the others on the team. He knows how to play best, and they should listen to him, because if they don't they'll find themselves right off the team.

Now it is likely that the statements paired above may sound fundamentally similar upon first hearing them. Perhaps most salient is that each of the paired statements arrives at a conclusion or decision identical to that of its mate. In the first case, both statements agree that the money spoken of should be evenly divided and in the second case, that the authority figure knows best and should be obeyed. But underlying these striking similarities, there are some profound differences in the ways that these statements are justified and organized. In the first pair, statement A proposes equality (and the resulting "fairness") as a means of avoiding the consequences of dissension and turmoil. Statement B, on the other hand, proposes equality as a means of giving everyone his just desserts: since everyone worked the same, they should all be paid back the same. The first statement is constructed and organized on the basis of the following principle: equality of treatment = fairness = the only way to avoid unpleasant consequences. The second statement is organized by a principle of just reciprocity, namely that persons should be paid back in kind for their actions. The next pair of statements above may be distinguished from each other in a similar manner. Statement A proposes that one should obey authority because the authority figure probably knows how to run a team (who goes where, and so on); on the other hand, if the authority figure proves incompetent in this regard, he may be replaced. The organizing principles here are that (1) the ability that legitimizes authority is specifically the knowledge of how to govern; and (2) that the authority relation is reversible in the sense that the authority figure may be replaced if he proves deficient in the knowledge that legitimizes authority. There is also the sense here that one submits to authority voluntarily. Statement B, to the contrary, claims that authority is obeyed (1) because the authority figure is generally superior in a number of abilities to those he leads, and (2) because the consequences of disobedience are unpleasant.*

Because structuralists focus on organizational similarity in behaviors rather than on "surface" or "content" similarity, they will often find consistency where others see only diversity. The consistency noted by structuralists does not imply that an individual's behavior must be constant or identical across different settings. The only implication is that the individual's behavior maintains a basic coherency as life situations vary. This coherency is established by the similar organizing principles underlying all aspects of the individual's behavior. It is the nature of these organizing principles that remains constant, not the individual's specific actions or behaviors.

That structuralists focus on organization rather than on the content of behavior does raise a problem when it comes to making specific predictions concerning how an individual will act from one moment to the next. Although a good structuralist may be able to describe richly and accurately a person's mode of dealing with the social world, the structuralist cannot hope to predict all aspects of the person's behavior. The structuralist, in his or her descriptions, focuses on the general pattern of the individual's behavior rather than on the person's specific deeds or acts. In fact, structuralists have no assumptions concerning the consistency of behavioral content, since their investment is only in the coherence of behavioral organization across situations. This may certainly be seen as a potential weakness in the structuralist approach. By definition, only the crudest of behavioral predictions can be made by knowing a person's basic mode (or modes) of structuring the world. On the other hand, a structuralist would argue that this is the best that one can hope to do. Given the complexity of human behavior, and given the diversity of the situational features that influence human behavior, it is a remarkable achievement indeed even to predict behavioral tendencies in individuals across different contexts. Although the structural-developmental approach to the problem of individual moral consistency is therefore less than totally ambitious, it has succeeded like no other approach in establishing the fundamental continuity of individual moral behavior in both children and adults.

*From *The Social World of the Child* by W. Damon. San Francisco: Jossey-Bass, Inc., Publishers, 1977.

Developmental principle.   Childhood, as we all know, is a very dynamic period developmentally. It is characterized by constant change, reorganization, and progressive movement in a child's knowledge and abilities. In fact, one of the greatest problems in the structuralist approach has been to adequately capture such dynamism in a model that lends itself to static descriptions (stages, levels, and so on). Many in the structuralist tradition are themselves grappling with this very problem. For the topic at hand, the message here is that we should not expect to find great consistency during periods characterized by developmental dynamism. In fact, inconsistency may actually serve progress, in the sense that an awareness of contradiction on the part of an individual may lead the individual toward movement and reorganization. According to this *developmental* proposition, we should expect to find mixture and inconsistency during any transitional phase of development. Turiel, in fact, has described moral transition periods in precisely this manner, "Transitional states are characterized by disequilibrium, as manifested in conflicts, contradictions, and inconsistencies" (Turiel, 1974, p. 25). Since childhood is a series of fleeting transitions, it is not surprising that we see marked fragmentation in children's moral behavior. Such inconsistency should pass, however, as moral knowledge begins to stabilize at the higher levels of behavior. This seems to be exactly what the research noted (Damon, 1977) has found. Only in instances of pathology should we find extreme inconsistency as a permanent feature of an individual's moral knowledge.

Functional principle.   Although we should find the greater part of moral fragmentation disappearing with advanced development, I doubt that we should ever expect total coherence or consistency. Nor should we desire it. There is also a *functional* explanation for moral inconsistency that derives from the notion that all social situations and social issues are not identical. For optimal functioning in a diverse social world, different moral principles must be applied to different settings. These different principles will not always be a part of one coherent system; in fact, they may at times be contradictory or conflicting. This is the notion of "*partial systems*" which Piaget (1967) introduced and which was described earlier in this chapter in relation to the different issues manifest within the social and moral domain (*see* page 52). Put simply, different kinds of behavior are appropriate in different kinds of social contexts, and a good moral life demands a certain degree of inherent inconsistency. Perhaps this point has been made most forcefully in literature. Boris Pasternak, describing the idealist revolutionary, Strelnikov, in the novel *Dr. Zhivago*, wrote:

> And if he were really to do good, he would have needed, in addition to his principles, a heart capable of violating them—a heart which knows only of the particular, not of general cases, and which achieves greatness in little actions.

THE ORDERING OF
INDIVIDUAL MORALITY

Each of the structural-developmental moral judgment models that has been described here rests on some controversial assumptions about primitive versus advanced modes of behavior. Implicit in each of these models are the assumptions that early stages represent primitive modes of behavior and later stages represent advanced modes, that the primitive modes tend to be replaced with the advanced modes as an individual develops, and that the advanced modes tend to work better than do the primitive ones. "Working better" can mean a number of things, depending upon the exact type of behavior that is developing. In the case of moral behavior, as Kohlberg (1971) has written, working better means being able to apply universal and consistent principles of justice to an ever greater range of social problems.

Individuals with egalitarian beliefs often react against this developmental perspective. Although willing to recognize that there are differences in the way individuals respond to moral events, many egalitarian-minded persons would hesitate to call some individuals' moral behavior *primitive* and others' moral behavior *advanced*. They are even less pleased about such labeling when it is implicit that advanced is somehow better than primitive.* Especially provocative has been the tendency of many developmentalists to compare the thinking of individuals in other cultures to that of individuals in our own society. Kohlberg (1969), for example, has compared the moral judgment of adults in other societies (Turkey, Taiwan, rural Mexico) to that of children and adolescents in the United States. He has gone as far as to suggest that the upper stages of his moral judgment system may never be reached in these "primitive" cultures. Such cross-cultural comparisons derive from a rich developmental tradition that has included speculations about mental growth in general by Piaget (1929), Werner (1948), and also by the anthropologist Levi-Bruhl (1910). Even more than the others, however, Kohlberg has tempted storms of controversy by bringing such speculation into the emotional realm of morality and ethics. Speaking for many with similar doubts, Simpson has written, "...the definition of [Kohlberg's] stages and the assumptions underlying them, including the view that the scheme is universally applicable, are ethnocentric and culturally biased" (1974, p. 81). In an impassioned plea for respecting cultural differences in moral judgment, she concluded:

*Many are particularly infuriated by the notion that individuals *themselves* may be ranked on a scale from primitive to advanced. But structural-developmental theory does not stage *individuals*, but rather, their *behavior*. Describing an individual's performance as primitive during a particular event does not necessarily imply anything about that person; although it may be of interest to determine whether or not the individual is *capable* of more advanced behavior in other contexts.

We would do better to explore and analyze differences wherever found, to borrow and adapt, and to nurture invention and cultural mutation as it occurs than to perpetuate the ideology of a suicidal world trying to reconcile its differences through the use of a theoretical framework ill-suited for containing and ordering real human diversity. (p. 103).

Probably the most renowned attack on such cross-cultural comparisons, and ultimately on the very distinction of primitive/advanced itself, has come from the anthropologist, Levi-Strauss (1969). He made two main points. First, he pointed out that there was more similarity than meets the eye between "primitive" and "advanced" thinking. For example, all persons, whether child or adult, savage or civilized, organize their world according to basic forms of categorization, such as grouping things on the basis of similarity and constructing oppositions on the basis of contrast. Second, he claimed that the differences that do exist are best conceptualized as distinct yet *parallel* means of coping with different kinds of environments, rather than as more adequate or less adequate modes of dealing with the world in general. (*See* Damon [1977, pp. 8-14] for a critique of Levi-Strauss's position.)

In a capsule, my own view is that there is more validity to this sort of antidevelopmental critique when it is applied to cross-cultural comparisons than when it is applied to comparisons between different periods of ontogenesis. Comparing the developmental status of different societies is certainly a tricky business, particularly when we must evaluate these societies through the filters of our own linguistic and cultural limitations. But as for the study of different individuals of different ages within our own society, it does seem that, with the aid of carefully planned methodologies, we should be able to witness developmental improvements in individuals' moral behavior during the course of ontogenesis. In such cases, the dimension of primitive/advanced is a useful and necessary means of describing key differences between different behavioral patterns. But the phrase *carefully planned methodologies* must be emphasized here. In studying young children, we must not make the mistake that has marred cross-cultural research—that is, we must not allow the incidental features of our own adult social world to distort the way in which we view childhood social knowledge. We must not, for example, overlook the genuine competencies of young children by observing only their responses to adult-centered tasks. This was the gist of my earlier criticism of Kohlberg's methodology. For a valid developmental analysis, each ontogenetic period must be studied on its own terms, in the context of the social problems, issues, and concerns normally dealt with by individuals during that age span. Only then may types of behavior representative of different age groups be ordered by a sequence of stages ranging from primitive to advanced.

In fact, recent research with children, adolescents, and adults has provided evidence that moral behavior can be objectively ordered on a scale from primitive to advanced during the course of ontogenesis. The first such evidence has been a number of studies establishing the greater logical adequacy of higher moral stages in comparison to lower moral stages. Some of these studies—such as that of Lee (1971)—show that the development of higher forms of moral judgment correlate with the development of higher levels of logical thinking as the child grows older. Other studies demonstrate even stronger and more specific bonds between advanced logical reasoning and advanced moral judgment. Kuhn, Langer, Kohlberg, and Haan (1977) and Tomlinson-Keasy and Keasy (1974) have reported results indicating that certain levels of logical thinking may actually be necessary for the emergence of higher moral stages. Specifically, both studies suggest that Piaget's stage of formal operations may provide a necessary condition for Kohlberg's Stages 5 and 6. I have also found great synchrony between children's positive-justice development and their early logical development. This synchrony has been demonstrated by empirical evidence of predictable parallels between children's performances on my positive-justice interview and these same children's performance on Inhelder and Piaget's concrete-operational tasks (Damon, 1975). Such studies show that logical development and moral development go hand in hand as the individual grows. This association between advanced logical abilities and the upper stages in structural-developmental stage models is one piece of objective evidence suggesting that the upper moral stages are, in some sense, improvements over the earlier stages, if only because they may be logically superior.

Aside from the data reported in these correlational studies, the logical superiority of higher moral stages over lower ones may be demonstrated by comparing low-level moral statements with high-level ones. In many cases, it can be directly observed that low-level moral statements contain logical incompatibilities that are resolved by higher-level reasoning. As examples, consider the following three statements drawn from my positive-justice research (Damon, 1977). These examples are drawn from children's responses to a story in which a teacher must decide who to give more "stars" to, a child who does well on a test but is too lazy to do homework, or a child who works hard but is not bright enough to do well on the test.

Maureen (4 years, 10 months)

Rebecca will get four stars.

And what about Peter?

I will not give him any.

Why not?

Because he doesn't act right, he did not do very well on his paper.

So Rebecca will get more stars than Peter?

And another thing is that she is bigger than Peter. Peter looks kind of funny.

What do you mean, "kind of funny"?

Well I'll bet he fools around a lot like the other boys do and runs around all the time. The girls . . . the boys aren't so nice sometimes.

Well what does that have to do with the stars on the papers?

Rececca will get the stars because she's biggest and she's a nice girl.

Why do teachers put stars on kids' papers?

Because the kids like them.

Steven (6 years, 6 months)

If Peter worked so hard, he should get two stars, and Rebecca should get two too because she did so well.

So they should both get the same amount of stars?

Yes, I think so.

Why is that?

Because they both did something good. He was a good worker, studying all night long and stuff, I'll bet he really did a lot of homework . . . Rebecca got all the answers right, you've got to give her something for that.

So if you were the teacher you would give them both two?

Yes.

Why do teachers put stars on papers in the first place?

They want to let the kids know how well they did. Parents want to know sometimes too, so they know if their kid is learning something in school

Sally (9 years, 0 months)

Rebecca will get one star for each answer she got right and Peter won't hardly get any.

Why would you do it that way?

Because Rebecca . . . well, because the stars are for getting answers right, not just for trying hard. The teacher might give Peter a special "E for effort" or something like that, that doesn't really count.

Is that the fair way to do it?

Sure, Rebecca got them all right and Peter didn't. She [the teacher] could still get mad at Rebecca for never doing any work, and then she [Rebecca] could still do better next time. But Peter can't get any stars because he got them all wrong.

Why do teachers put stars on papers?

To tell the kids in their class that they're doing all right, or that they're not doing so hot. If the kids don't know anything they can't give them stars.

Why not?

Well, if Peter knows that he got everything wrong maybe he can talk with Miss Townsend and try to learn the right way, but if he doesn't know then he won't ever do any better.

    In these three examples of children's positive justice reasoning, we can witness the logical progress that is concomitant with children's advances in moral judgment. In the first example quoted, Maureen's justice reasoning shows many features of primitive logical thought as it has been described by cognitive psychologists like Piaget and Vygotsky. For example, there is a chain-logic quality in Maureen's skipping from one criterion to another in justifying her decision to give Rebecca four stars and Peter none. First Maureen notes that Peter did poorly, then she introduces Rebecca's size, then Peter's bad conduct (or rather the bad conduct of boys in general!), and then, Rebecca's niceness. None of these criteria are coordinated in any logical fashion with each other or with the rationale behind giving stars ("Because the kids like them."). This fluctuating, inconstant use of justification is typical of the transductive logic of preoperational thought (Inhelder & Piaget, 1958). Steven's reasoning is certainly more constant, since he focuses steadily on the criteria of doing "something good" as a justification for rewarding both Rebecca and Peter with stars. But there is nevertheless an incompatibility between Steven's decision and the rationale that he presents for awarding stars to students. If, as Steven says, stars are to let students (and their parents) know how well the students are doing, logically Peter should not receive as many stars as Rebecca. Among the children quoted, only Sally is able logically to coordinate her decision with her conception of why stars are given. For Sally, it is perfectly fair to reward Rebecca and not Peter, since this is the only course that is compatible with the educational function of giving stars (as Sally sees it). Although we may or may not agree with Sally's justice decision, we cannot fault her reasoning on logical grounds. This is a clear and objective improvement over the statements made by the younger Maureen and Steven.

    Other evidence that higher moral stages represent a genuine advance over lower stages may be found in experimental moral-judgment training studies. Studies by Turiel (1966), Rest, Turiel, and Kohlberg 1969), and Rest (1973) presented subjects with moral-judgments below, at, and above the subjects' own stages. Results from these studies support the ordering of moral judgment as proposed by Kohlberg's stage system. In the first study, it was found that "subjects exposed to the stage directly above their own showed a significant use of that stage, exposure to the stage two above had no effect, and exposure to the stage below had significantly less effect than exposure to stage one above" (Turiel, 1969, p. 102). Therefore, subjects seemed to reject lower modes of moral judgment, to use modes that were at or slightly in advance of their own level, and to be unable to employ modes that were significantly ahead of their own. The other studies (Rest, Turiel, & Kohlberg, 1969; Rest, 1973) show that children preferred moral judgments one and two stages above their own to judgments one or more stages below their own. The lower-level judgments were generally rejected and even ridiculed, although these lower levels were clearly understood. In contrast, the higher-level judgments were often appreciated, but not fully comprehended: children had trouble recapitulating moral arguments two or more stages in advance of their own, even though many thought the two-stages-higher arguments to "sound" the best. Taken together, these studies indicate that, during development, children move forward along an ordered sequence of moral stages largely because the higher stages seem inherently more adequate and more attractive than do the lower stages. There are limits to this forward developmental movement, however, since children are unable to understand modes of behavior too far in advance of their current stages. Change is, thus, an orderly process, occurring one step at a time. Longitudinal data reported by Kuhn (1976) and Damon (1977) also confirm the ordered, sequence-like nature of moral change in individual children observed over a period of naturally occurring development.

Empirical evidence derived from the two types of studies described —the logical-moral studies and the moral change studies—suggests that the moral sequences proposed by structural-developmental theorists are not entirely arbitrary, subjective, or value-laden. But it should not be taken to suggest that these sequences are universally applicable to all people for all time, or even that these sequences are entirely adequate to describe moral development in our own Western society. Describing developmental structures formally and accurately is a task that has only just begun. Hopefully the future of psychological science will see improvements, revisions, and even reorganizations and "progressive rejections" of the structural descriptions on which we now rely. Developmental psychology is still a young science, and we now have at best a good first approximation of the nature and course of moral development in the individual.

CONCLUSIONS AND APPLICATION

A number of direct and indirect educational techniques have grown out of the structural-developmental study of moral development. Kohlberg has founded a Center for Moral Education at Harvard University and has produced filmstrips, discussion guides, and a wide variety of other aids for teachers. Kohlberg himself has turned a Cambridge, Massachusetts, high school into a "just school" that teaches moral concepts to its students by allowing them to make important administrative decisions and then encouraging them to discuss and reflect upon these decisions. In addition, Kohlberg has designed remediation techniques for delinquents and criminals. These techniques are currently being used in a number of prisons and half-way houses throughout the country. Sullivan, in Chapter 8, reviews these and other attempts to "teach values" by the application of psychological principles to the moral development of individuals. Whatever else can be said about these educational techniques, it is clear that we do not know nearly enough about the mysteries of moral development to be able to train all individuals to behave according to the highest principles of moral knowledge. Moral education is itself a new and almost totally untested enterprise.

My own view is that we do not need specific educational techniques to justify the scientific study of moral development. Important "application" of scientific findings can be found simply in the understanding that these findings engender. In structural-developmental writings, the stages through which moral behavior develops have been richly and carefully described. These descriptions are invaluable for anyone working with children, adolescents, or adults, or even for anyone wishing to understand more about his or her own developmental roots. Such understanding has a subtle but unmistakable influence upon the way one deals with everyday problems. A teacher recognizing early forms of moral behavior in her students, as one example, will be better able to place this behavior in perspective than will one who sees it merely as an aberration from "acceptable" standards. This does not necessarily mean that the teacher will directly apply moral-educational principles (such as conducting discussions exactly one level higher than the levels of her students). Rather it means that she will better be able to establish an atmosphere in her classroom that is sympathetic to early developmental levels, and that introduces children to alternative (and more advanced) means of resolving social problems. It may also mean that the teacher will feel more comfortable with his or her students; and that he or she will be able to distinguish normal primitive behavior from true deviation.

My favorite example of the value of such understanding comes from a story told to me by an elementary school teacher from upstate New York. The incident began with a first-grade project in which each child raised and cared for his or her own pet fish. The pet fish of one little girl died, and she was upset. She asked the teacher what would become of the fish, now that it was dead. The teacher was very sensitive to the religious implications of this question, particularly since her local school board was quite strict about keeping religion out of the classroom. The teacher said that she answered quite carefully to the effect that the fish was in no pain, but that it would no longer be with us. It would be buried, and that would be the last we would see of it. The teacher suggested that the girl raise a new one.

The very next day the teacher confronted a stern and angry principal. How, he demanded, could she tell her pupils that fish go to heaven when they die? The stunned teacher managed to get the principal to relay the following events: The little girl's irate mother had called the principal at home the previous night to complain that her daughter had come home from school making statements to the effect that, "Joey, my pet fish, died in his sleep, but Miss Henry says that it's all right—he's going to Heaven because we all love him, and he'll be happy there always." What had upset the mother so was that in her Roman Catholic tradition, there is a clear discontinuity between animals and humans. Humans have souls, animals do not; humans have afterlives, animals are gone when they die. Suggesting the existence of a heaven for fish denigrates the unique sacredness of the human soul.

Since this incident, the teacher admitted feeling persecuted and very bitter toward her pupil. Was the little girl "out to get her"? Was she being vicious and dishonest? The teacher had not a clue as to what the little girl could have against her, or why she would tell such a "malicious" (the teacher's word) lie.

My own speculation about this event is that such a story, coming from a six-year-old, should surprise no one familiar with childhood thinking. Piaget long ago described the magical and supernatural notions that underlie the thinking of young children. It is difficult to imagine how a six-year-old girl would organize her knowledge about the period after life without employing some notion of a heaven or a hell. Clearly these notions will be realistic (in the sense that heaven and hell are seen to be real, physically constituted places). A young child is incapable of more abstract versions of such notions. In addition, it is not surprising that conceptual boundaries like the difference between the supernatural and the natural, or the difference between creatures with souls and creatures without souls, might be blurred in early childhood. In short, there was no need whatsoever for the teacher to introduce the concept of a heaven for fish to her six-year-old pupil (once the girl had already been introduced to the notion of heaven in general). The girl was entirely capable of inventing this idea herself, as a function of the way that she quite naturally organized her thinking about afterlives and living creatures. In fact, not only was the child capable of such an invention; in some sense it was inevitable that she would construct this or a similar invention, regardless of what an adult would tell her. I believe that an awareness of this and other idiosyncrasies of early development enables adults to work more comfortably in their relations with children and adolescents. It is just such an awareness that developmental psychology, at its best, is able to offer.

REFERENCES

Berkowitz, L. *Development of motives and values in the child.* New York: Macmillan, Inc., 1964.

Blurton-Jones, N. (Ed.). *Ethological studies of child behavior.* Cambridge, England: Cambridge University Press, 1972.

Brown, R., & Herrnstein, R. *Psychology.* Boston: Little, Brown & Company, 1975.

Burton, R. V. The generality of honesty reconsidered. *Psychological Review,* 1963, *70,* 481-499.

Damon, W. Early conceptions of positive justice as related to the development of logical operations. *Child Development,* 1975, *46,* 301-312.

Damon, W. *The social world of the child.* San Francisco: Jossey-Bass, Inc., Publishers, 1977.

Gibbs, J. Kohlberg's stages of moral judgment: A constructive critique. *Harvard Educational Review,* 1977, *47,* 43-61.

Hartshorne, H., & May, M. S. *Studies in the nature of character.* New York: Macmillan, Inc., 1928-1930.

Hoffman, M. Moral development. In P. Mussen (Ed.), *Carmichael's manual of child psychology.* New York: John Wiley & Sons, Inc., 1970.

Hogan, R. A dimension of moral judgment. *Journal of Consulting & Clinical Psychology,* 1970, *35,* 205-212.

Inhelder, B., & Piaget, J. *The growth of logical thinking from childhood to adolescence.* New York: Basic Books, 1958.

Inhelder, B., & Piaget, J. *The early growth of logic in the child.* New York: Harper, 1964.

Kohlberg, L. The development of children's orientation toward a moral order. *Vita Humana,* 1963, *6,* 11-33.

Kohlberg, L. Stage and sequence: The cognitive-developmental approach to socialization. In D. Goslin (Ed.), *Handbook of socialization theory and research.* New York: Rand McNally & Company, 1969.

Kohlberg, L. From is to ought: How to commit the naturalistic fallacy and get away with it in the study of moral development. In T. Mischel (Ed.), *Cognitive development and epistemology.* New York: Academic Press, 1971.

Kohlberg, L., & Kramer, R. Continuities and discontinuities in childhood and adult moral development. *Human Development,* 1969, *12,* 93-120.

Kuhn, D. Short-term longitudinal evidence for the sequentiality of Kohlberg's early stages of moral judgment. *Developmental Psychology,* 1976, *12,* 162-167.

Kuhn, D., Langer, J., Kohlberg, L., & Haan, N. The development of formal operations in logical and moral judgments. *Genetic Psychology Monographs,* 1977, *95,* 97-188.

Kurtines, W., & Greif, E. B. The development of moral thought: Review and evaluation of Kohlberg's approach. *Psychological Bulletin,* 1974, *81,* 453-470.

Lee, L. C. The concomitant development of cognitive and moral modes of thought: A test of selected deductions from Piaget's theory. *Genetic Psychology Monographs,* 1971, *83,* 93-146.

68   *Structural-Developmental Theory and Moral Development*

Levi-Bruhl, C. *How natives think.* New York: Washington Square Press, 1910.

Levi-Strauss, C. *Elementary structures of kinship.* Boston: Beacon Press, 1969.

Lieberman, M. Introduction to standard scoring manual (Kohlberg's moral judgment system) Manuscript in preparation, Harvard University.

Loevinger, J. *Ego development.* San Francisco: Jossey-Bass, Inc., Publishers, 1976.

Nucci, L. & Turiel, E. Social interactions and the development of social concepts in preschool children. *Child Development,* 1978, *49,* 400-407.

Piaget, J. *The child's conception of the world.* London: Routledge and Kegan Paul, 1929.

Piaget, J. *The moral judgment of the child.* New York: Harcourt, Brace, 1932.

Piaget, J. *Plays, dreams and imitation.* New York: W. W. Norton & Co., 1951.

Piaget, J. *Six psychological studies.* New York: Random House, Inc., 1967.

Piaget J. *Le problème de stade en psychologie de l'enfant.* Paris: Presses Univ. de France, 1968.

Rest, J. Patterns of preference and comprehension in moral judgment. *Journal of Personality,* 1973, *41,* 86-109.

Rest, J., Turiel, E., & Kohlberg, L. Relations between level of moral judgment and preference and comprehension of the moral judgment of others. *Journal Personality,* 1969, *37,* 225-252.

Saltzstein, H. D., Diamond, R. M., & Belenky, M. Moral judgment level and conformity behavior. *Developmental Psychology,* 1972, *7,* 327-336.

Simpson, E. Moral development research: A case of scientific cultural bias. *Human Development,* 1974, *17,* 81-106.

Tomlinson-Keasy, C., & Keasy, C. B. The mediating role of cognitive development in moral judgment. *Child Development,* 1974, *45,* 291-298.

Turiel, E. An experimental test of the sequentiality of developmental stages in the child's moral judgments. *Journal of Personality & Social Psychology,* 1966, *3,* 611-618.

Turiel, E. Developmental processes in the child's moral thinking. In P. Mussen, J. Langer, & M. Covington (Eds.). *Trends and issues in developmental psychology.* New York: Holt, Rinehart, and Winston, 1969.

Turiel, E. Conflict and transition in adolescent moral development. *Child Development,* 1974, *45,* 14-29.

Turiel, E. The development of social concepts. In D. DePalma & J. Foley (Eds.), *Moral development.* Hillsdale, N.J.: Lawrence Erlbaum Associates, 1975.

Turiel, E., & Rothman, G. The influence of reasoning on behavioral choices at different stages of moral development. *Child Development,* 1972, *43,* 741-756.

Werner, H. *Comparative psychology of mental development.* New York: Science Editions, 1948.

Wohlwill, J. *The study of behavioral development.* New York: Academic Press, 1973.

3

The Development
of Social-Conventional
and Moral Concepts

ELLIOT TURIEL

The topic of this chapter is somewhat different from those of the other chapters in this volume. While all the others deal mainly with moral development, the primary emphasis here is on the development of concepts of social convention and on the basis for distinguishing social convention from morality. Concepts of social convention stem from the child's efforts at understanding social systems. From a relatively young age, children partake in social groups and social organizations. In the process of such interactions, children develop a sociological orientation through which they form concepts of culture and social organization. A central aspect of interaction in social systems is the normative regulation reflected in *conventionally* shared behaviors; as part of their understanding of social organization, children develop concepts of social conventions. Through their social interactions children also develop moral judgments, which are prescriptions about behavior.

Therefore, two separate questions require investigation: (1) How does the individual think about culture and social organization? (2) How does the individual make moral judgments? In turn, these two questions require separate developmental analyses. This chapter deals with theory and research pertaining to these two issues, from the perspective of a structural-developmental approach. The structural-developmental approach is also represented in this book by Damon (*see* Chapter 2) and Rothman (*see* Chapter 4) in their discussions of moral judgment and behavior. Basic to this framework are the following propositions, which apply not only to social development but also to other aspects of cognitive development (cf. Kaplan, 1966; Langer, 1969a; Piaget, 1947/1950, 1970; Piaget & Inhelder, 1969; Strauss, 1972; Werner, 1948): (1) The individual's development progresses through a series of organized structures of thought and action, which (2) are transformed in an ordered way through (3) interaction with the social and physical environments. This approach is termed *structural-developmental* because it rests on analyses of the organization of thought and action and of the transformations that structures undergo in development. Mental structures define the ways the child actively organizes experiences, and out of efforts at active organization of experience, structural changes occur (Inhelder, Sinclair, & Bovet, 1974; Langer, 1969b; Snyder & Feldman, 1977; Strauss, 1972; Turiel, 1973, 1974, 1977).

Approaching the development of social concepts from a structural viewpoint implies that children construct social concepts that form organized patterns. Social judgments are not determined by environmental content, but are constructions stemming from the individual's *interactions* with the environment. Development involves progress through a series of organized structures, not derived directly from the environment, but generated out of interaction with the environment. This interactional thesis was formulated by Piaget: "Knowledge, at its origin, neither arises from objects nor from the subject, but from interactions—at first inextricable—between the subject and those objects" (Piaget, 1970, p. 704). Piaget's proposition is that the development of knowledge is not a function of direct instruction: "Each time one prematurely teaches a child something he could have discovered himself, that child is kept from inventing it and consequently from understanding it completely" (Piaget, 1970, p. 715).

As both Damon and Rothman maintain in their chapters, within the structural approach, moral development is not seen as a process of internalizing socially acceptable behaviors or cultural values. Rather, it is seen as a construction of concepts of right or wrong or of justice. Moreover, I take the position that if morality is to be viewed as involving judgmental processes, then it is necessary that moral judgments be distinguished from other forms of social judgments, particularly from judgments about the conventions of social systems.

The role of convention in social organization has been differentiated from that of morality by the sociologist, Max Weber (1922/1947). Weber actually identified three categories of social action: custom, convention, and ethics. He used the term *custom* to refer to actions that are performed with some regularity, but that do not serve a social-organizational function and are, thus, readily alterable. Consequently, customs are not regulated by external sanctions: "Today it is customary every morning to eat a breakfast which, within limits, conforms to a certain pattern. But there is no obligation to do so" (Weber, 1922/1947, p. 122). In contrast, conventions are a significant aspect of the "legitimate order" of social organization and are regulated by sanctions:

The term *convention* will be employed to designate that part of the custom followed within a given social group which is recognized as "binding" and protected against violation by sanctions of disapproval . . . . Conformity with convention in such matters of the usual forms of greeting, the mode of dress recognized as appropriate or respectable, and various of the rules governing the restrictions on social intercourse, both in form and in content, is very definitely expected of the individual and regarded as binding on him. (pp. 127-128).

In turn, the conventional is distinct from the ethical:

Every system of ethics which has in a sociological sense become validly established is likely to be upheld to a large extent by the probability that disapproval will result in its violation, that is, by convention. On the other hand, it is by no means necessary that all conventionally or legally guaranteed forms of order should claim the authority of ethical norms. (p. 130).

SOCIAL CONVENTION AS DISTINCT
FROM MORALITY

At this point brief definitions of the terms *social convention* and *morality* are in order. By social convention I am referring to behavioral uniformities that coordinate interactions of individuals within social systems. Thus, social conventions constitute shared knowledge of uniformities in social interactions and are determined by the social system in which they are formed. Some illustrative examples of social-conventional acts include uniformities in modes of dress, usages of forms of address (e.g., first name or titles plus last name), and modes of greeting. Research has shown that these types of conventional uniformities are based on accepted usage and are regulated by social organization. For instance, it has been found (Brown & Gilman, 1960; Slobin, Miller, & Porter, 1968) that usage of forms of address reflects the relative social status of individuals within a social organization. Forms of address are regulated by the social relations between the speaker and addressee, which in turn are partially regulated by the social structure. These conclusions are based on analyses of pronouns of address (e.g., *tu* or *vous* in French) in a number of languages in different historical contexts (Brown & Gilman, 1960), as well as on uses of first names or titles (Brown & Ford, 1961) in a variety of contexts (e.g., usage in modern American plays and in business firms). Furthermore, it has been shown that modes of greeting in Mexican (Foster, 1964) and African (Goody, 1972) societies serve to affirm social status and maintain different levels of social distance between individuals.

Social conventional acts in themselves are arbitrary, in that they do not have an intrinsically prescriptive basis—in other words, alternative courses of action can serve similar functions. A conventional uniformity within one social unit may serve the same function as a different conventional uniformity in another social system. Consider, for example, conventional uniformities regarding modes of dress. Typically, formal attire (e.g., suit and tie) is worn in certain social contexts (e.g., a business firm or place of religious worship) and the content of this conventional uniformity is arbitrarily designated. Uniform modes of dress other than a suit and tie could just as well be designated as appropriate for the business office or church.

In the case of conventions, therefore, the content of the regularity can be varied without altering the functions served; conventional uniformities are defined relative to the social-situational context. Accordingly, within the conventional domain, only violations of implicit or explicit regulations would be regarded as transgressions. For an individual to regard a particular act as a transgression, he or she would have to possess culture-specific information about the act's status as a socially determined regularity. This is not the case in the moral domain. Within the moral domain, actions are not arbitrary, and the existence of a social regulation is not necessary for an individual to view an event as a transgression. For example, when one person hits another, thereby causing physical harm, perception of that event as a transgression stems from features intrinsic to the event (e.g., from a perception of the consequences to the victim). Thus, moral issues are not relative to the social context, nor are they determined by social regulations.

The distinction between convention and morality implies a narrow definition of morality as justice. The proposition is that children develop concepts of justice, which apply to a relatively limited range of issues, including the value of life, physical and psychological harm to others, trust, and responsibility. In contrast to convention, moral considerations stem from factors intrinsic to actions, such as their consequences (e.g., physical and psychological harm to others, violation of rights, effects on the general welfare, etc.). On this basis we can distinguish between (1) convention, which is part of social systems, as structured by an underlying conceptualization of social organization: and (2) morality, which is structured by an underlying conceptualization of justice (cf. Damon, this book; Piaget, 1932/1948; Kohlberg, 1969; Turiel, 1974).

Theories of Moral Development

Research into the development of concepts of social convention is important in its own right as a means of explaining a central aspect of the child's understanding of the social world. In addition, such study has a bearing upon our understanding of moral development. As Richard Brandt stated in his philosophical overview of *Ethical Theory:*

Some branches of the more experimental social sciences also do, or should, draw on the concepts and distinctions that metaethics aims to criticize and clarify, particularly those parts of anthropology, sociology and psychology that are concerned with values and attitudes and conscience . . . . Some scientists have no criterion for distinguishing between ethical beliefs or judgments and nonethical ones. Hence, in their descriptive work they mix the two together indiscriminately, missing many opportunities for observations of theoretical importance . . . . Some social scientists ignore the difference between beliefs about the good or desirable and beliefs about duty and obligation, and thereby overlook the possibility that quite different accounts of the genesis of the two may be in order. (1959, p. 12).

Carrying Brandt's position even further, it is my contention that students of moral development have traditionally failed to distinguish social convention from morality, and that this failure has been a major obstacle in social scientific explanations of morality. There have been two main trends in social scientific analyses of moral development from at least the 1920s until the present time. One trend is represented by internalization theories and the other by structural-developmental theories. In the 1920s and 1930s, some of the prominent social scientists maintaining internalization positions were Durkheim (1924/1974, 1925/1961), Freud (1923/1960, 1930/1961), and Hartshorne and May (1928-1930). The structural view, at the time, was represented by Piaget (1932/1948). More recently, the neo-behaviorists (Sears, Maccoby, & Levin, 1957; Whiting, 1960) and the social-learning theorists (Aronfreed, 1968, 1976; Grinder, 1962; Mischel & Mischel, 1976) have maintained the internalization position, while followers of Piaget have extended his explanations of moral development (Kohlberg, 1969, 1976; Lickona, 1976; Rest, 1976). Although doing so in rather different ways, both approaches have assumed that convention and morality are part of one domain and that they do not develop independently of each other. Internalization theorists, for instance, have maintained that moral development is the learning of socially acceptable behavior and the incorporation of transmitted values. By viewing social behaviors and values as the incorporation of externally determined and imposed content, theorists taking this view make no conceptual distinction between different social behaviors.

While structural theorists have maintained that moral development is *not* an internalization of values, the specific stage formulations proposed by Piaget (1932/1948) and, more recently, by Kohlberg (1969) have been based on the presumption that moral judgments apply to *all* forms of social behavior. Thus, those explanations have also fused the moral and social-conventional domains: convention is treated as a subclass of the moral domain. Piaget originally proposed that moral development proceeds through two stages (following a nonmoral or premoral phase). The first is labeled *heteronomous* (generally corresponding to ages three to eight), and the second is labeled *autonomous*. According to Piaget, the child's moral orientation develops from an attitude of unilateral respect for adult authority to relationships of mutual respect among equals. At the heteronomous level, morality is based on a nonmutual, but unilateral, respect the child feels toward adults (regarded as authority). Rules are viewed as fixed and unalterable. In turn, the social order and its adult authorities are regarded as sacred. Developmentally, the young child's morality of unilateral respect becomes transformed into a morality of cooperation and mutual respect (the autonomous level). The basis for this stage is the emergence of the concepts of reciprocity and equality. Rules are no longer regarded as fixed or sacred; rather, they are viewed as products of mutual agreement, serving the aims of cooperation, and are, thus, regarded as changeable.

Piaget's two-stage system was modified and extended by Kohlberg (1958, 1969) into a six-stage system. Summary definitions of those six stages are presented elsewhere in this book (*see* Chapter 8), and need not be repeated here. It should be noted, however, that the major modifications of Piaget's moral stage scheme made in the stages formulated by Kohlberg are: (1) at the earliest levels (Stages 1 and 2), moral judgments are based not on respect for authority and rules, but on an orientation to punishment; and (2) those early stages are followed in adolescence by levels (Stages 3 and 4) in which there is an orientation toward maintaining the rules of social groups and society. At the next levels (Stages 5 and 6), moral judgments are autonomous and based on principles that are "universal principles of justice: the equality of human rights and respect for the dignity of human beings as individual persons" (Kohlberg, 1976, p. 35).

In spite of their differences, both Piaget's and Kohlberg's formulations are based on the assumption that moral development progresses from (1) judgments in which morality and convention are undifferentiated, to (2) judgments in which the two are differentiated, with convention subordinate to morality. In both stage sequences, the most advanced forms of morality are defined as ones in which concepts of justice are differentiated from and *displace* concepts of convention. Correspondingly, in both stage sequences, lower levels of judgment are ones in which justice is undifferentiated from convention. This was stated explicitly by Piaget in the way he contrasted the heteronomous and autonomous stages:

> Law now [autonomous stage] emanates from the sovereign people and no longer from the tradition laid down by the Elders. And correlatively with this change, the respective values attaching to custom and the rights of reason come to be practically reversed. In the past [heteronomous stage] custom had always prevailed over rights. (Piaget, 1932/1948, p. 64).

> For very young children, a rule is a sacred reality because it is traditional; for the older ones it depends upon mutual agreement. (Piaget, 1932/1948, pp. 96-97).

There are two points to be noted here. One is that morality and convention are treated by Piaget as closely intertwined within one domain.

The second is that Piaget attributes a great deal to the young child; the six year old is seen as having a sense of culture, custom, and tradition.

Classification of Stimulus Events
Used in Research

If social convention is to be distinguished from morality, then it is necessary that stimulus events used in research be appropriate to the domain being investigated. That is, the use of events in the social-conventional domain would be inappropriate in research on moral judgment or behavior. This point can be illustrated through an example from a domain clearly different from the moral. Suppose that in order to investigate moral reasoning a researcher posed a series of mathematical problems to subjects of different ages. Of course, such a procedure would be questionable; we could not be at all confident that subjects in the study had engaged in moral reasoning. The inadequacy of using mathematical problems to study moral development is quite apparent, and as far as I know no one has done so. Similarly, the adequacy of many types of social situations used by moral development researchers is open to question. As one example, in an experiment (Stein, 1967) on the role of imitation in moral development, children were assigned to do a boring task while a very attractive film was being shown in the same room. Children who left their assigned task to look at the film were considered to have violated a moral standard. The researcher classified "duty and responsibility in performing a job" as a moral standard on the grounds that such behavior reflects a moral value of the society. It is not self-evident, however, that the performance of an assigned task is a valid measure of moral behavior. Does it reflect a moral standard or a nonmoral standard which relates to social and economic organization?

Another example comes from an often-used experimental paradigm for studying children's acquisition of moral behavior. Children's behaviors in response to a prohibition against playing with designated toys are measured. This paradigm has been labeled the *forbidden toy paradigm*. The basic experimental event is one in which the child is prohibited by an experimenter from touching or playing with certain toys that are available in the experimental room. (Generally, the subject is prohibited from playing with the more attractive of pairs of toys.) The effects of a number of variables on the internalization of the (presumed) moral prohibition have been studied. These have included nurturance (Parke, 1967; Parke & Walters, 1967), modeling (Parke & Walters, 1967; Slaby & Parke, 1971; Walters, Parke & Cane, 1965), intensity and timing of punishment (Aronfreed, 1966; Aronfreed & Reber, 1965; Parke & Walters, 1967; Walters, Parke, & Cane, 1965), and verbal instructions (Aronfreed, 1966; Cheyne, 1971; Cheyne, Goyeche, & Walters, 1969; Cheyne & Walters, 1969; Stouwie, 1971). In the usual procedure, the child is left alone with the toys used in the experimental treatments; thereby, a measure is obtained of the degree of internalization of the response (i.e., resistance to the temptation to play with the prohibited toys). From the viewpoint of the convention/morality distinction, the forbidden toy paradigm would not be classified as a moral situation. The prohibition against playing with a designated toy is an arbitrary restriction established by the experimenter for the experimental situation. An experimenter could just as well, without altering the moral value of the act, establish the opposite prohibition and restrict the child from playing with the less attractive toys. The restrictions placed upon the child are related solely to the scientific aims of the experiment: how the child responds to a prohibition when there is presumably some temptation to violate it. Given the arbitrary (nonmoral) nature of the restriction imposed, it is likely that children would view the restriction as a rule or convention specific to the social interactions of the experimental situation.

Several other events of questionable status have been used ostensibly to study moral judgment and behavior. In one case, children's concepts of game rules were used as a means of assessing moral judgments (Piaget, 1932/1948). In other cases, events involving material damage to objects were used to study moral judgments (Piaget, 1932/1948), as well as the moral emotion of guilt (Aronfreed, 1963; Aronfreed, Cutick, & Fagen, 1963).

In sum, an adequate understanding of the individual's social development requires both delineation of domains of social concepts and specification of the domain of social stimulus events. When faced with a social stimulus, the subject's response is, in part, determined by the nature of the event. Generally, the individual applies social-conventional concepts to certain types of events and moral concepts to other types of events. The use of stimuli that do not correspond to the conceptual domain being studied (as has often been the case) is likely to produce inaccurate results. Consequently, the choice of stimulus events in research should be based on criteria (Turiel, 1978a) for their appropriateness to the domain of the social concept or behavior under investigation.

SOCIAL DOMAINS AND CONCEPTS OF SOCIAL RULES

As stated earlier, previous structural-developmental explanations of moral development (i.e., those of Piaget and Kohlberg) have not distinguished between morality and social convention. It is my contention that those explanations have defined the moral domain in too broad a fashion. An adequate application of the principles of structural-developmental theory requires that distinctions be made between different aspects of social concepts. It will be recalled that one of the premises of the structural approach is that concepts are constructions stemming from the individual's interactions with the environment. This is to say that the child's concepts are formed out of his or her actions upon the environment; to form concepts about objects and events, the child must act upon them. In turn, interactions with fundamentally different types of objects and events would result in the production of different conceptual frameworks (Turiel, 1975). More specifically, social-conventional concepts originate from experiences that are distinguishable from experiences that produce moral concepts. For instance, experiences with distribution of goods and infliction of harm or theft would relate to moral development, while experiences with social order, rules, or being different from the group would relate to developing concepts of social convention.

A recently completed study (Nucci & Turiel, 1978) demonstrates how young children's social interactions revolving around social-conventional events may differ from their interactions around moral events. In this study, observations of social behaviors were made in ten different preschools. In these schools the social class backgrounds of the children and the teachers' instructional and socialization practices varied. At each school an observer tape-recorded narrative descriptions of a series of naturally occurring events that entailed social-conventional and moral transgressions. (The described events were reliably classified as social-conventional or moral.) For each of these events, the observer rated the responses made by children and adults to the transgressions. These ratings were done on a checklist that contained a listing of categories of potential responses (statements pertaining to injury or loss, emotional reactions, rationales; statements about feelings of others, physical reactions; statements about disorder, rules and sanctions, and commands). The observer tallied the number of responses displayed in each observed event.

The frequencies of responses on the category checklist showed that the types of social interactions associated with moral transgressions differed from those associated with social-conventional transgressions. In the first place, children were much more likely to respond to moral transgressions than to social-conventional transgressions; children and adults responded at about equal frequencies to moral transgressions. Moral transgressions frequently produced direct communications (regarding injury or loss and emotional reactions) by the victim to the transgressor. The children's responses revolved around the intrinsic consequences of actions and often resulted in direct feedback regarding the effects of the acts upon the victim. Adult responses to moral transgressions complemented the responses initiated by children. Adults often responded either by pointing out to the transgressor the effects of his actions upon the victim or by encouraging the victim to do so.

Adults responded to children's social-conventional transgressions differently from the way they responded to children's moral transgressions. Adult responses to social-conventional events consisted mainly of communications focusing on aspects of the social order of the school. In large part, such communication entailed commands to refrain from violating norms and statements specifying school rules. Adult responses to social-conventional transgressions also focused on the maintenance of classroom order.

These findings suggest that the social context for learning social-conventional concepts may differ from that related to the learning of moral concepts. In other words, the types of social interactions experienced by the children differed according to the domain of the transgression. However, these findings do not demonstrate that the two domains constitute different conceptual systems in children's development. In that regard, it is necessary to show that children of different ages indeed do make the distinction. In explaining conceptual development, it is not sufficient (although it is necessary) to draw distinctions on definitional or philosophical grounds. As the concern here is with structure and development in ontogenesis, the issue in question requires empirical investigation.

A recent series of studies on individuals' concepts of rules pertaining to moral and social-conventional acts provide support for the proposition that the distinction between the two domains is made across developmental levels. The findings of these studies speak to a second issue as well: namely, how do children understand social rules. Social rules and regulations constitute a pervasive and important aspect of the child's social environment. From an early age the child deals with rules—in the home, in the school, among peers, and in the broader societal context. Undoubtedly, social rules influence the child's behavior and contribute to development. To understand the influence of rules on development, it is necessary to keep in mind that a rule always pertains to an action (or class of actions) and, as I have maintained, actions can be classified according to domain. It follows, therefore, that the meanings and functions attributed by individuals to rules would vary on the basis of the act to which the rule pertains; the meaning attributed to moral acts would be different from the meaning attributed to rules pertaining to social-conventional acts.

This point can be illustrated by considering an example of a child's responses to questions about rights to possessions. It will be recalled that social-conventional acts, in themselves, are defined as arbitrary and as having no intrinsically prescriptive basis independent of social organization. Rules related to moral acts, however, are not defined by their social context, but by factors intrinsic to actions. Consider the following responses made by a ten-year-old boy who was questioned about a story in which an adolescent had cheated an old man out of money (taken from Turiel, 1979). The subject was asked whether or not taking the man's money would be wrong if no rule prohibited such cheating and if everyone agreed it was acceptable.

I still think that would be wrong.

Why?

Because you're still cheating the old man. It doesn't matter whether he's stupid enough or not, and it's not really fair to take the money.

What do you mean, it's not fair to steal?

It's not nice to do it, because maybe he needs it too.

What if the rule were changed about calling people by their first names so that everybody could call their teachers by their first names? Do you think it would be right or wrong in that case to do it?

I think it would be all right then because the rule is changed. Right? And everybody else would probably be doing it too.

How come the two things are different?

Because it's sort of a different story. Cheating an old man, you should never do that, even if everybody says you can. You should still never cheat off an old man.

These responses illustrate that the relation between a moral act and a rule is conceptualized differently from the relationship between a conventional act and rule. In the moral domain, the regulations are explicit formulations of prescriptions, and thus the rule stems from the act to which it pertains. Consider as an example, a rule prohibiting theft. Such a rule stems from the judgment that it is wrong to take someone else's possessions. The rule, therefore, is an explicit formulation of a prescription regarding the justice or injustice of an action. If an act is intrinsically valued, then a rule pertaining to the act will be viewed as unchangeable and universally desirable. Furthermore, the aims served by the rule will not be regarded as specific to a given social context.

In the social-conventional domain, in contrast, the rule does not stem from the act to which it pertains. A rule is an explicit formulation of the convention. Thus, the uniformity leads to the rule, which guides the action. Since this aim can be served by a variety of actions, such rules will be viewed as changeable and relative to their social context.

Studies have been done with subjects of various ages on the ways they view the relation between acts and rules. One finding comes from the Nucci and Turiel study (1978). Preschool children were questioned about the spontaneously occurring moral and social-conventional events that they had witnessed. The children were asked whether or not the act would be wrong if there were no rule in the school pertaining to the act. When questioned about social-conventional events, in 81 percent of the cases the children stated that the act would be all right if no school rule existed. When questioned about moral events, in 86 percent of the cases the children stated that the act would not be right even if no rule existed.

In a study by Nucci (1977) the subjects were of a wider age range—from 7 to 19 years. They were presented with a series of statements describing transgressions of rules pertaining to moral and social-conventional acts. Subjects were then requested to select those statements which described acts that they considered "wrong regardless of the absence of a rule." At all ages, subjects selected almost all the statements depicting moral transgressions and only a very few of the statements depicting social-conventional transgressions.

One additional study (Turiel, 1978b) dealt with conceptions of the relativity of rules. Subjects ranging from 6 to 17 years of age were interviewed about a variety of moral and social—conventional rules, some of which they themselves had generated (e.g., rules in their homes and schools) and some of which the experimenter had presented (e.g., a rule prohibiting theft). They were questioned about their view of the relativity of those rules (e.g., suppose there is another country in which the rules do not exist?). As expected, it was found that subjects discriminated between the two types of rules. Most subjects, at all ages, regarded the conventional rules as legitimately changeable from one setting to another. But they did not regard the moral rules as legitimately changeable from setting to setting. The most striking finding was that the large majority of subjects at every age stated: (1) that it would *not* be right for a social system to have no rule regarding theft, and (2) that it would be wrong to steal even if there were no rule prohibiting stealing.*

Taken together, the findings from these studies on social rules demonstrate that the distinction between morality and convention is made across developmental levels. It appears, therefore, that concepts of social convention and moral concepts develop in parallel fashion. Having thus presented some evidence regarding the ways in which the two domains are distinguished, I can now turn to other research which has focused directly on the form and development of concepts of social convention.

CONCEPTS OF SOCIAL CONVENTION

The development of concepts of social convention has been studied through interviews with children, adolescents, and young adults. In that research, the method termed the *clinical method* by Piaget (1928) was used. In the clinical method the subject is administered a semi-structured interview designed to obtain information about the form of reasoning, rather than just the conclusions or attitudes held (content). The interview

---

*In the Turiel (1978b) study, subjects were also questioned about rules in games. Regardless of age, subjects stated that game rules were changeable and specific to the functions of the game. Therefore, the meaning and function attributed to game rules by children is different from the meaning and function attributed to moral rules. As was stated in the previous section, assessments of children's concepts of game rules have been used as a means of assessing moral judgments (Piaget, 1932/1948). However, these findings show that the use of game rules is not an appropriate way to study moral development. *See* Turiel, 1978a for further discussion.

contains questions aimed at stimulating the subject to explain the basis for his or her conclusions as fully as possible. Accordingly, the interviewer probes in such a way as to obtain the type of information adequate to an analysis of the organization of thought.* (For more extensive discussions of the rationale behind the clinical method, *see* Damon, 1977; Piaget, 1928/1960; Turiel, 1969; and Chapter 2 in this book.)

In the study of social convention (Turiel, 1978a), 110 subjects aged 6 to 25 years were administered an interview that revolved around a series of hypothetical stories. Each of these stories dealt with a form of conventional usage, about which subjects were extensively probed. The stories dealt with: (1) forms of address (a boy who wants to call teachers in school by their first names), (2) modes of dress (dressing casually in a business office), (3) sex-associated occupations (a boy who wants to become a nurse caring for infants when he grows up), (4) patterns of family living arrangements in different cultures (fathers living apart from the rest of the family), and (5) modes of eating (with hands or with knife and fork). I can provide a concrete example of the type of story used in the interview by referring to the situation dealing with forms of address. The story concerns a boy, brought up by his parents to call people by their first names, who is expected to address teachers in his new school by their formal titles. He comes into conflict with the teachers and the principal who insist that he use titles and last names rather than first names.

---

*It is essential to understand that the clinical interview method is based on different methodological criteria from those of the method of standardized testing (i.e., the method used in IQ tests and most personality tests). Unlike the clinical method, standardized tests are designed to elicit answers from the subject (such as an answer to a mathematical problem), without analysis of the form of reasoning that produced the answer. Again unlike the clinical method, standardized tests yield a score reflecting some quantitative assessment of the testee's capacity or trait (such as an IQ score). The clinical method, and the theory from which it stems, is based on contrasting assumptions. For instance, early in his career Piaget concluded that standardized tests did not yield sufficient information regarding the reasoning used by the individual to arrive at his or her answers. Piaget concluded that investigation of the nature or form of thinking required an alternative method to standardized testing and, thus, he formulated the "clinical method."

Clearly, the differences in theoretical assumptions and methodological criteria between the clinical method and standardized tests are fundamental ones. Unfortunately, these differences are not always understood. I have in mind an article by Kurtines and Greif (1974) in which they purport to critically evaluate Kohlberg's methods for assessing moral judgments. However, Kurtines and Greif evaluated Kohlberg's structural theory, which is based on data obtained through the clinical method, using criteria derived from standardized testing. They committed a major fallacy by evaluating one methodology with criteria from an alternative methodology. Moreover, they evaluated a structural theory with some criteria explicitly rejected by structural theorists in their alternative methodology. I do not mean to say that is is not legitimate to debate the relative merits of the criteria of one approach over those of another. But Kurtines and Greif did not do this. Instead, they accepted the tenets of one approach as if they were absolute, and then mechanically applied them to another (contrasting) approach. This procedure is scientifically untenable since the methodology evaluated was designed to meet empirical objectives different from most of the criteria used in the evaluation. It can be safely assumed that conclusions derived from scientifically illegitimate procedures hold no scientific weight.

The analyses of responses to the interview showed that there is a progression in social-conventional concepts from childhood through early adulthood. This progression is characterized through the seven ordered levels that are summarized in Table 3-1. It should be noted that the progression, represented by the levels summarized in Table 3-1, is not one of straightforward linear development. Rather, the pattern of development is one in which there is a series of oscillations between *affirmation* and *negation* of convention and social structure. Each affirmation entails a construction of concepts of conventions and social structure. Each phase of affirmation is followed by negation of the validity of that construction. In turn, each phase of negation leads to a new construction of concepts of convention and social structure.

The forms of affirmation and negation vary from level to level. At all of the levels, however, conventions are understood to be social constructions. Throughout the levels, two factors are salient: one is the conceived arbitrariness of social-conventional acts, and the other is the conceptual connections made between such acts and the social context. At each of the levels, conventional acts are (1) viewed, in some sense, as arbitrary, and (2) related to a conception of social structure. The phases of affirmation of convention entail the formation of concepts of social structure. The phases of negation of convention entail reevaluation of the social structure conception of the previous level. Development within this domain progresses toward viewing conventions as shared knowledge of uniformities in interactions within the social systems and toward viewing such uniformities as functional to the coordination of social interactions.

In what follows, each of the levels is described and corresponding illustrative responses are provided. I will keep the descriptions brief and limit the number of subject responses (all of which are taken from Turiel, 1978a) used to illustrate the levels. A fuller description can be found in Turiel (1978a).

First Level: Convention as Descriptive of Social Uniformity

It is necessary to begin the description of the first level with a cautionary statement. The data supporting an explanation of the social-conventional concepts of six or seven year olds are still quite limited. The younger children in this sample were administered a short interview containing only two of the hypothetical stories. (This caution applies to the description of the second level, as well.) Those subjects were given a less extensive interview than the rest because a highly verbal procedure could only be used in limited ways with children of those ages. (Young children's thinking is currently being studied by using methods less dependent upon verbal explanations.)

Table 3-1. Major changes in social-conventional concepts.

Level	Description	Approximate Ages
1	*Convention as descriptive of social uniformity.* Convention is viewed as being descriptive of uniformities in behavior. Convention is not conceived as part of the structure or function of social interaction. Conventional uniformities are descriptive of what is assumed to exist. Convention is maintained to avoid violation of empirical uniformities.	6-7
2	*Negation of convention as descriptive of social uniformity.* Empirical uniformity is not seen as a sufficient basis for maintaining conventions. Conventional acts are regarded as arbitrary. Convention is not conceived as part of the structure or function of social interaction.	8-9
3	*Convention as affirmation of the rule system; early concrete conception of the social system.* Convention is seen as arbitrary and changeable. Adherence to convention is based on concrete rules and authoritative expectations. One's conception of conventional acts is not coordinated with the conception of rules.	10-11
4	*Negation of convention as part of the rule system.* Convention is now seen as arbitrary and changeable regardless of the rules. Evaluation of rules pertaining to conventional acts is coordinated with evaluation of the act. Conventions are "nothing but" social expectations.	12-13
5	*Convention as mediated by the social system.* Systematic concepts of social structure emerge. Convention is regarded as normative regulation in a social system built on uniformity, fixed roles, and static hierarchical organization.	14-16
6	*Negation of convention as societal standards.* Convention is regarded as codified societal standards. Uniformity in convention is not considered to serve the function of maintaining the social system. Conventions are "nothing but" societal standards that exist through habitual use.	17-18
7	*Convention as coordination of social interactions.* Conventions are regarded as uniformities that are functional in coordinating social interactions. Shared knowledge, in the form of conventions, among members of social groups facilitates interaction and operation of the social system.	18-25

One of the stories used with these young subjects dealt with forms of address (described earlier in this section). The other story dealt with a young boy who claims that he wants to become a nurse and care for infants when he grows up; his father thinks that he should not do so.

Let's begin the description of this level with presentation of some responses made by a six year old. The basis of conventional thinking at this level is in the assumption, and interpretation, of the existence of descriptive social uniformities.

First the responses to the story dealing with forms of address:

Joan (6 years:10 months)

Should Peter call his teachers by their first names?

He is wrong because if like if everyone called her Mrs. Loomis, and he called her by her first name, she expects to be called Mrs. Loomis instead.

Why is that better than by her first name?

Because it sounds a little bit better and everyone else calls her Mrs. Loomis.

What if he wants to do something different than everyone else does, do you think he would be right or wrong in calling her Carol instead of Mrs. Loomis?

No, wrong. Because if everyone else calls her Loomis, she would want him to call her Loomis and like when he says hey Carol, and not Mrs. Loomis, it would sound different.

Do you think it matters if you call people by first names or Mr. or Mrs. or doctor, do you think it makes a difference?

Yes. If you were Mrs. and they called you Miss, it would be wrong because you would be married.

What if they called me Helen instead of Mrs., what would you think of that? Does it make a difference?

Yes. Helen is a girl's name.

The following responses were made to the story dealing with the boy who wants to become a nurse.

Joan

Should he become a nurse?

Well, no because he could easily be a doctor and he could take care of babies in the hospital.

Why shouldn't he be a nurse?

Well, because a nurse is a lady and the boys, the other men would just laugh at them.

Why shouldn't a man be a nurse?

Well, because it would be sort of silly because ladies wear those kind of dresses and those kind of shoes and hats.

What is the difference between doctors and nurses?

Doctors take care of them most and nurses just hand them things.

Do you think his father was right?

Yes. Because well, a nurse, she typewrites and stuff and all that.

The man should not do that?

No. Because he would look silly in a dress.

Insofar as social convention has relevance to the thinking of subjects at this level, it is related to the meaning attributed to what they perceive to be uniformities in behavior. Uniformities in social behavior are not understood to be regulations or coordinations of social interactions or part of a social system. Uniformities in behavior are descriptive of what is assumed to exist. In turn, what is assumed to exist uniformly is interpreted as necessary and requiring conservation. For instance, these subjects stated that titles are necessarily associated with certain classes of people and that occupations (nurse, doctor) are necessarily associated with the class of male or female. Thus, for these subjects, titles are not signs of role or status, nor do they serve communicative functions. Rather, titles are descriptive of the person. Titles may describe the marital status or age of an individual.

Similarly, observed behaviors or physical traits of classes of persons are interpreted as fixed and necessary for individuals within the classification. This notion was most clearly apparent in the subjects' consideration of whether or not a male could become a nurse. It was maintained that two types of (nondesirable) violations of empirical uniformity would result if a male became a nurse: type of activity and type of dress. Activities and physical characteristics (e.g., dress) serve to classify roles and persons for these subjects. The role of a nurse is defined by: (1) activities like taking care of babies, giving injections, typewriting, etc., and (2) wearing a particular kind of dress. In turn, females are defined by similar activities and types of dress. According to subjects at this level, if a male were to become a nurse, the necessary associations of activities or dress to the classes male and female would be violated because a male would be engaging in female activities and wearing female dress.

We shall see that at the next level—one of negation of social convention—it is asserted that empirical uniformity is not sufficient for judging behaviors as necessary, fixed, or requiring conservation.

Second Level: Negation of Convention as Descriptive of Social Uniformity

By about the age of eight or nine, there is a shift in children's thinking about uniformity and convention. While at the first level perceived empirical regularities are regarded as requiring specified behavior by individual actors, at the second level children cease to see empirical uniformities as implying fixed or necessary behaviors. Furthermore, children at the second level have yet to construct notions of social structure or of the functions of convention as a means for coordinating social interactions. Consequently, at this level there is a negation of the necessity for adherence to convention.

Susan (8:6)

Right, because it doesn't matter. There are men nurses in the hospitals.

What if there were not any in Joe's time, do you still think he should have done it?

Yes. It doesn't matter if it is a man or woman it is just your job taking care of little children.

How come it doesn't matter if you are a man or woman?

Like we talked about before, a man is the same as a woman.

Why do you think his parents think he should not take care of little kids?

Because his father might be old fashioned and he would think that men could not take care of babies.

Why do you think he thinks that?

Because it is a lady's job, because ladies know what babies are because they have them.

You don't think that is true?

No. Because ladies are the same and men might know a lot about babies too.

What about the fact that women have them and know more about them, do you think that is true?

No. Men might take care of babies when the mother is not home.

It can be seen from these responses that empirical uniformities in behavior no longer have the force that they did at the previous level. Subjects at the second level understand that there may exist (or at one time there may have existed) uniformities in these behaviors. Uniformity does not imply necessity. The empirical associations of activities, roles, or labels

(e.g., titles) with classes of person are no longer seen as necessary associations. Viewing uniformities as implying social necessity is attributed to
others; but it is not accepted by these subjects. One eight-year-old boy
stated the following:

> *Why do you think his parents see that job as for women only?*
>
> Because most women do it. But on my baseball team there is a girl.
> So you can't say he can't. She is a good player in fact.

    The most salient feature of social-conventional thinking at this level is
that the acts are regarded as arbitrary. It is assumed that there is no intrinsic
basis for acting one way or the other. It is on the basis of the assertion of
the arbitrariness of these actions that subjects at the second level negate the
necessity for convention. However, there is no awareness of the coordinative functions of convention, except at the level of the need to determine
others' specific preferences.

Third Level: Convention as Affirmation of the Rule System

For the first time, social convention is related to elements of the social system at the third level. Subjects at this level still regard social-conventional
acts as arbitrary—in the sense that it is assumed there is no intrinsic basis
for the action. The basic change at this level is that concrete conceptions of
social structure begin to emerge. Subjects evaluate social-conventional acts
in relation to the rules and authoritative expectations which are part of a
social system or institution.

    The responses that follow illustrate these changing conceptions. The
first set of responses were in reply to questions pertaining to the story dealing with forms of address. The second set of responses were to questions
dealing with formal and informal dress. In the latter story, one lawyer
(Ken) decides to dress informally in the law office despite objection from
his partner (Bob).

Bruce (11:5)

*Do you think Peter was right or wrong to continue calling his teachers
by their first names?*

Wrong, because the principal told him not to. Because it was a rule.
It was one of the rules of the school.

And why does that make it wrong to call a teacher by his first name?

Because you should follow the rules.

*Do you think if there weren't a rule, that it would be wrong—or
would it be right to call teachers by their first names?*

Right. Because if there wasn't a rule, it wouldn't matter.

What do you mean, it wouldn't matter?

It wouldn't matter what they called her if there wasn't a rule.

What about the rule makes it wrong?

They made the rule because if there wasn't any rules, everybody would just be doing things they wanted to do. If they didn't have any rules everybody would, like, be running in the corridor and knocking over people!

Bruce

I guess it was all right to wear sports clothes.

How come?

Because—he shouldn't wear rags or anything, but I think it's all right to wear sports clothes.

What about Bob's concern for it not looking professional? Do you think that doesn't matter?

Well, I guess he should look some professional. But you don't judge by his clothes, you judge by what he does.

Could you explain what you mean by that?

Well, you don't go judging a person by what he wears, you should see whether he's good at it.

Do you think it's right or wrong for Bob to expect Ken to dress in a particular way?

Wrong. Because he should be able to wear what he wants to the office.

What if it's an office rule to wear a suit and tie to the office? Is Ken right or wrong in breaking the rule?

If it's a rule to wear a tie, I guess you should.

Why is that?

Because that's one of the rules.

It is clear that in one sense these subjects regard social-conventional acts as arbitrary and changeable. Apart from concrete rules or specific demands for compliance from authorities, conventional acts are not seen as necessary. In the absence of rules or authoritative expectations, conventions, like forms of address, modes of dress, or manner of eating, "do not matter."

The third level represents the beginning of conceptions of social structure. Three notions of social structure are related to convention at this level: (1) authority, (2) adherence to rules, and (3) maintenance of social order. Social relationships are now seen as governed by a system in which individuals hold positions of authority, such as principals or teachers in a school or employers in a business firm. The authority is seen to come primarily from the power of individuals in such positions. Rules pertaining to conventions (i.e., acts otherwise regarded as arbitrary) are viewed as requiring adherence. Additionally, rudimentary notions of social order emerge at this level. It is assumed that maintenance of an existing social order is based on conformity to rules and authoritative expectations. At this level, therefore, conventions are contingent upon the social context: rules and authoritative expectations require adherence to the conventions. The demands of authority or existing rules may vary from one context to the next—as from one school to another.

For subjects at this level, therefore, the evaluation of what are regarded as arbitrary conventional acts is dependent upon whether or not a rule exists. This means that the subject's conception of convention is not coordinated with his or her conception of rules or social context. That is, the rule is treated as obligatory and invariable even though it pertains to an act which is otherwise treated as variable. At the next level, which takes the form of negation of convention, there is a coordination of rules and action.

Fourth Level: Negation of Convention as Part of the Rule System

At the fourth level, the basic conception of conventional acts as arbitrary is maintained, as was the case with subjects at the previous two levels. Unlike subjects at the third level, however, subjects at the fourth level coordinate their evaluation of an act with the evaluation of the rule or expectation to which the act pertains. Viewing conventional acts as arbitrary, subjects at the fourth level maintain that rules or expectations about such acts are not valid. This level, therefore, represents another form of negation of convention.

<u>Bill</u> (12:11)

Do you think Peter was right or wrong to continue calling his teachers by their first names?

I think it is up to him what he calls them because a name is just like a symbol or something and it doesn't really matter, just as long as the teacher knows or everybody else knows who you are talking about.

What about the rule, do you think it would be wrong to disobey it in the school?

No.

In some schools it is generally accepted to address teachers by their first names. Do you consider it wrong to call a teacher by his name even in a school where it is allowed?

No.

Is there a difference in doing it in a school where it is allowed and in a school where it is not allowed?

. I don't think so.

How come?

I don't really think it makes that much difference. I think that kids should call teachers by their first names, so I don't see any difference in it.

Why do you think kids should call teachers by their first names?

They call everybody else by their first names, and it seems more friendly, too.

Some people might argue that it shows a lack of consideration and respect to call a teacher by his first name. What would you say to that?

I think that is stupid. There is nothing wrong with a name no matter which you say. It doesn't really matter.

The distinguishing features of thinking at the fourth level are: (1) social-conventional acts are regarded as arbitrary; (2) rules and authoritative expectations are evaluated on the basis of the acts involved; and therefore, (3) those rules pertaining to social-conventional acts are unnecessary and unduly constraining. The use of titles or modes of dress, for instance, are regarded as arbitrary. It is the ability to communicate with others that these subjects regard as important. Names are seen as ways of identifying people and it is thought that communication can be achieved via the use of first names or titles. Similarly, modes of dress have little meaning to these subjects. It is believed that these kinds of decisions are up to individual choice. Therefore, each individual has the right to make his or her own choice of how to address teachers or how to dress.

The changes from the third to the fourth level in the conception of rules pertaining to conventional acts result in the view that conventions are *nothing but the expectations of others.* This nothing-but-the-expectations-of-others orientation stems from an awareness that, indeed, expectations do exist regarding what appear to these subjects as arbitrary acts. Consequently, social expectations are rejected as an insufficient basis for prescriptions of behavior.

At this level, therefore, expectations of authorities regarding conventional acts are not regarded as sufficient justification for adherence to convention. At the previous level, such expectations or rules were regarded as sufficient justification. The fourth level is different because such rules or ex-

pectations are regarded as arbitrary labels of expected and unexpected behavior. In addition, the necessity for adherence to a rule is evaluated prag-
matically. But, the role and function of convention in social organization is
neither negated nor affirmed at this level.

Fifth Level: Convention as Mediated by the Social System

The previous two levels can be viewed as forming the foundations for concepts of convention as mediated by social structure. At the third level, conventions formed part of the individual's uncoordinated concepts about
concrete rules and authoritative expectations. The fourth level constitutes
a negation of convention through the coordination of conventional acts
and prescriptions (rules and expectations). This phase of negation of convention leaves the adolescent without a systematic understanding of the
organization of social interactions. It is at the fifth level that we see the formation of systematic concepts of social organization.

The basic change at this level, therefore, is the formulation of conceptions of society as a system. Notions about individuals as part of more
general social units or of a collective system have been formed. Social units
are defined as systems of individuals interconnected in an organization
with a hierarchical order.

At this level, convention is defined as shared behavior mediated by
common concepts of society. Normative characteristics are viewed as central to social units. Therefore, one of the defining characteristics of a social
system is uniformity. Conventionally shared behavior is necessary because
of the function served by uniformity in the social system. At this fifth level,
therefore, convention is normative regulation in a system with uniformity,
fixed roles, and static hierarchical organization.

There are two phases to the fifth level. During the first phase uniformity is a defining characteristic of a collectivity, and adherence to conventional uniformities is necessary for participation. In the second phase
uniformity represents a general consensus that is codified and that functions to maintain the social order. First, let's consider examples of the first
phase.

Richard (17:1)

*Do you think Peter was right or wrong to continue calling his teachers
by their first names?*

I think he was wrong, because you have to realize that you should
have respect for your elders and that respect is shown by addressing
them by their last names.

Why do you think that shows respect?

Informally, you just call any of your friends by their first names, but you really don't have that relation with a teacher. Whereas with parents too, you call them Mom and Dad and it's a different relation than the other two.

What if Peter thought it didn't make any difference what you called people, that you could still respect them no matter what you called them?

I think he'd have to realize that you have to go along with the ways of other people in your society.

Why do you have to go along with the societal part of it in this case?

I think in society when you talk to an elder or teacher you have a more formal—you do it more formally, whereas a first-name basis would be informal and it would be just ordinary, really. As if it was just anybody.

Richard

Do you think Ken was right or wrong in his decision to continue wearing sports clothes to the office?

I think he was wrong, because you have to sacrifice some things if it would be better for the company. But if he really felt that strongly about it, I guess it's his prerogative to do it.

Do you think he'd be right in doing it, sticking to his beliefs?

I don't know, I think he should go along with what is set up, really, by the office to begin with, because when he first worked there he did dress up. So he's working on the understanding that you should dress up because it's a professional service.

Why do you think you should dress up in a professional service?

Your appearance sometimes makes them either for you or against you, and if you saw someone dressed up in dungarees you'd think less of him than if you saw someone in a tie and suit.

Why is that?

Because people feel that if he has that much pride in the way he dresses, he'd be apt to have pride in the other things he does.

In a general sense, these responses illustrate the changes at the fifth level. Social acts are now judged in relation to a group or social system in which the individual is subordinate. Social systems are viewed as providing a context for rules and expectations. More specifically, Richard made clear distinctions between different social units and defined social units by the specified uniform behavior. For subjects at the first phase of the fifth level, the individual's adherence to uniformities is a necessary accommodation to the group in order to be a participant. Participation in group or collective life is not considered an obligation for the individual. However, if an individual is part of the group, then adherence to its uniformities is necessary. Deviance from the prescribed behavior is a violation of the legitimate expectations of others who are part of the group.

That these subjects view conventions as social constructions of group life is demonstrated by the fact that they maintain that sanctions for deviations should take the form of exclusion from the group. The following response illustrates this point:

Mike (14:6)

I don't think he should be punished just because it's an accepted custom. If there's some reason that this custom is terribly bad there's a law against it, so that you won't be doing it. But if there's no law, I think that the punishment itself comes from society, and that's why you don't find a lot of people eating with their hands, because society has taught them not to. And those that have learned to, which are very few, you know, from their families or something, learn not to because society itself punished you by regarding you as an outcast.

In the second phase of the fifth level, there is an extension of the subject's conception of social systems. While in the first phase uniformity is related to group participation, in the second phase it is also assumed that conventional uniformities in social groups, particularly at the societal level, are also necessary for the maintenance of the society. During the first phase, variance in an individual's behavior results in group exclusion for that person; at the second phase variance or diversity can additionally imply a breakdown of the social unit.

James (15:11)

I think he's wrong, because in his family he can call his mother and father by their first names. But when he's in public he's got to respect the rules of the school.

Why does he have to respect the rules of the school?

How can you be one individual? If everyone else—he's one individual and his family is brought up with first names. In school, it's a rule to call people by their last names, and if it's a rule he can't be the only one who's not going to do it. He's just going to have to live with it. Even if his family taught him like that, he doesn't have to tell them . . . he cannot do it. It's just the principle of the thing. Because it's different if a lot of families did it, but I think he probably is just one exception. And he should obey the rules of the school.

How would it be different if a lot of families brought their children up that way?

It depends. Usually in schools they allow the parents to have some opinion on how the school is run. And so if there's umpteen million families that are brought up like this, like I know, most of the time (maybe this is an exception, but it's a good example), most families I think will teach kids to call adults and older people by their last names. But if it's the other way around—say, it was more polite to call them by their first names now, and there was a lot of people and say the principal said, "if you don't call me by my last name," I guarantee you if they—they'd finally take a vote through the town, and it would probably be passed that they would call them by first names. So it really depends on what the customs are. Like I know right now that usually it's appropriate to call them by their last names. If he's only one in twenty maybe, even more than that, then he should call them by their last names.

We can see from these responses that at this level conventions are codified. They represent common shared knowledge of the part of the members of a social system. Conventions are determined by general acceptance and are thereby binding on all members. Furthermore, the nature of relations between members of a social group are determined by social organization. For instance, the relation between student and teacher is determined by the social context of the school. Within the school context, the use of titles represents a uniform means for signifying the student-teacher relation.

Having formed systematic concepts of social organization, subjects at the fifth level now define society as hierarchically ordered. Individuals are thereby classified on the basis of their role and status within the system. Conventions symbolize both roles and status. An example of the way in which conventions symbolize roles can be seen in the following response:

Actually my answer would depend on what kind of firm it was, and actually I am not sure, but if it was an old established law firm and he had several law partners who dressed like lawyers do and then he came in wearing very casual clothes, I think he would be jeopardizing the people he worked with, compromising their willingness to wear clothes as part of their occupation. It would be unfair to them in the sense that since they are lawyers and dealing with people this guy would have certain responsibilities towards the company he worked for and by wearing casual clothes, he would create a bad impression that others would want to avoid; if he were a clerk and nobody ever saw him, then it wouldn't really matter.

Do you think it makes a difference if people dress appropriately or not for their job?

For your job, your dress, unfortunately, I guess people's first impression of you is on how you look, which I guess is only right because they have no other way of judging you. I guess most of how you look is what clothes you wear, so if you want to create a favorable impression you should wear clothes that create a favorable impression.

At this level, hierarchical distinctions are made between people of differing roles and status. Status distinctions are based on the roles and functions within the social system. Status distinctions place constraints upon relationships, and interactions between individuals of unequal status require conventional forms of address. In this sense, conventions regulate those relations between individuals which are determined by the social context and the relative status of the actors.

Sixth Level: Negation of Convention as Societal Standards

The sixth level represents another swing to the negation of convention. The previous form of negation (fourth level) entailed the assertion that conventions are "nothing but" social expectations. This was followed (fifth level) by the formation of social-system concepts where conventions were interpreted as societal standards providing necessary uniformity. The sixth level is, once again, a phase of negation—in this case conventions are regarded as "nothing but" societal expectations. Conventions are interpreted as codified standards. However, uniformity in convention is no longer considered to serve the function of maintaining the social system. The following responses provide examples of this sixth level:

Kevin (17:10)

Do you think Peter was right or wrong to continue calling his teachers by their first names?

Well, obviously he was right. Just the fact that teachers in schools have to be called Mr. and Mrs. is no valid reason for that. And also they simply refuse to acknowledge the fact that he's used to calling people by their first names, which is a natural thing to do.

Why is there no valid reason for calling teachers by . . .

Well, there is no good reason for it, the reason is to give the teacher in the classroom respect and give him a feeling of power and authority over the kids in the class.

And why don't you think that's a good reason?

Well because classroom situations don't turn into learning situations, they turn into situations where there is one person in the class who has all the knowledge and has all the controlling force over the class. And you have a bunch of students who are supposed to play a role

which is subservient to him. And it's a different situation when one
person obviously has more knowledge than the other people but he
doesn't require them to be subservient to him.

*What about calling people like doctors or professors by their first
names, would that be wrong?*

Well, I don't know whether it's right or wrong. I usually call people by
their first names. I don't think it's very important, the fact that teachers want to be called Mr. or Mrs. People want to be called Doctor or
Professor . . . . It's not a very urgent problem.

Jerry (17:9)

*Do you think Ken was right or wrong in his decision to continue
wearing sports clothes to the office?*

I don't know whether that is a place where you have to get dressed
up—in the sense of a coat and tie. Maybe he should wear whatever is
comfortable. Like in schools most dress codes are abolished and
there's a move to have faculty dress codes abolished. So in that
sense the strict coat and tie code is going out. So he's just a little bit
ahead of the time in that office.

*What if the style wasn't changing and people still had to dress pretty
traditionally. Do you think he'd be right or wrong in wearing casual
clothes?*

I think it's up to him to decide whether he should wear them. He will
probably in that case be a minority of one; he would be in the position where he would be forced to either conform to the rest of the
business or society or leave the business.

Why do you think it's up to him?

I don't see that it makes any difference for society to set the code. I
think a personal code is the ultimate that you should have for dress
that is possible.

The negation of convention at this level represents a rejection of the
reasoning of the previous level. Conventions are still regarded as part of
collective opinion or of the social system. Conventions are defined as codified societal standards that serve the purpose of providing uniformity of behavior within the group. At the sixth level, however, uniformity per se is no
longer regarded as a necessary condition for the adequate functioning of
social systems. Diversity or variation in the behavior of individuals is not
seen as incompatible with the organization of a social system. Changes in
conventions are interpreted to mean that uniformity within a social system
is not necessary. Without the uniformity requirement, conventions are regarded as arbitrary. Conventions are not yet understood to serve integrat-

ing or coordinative functions, and they are considered to be arbitrary dictates.

Bob (17:8)

Calling someone Professor or something isn't wrong because you are not doing physical harm. It is just a social rule, the way you have been brought up. Society says you call people Mr. and Mrs. That is not going to do anything to actual relationships, it is just something someone says—now you call him Mr. or Mrs.

For subjects at this level, conventions are societal standards for uniform behavior. Conventions are arbitrary, but habitual, forms of behavior that in some instances serve nonsocietal functions. Perceived changes in conventions over time are taken to support the idea that conventions are arbitrary and maintained through habitual use.

Seventh Level: Convention as a Coordination of Social Interactions

We have seen that by the fifth level, conceptual connections are made between convention and uniformities in social organization. At that level, it is assumed that uniformities are societal standards necessary of all members of the group. The negation of convention at the sixth level is based on the premise that conventional uniformities are not necessary for maintenance of a social system. Conventional concepts at the seventh level maintain conceptual connections between convention and the social system. The social system mediates convention, which is defined as uniformity that is functional in coordinating social interactions.

At this seventh level, conventions are conceptualized as integral elements of the interactions of groups of people in a more or less stable relationship (e.g., school, business firm, society) forming an organizational system. The basic function of convention is to coordinate interactions between individuals and to integrate different parts of the system. Conventional acts are regarded as arbitrary in that there is no principle intrinsic to acting in a particular way. Alternative (and perhaps opposing) courses of action may be equally valid. However, uniform or specified courses of action on the part of members of the social system are necessary. These are generally agreed-upon and known modes of behavior. The purpose of these uniformities is to coordinate interactions and thereby facilitate the operation of the social system. For subjects at the seventh level, such uniformities constitute social conventions.

It is also assumed that a system of conventions is based on general knowledge (shared norms) within the social system. The need for uniformity is based on the mutual expectations held by members of the social system that each individual will act in specified ways in order to achieve coordination. Achieving coordination entails recognizing that members interact in a way that makes conventional uniformities in behavior necessary. It is assumed that individuals adhere to convention on the basis of: (1) the expectation that others do so, and (2) the view that conventional acts are arbitrary (no intrinsic consequences to the act). Conventions are, therefore, based on the premise that there is common knowledge (by all likely participants) that individuals will adhere to the specified behaviors. In part, shared knowledge is based on the past behavior (the traditional and customary) of members of the social system.

Consider examples of this seventh level:

Joseph (26:8)

Well to the extent that conformity to these social norms is necessary probably even from the standpoint of his best interests, he has to get used to using the modes of address. They are social customs that are acceptable.

You said to the extent that social conformity is necessary, to what extent is it necessary?

Looking at it strictly from his point of view, he is going to be measurably better off if he learns to accept these things.

Better off in what way?

Well, from the standpoint of being able to get a job, just getting along with people. If he has some strong feeling about this in this matter, that would weigh in the balance on the other side. But it would probably be a mistake in our society today to allow a child to continue to deviate from the norms that he is going to be expected to follow, that are necessary in his success in anything that he would want to do.

Why do you think these norms are necessary?

I didn't say they were necessary. I said his conforming to them is necessary.

Why do you think his conforming is necessary?

Well, it doesn't matter to me, but probably every society has had some sorts of distinctions about what to call people under titles that are given, possibly meaningless or possibly they have some meaning. It goes back to the old sociology that people have to have some method of determining how they are expected to act, and they have to have some way of knowing how other people are going to act to them in order to carry on day to day interpersonal relations. They can't be carried on completely in the dark as to what other people are going to do.

Tom (19:0)

Do you think Peter was right or wrong to continue calling his teachers by their first names?

He was wrong.

Why?

Because the teacher didn't like to be called by his first name, and I think this was right, if that was how he wanted to be addressed. . . .

Why shouldn't the teacher just change for him, why should he change for the teacher?

Well, I'd say the teacher has to make a general—rules have to be accepted between teacher and student. If it was tutorial then the student would probably be able to convince the teacher that it would be all right to do that, as long as the student is not showing any lack of respect by addressing the teacher by his first name. The thing is, in a class that has several kids, assuming the rest of the kids have been brought up the same way we have, and they address the teacher formally, it would be breaking the generality of all the students addressing the teacher in the same manner if she lets this one student address her by her first name.

What do you mean showing respect for the teacher calling him by his first name?

I can see she would only be offended by the student calling her by her first name if she connected that with the students possibly thinking of her as a peer instead of someone with authority and a higher status.

Would that be wrong?

Would it be wrong for the student to think of the teacher as a peer? It wouldn't be wrong. It would only be inconvenient if the student thought he was just as authoritative on anything that comes up between the teacher and the student. Because in that case he would argue with the teacher who in the vast majority of the cases is bound to be right or would show better judgment because she is experienced a lot more. So it would be all right for the student to consider the teacher a peer as long as—the thing is it entails a definition of considering a peer, if you feel you have just as much authority when you say something as the other person. You can't, it isn't true. It would be wrong if the student considered himself just as authoritative as the teacher.

For subjects at the seventh level, convention is based on common or shared knowledge that facilitates social interactions. Violations of conventions produce the "inconveniences" stemming from the failure to coordinate interactions or to maintain a social organization. It is thought that to facilitate interactions the individual within social organizations needs to have ways of knowing how others will act in a given situation. This is accomplished through convention.

That convention is based on the shared knowledge and expectations is made more explicit in the following responses:

Tom

What would you prefer to be called or to call a teacher?

I don't really care, it is not what you call them, but what you think calling them a certain thing means. I would just address the teacher by what I thought was conventional and be thinking all the time or have established in my mind what my relationship with the teacher is. The name doesn't really matter.

Why would you do what was conventional?

Because it is the easiest thing to do. If I did something unconventional then I would have to stop and explain to the teacher why I am doing things that are unconventional and it is really trivial, the reason for it.

What are the reasons for conventions?

Well, conventions make things move along smoothly and also—are most consistently understandable communication. If something involved in the communication of two people involves a certain way, if you communicate with somebody about something, you probably have some conventional way of talking about the thing you want to communicate and the person you are trying to communicate to is also familiar with the general way of communicating this convention. Therefore he is able to follow you more quickly because he automatically is familiar with the way you start to do something, if it is the conventional way of doing something. So he doesn't have to stop and think how is that working, how is this thing said, because he has already been familiar with it. It shortens the process in many cases.

At this seventh level, therefore, the primary function of convention is to facilitate interactions. By utilizing conventions, shared forms of knowledge allow for smoother interactions. Each participant assumes a common understanding based on past experiences in similar situations.

CONCLUSIONS AND APPLICATION

The levels of social-conventional concepts just described demonstrate that social convention is structured by underlying concepts of social organization. At each level, conventions are seen in relation to social structure. The levels reflect changes in conceptions of the social system and changes in the understanding of the connections between convention and the social system. In other words, the individual, in taking a sociological perspective, develops a conception of society in which convention is an integral part. From this viewpoint, the individual's adherence to convention would not be regarded as the result of the acquisition of specific attitudes or habitual behavior. Rather, adherence to convention stems from the individual's conceptualizations of systems of social interaction. Conventions may vary in their specifics, but they are structured by the underlying concepts of social organization. As Dewey put it: "The particular form a convention takes has nothing fixed and absolute about it. But the existence of some form of convention is not itself a convention. It is a uniform attendant of all social relationships" (1938/1963, p. 59).

The findings on the development of concepts of social convention have direct bearing upon explanations of moral development. As discussed earlier, most explanations of moral development have failed to adequately distinguish between convention and morality. As a consequence, the development of moral concepts has not been described in a sufficiently precise way. For instance, in the moral development theories reviewed earlier (e.g., Kohlberg, 1969; Piaget, 1932/1948) a dichotomy is made between what is assumed to be the nonreasoning or conformist states of individuals at earlier developmental levels and the reasoning of individuals at advanced developmental levels. Within those formulations it is assumed that convention is equivalent to conformity, which constitutes a less advanced developmental level.

The proposition of a dichotomy between the "less developed" conformists and the "more developed" reasoners has its parallel in some anthropological explanations of "primitive" and "advanced" societies. That type of anthropological explanation has been characterized by Malinowski:

> Underlying all these ideas was the assumption that in primitive societies the individual is completely dominated by the group—the horde, the clan or the tribe—that he obeys the commands of his community, its traditions, its public opinion, its decrees, with a slaved, fascinated, passive obedience. (1926/1962, pp. 3-4).

Criticizing the assumption that individuals in primitive societies merely conform to the social system, Malinowski (1926/1962) argued that individuals from primitive societies reason about custom and law in ways that are not dissimilar from the reasoning of individuals in other types of societies. Similarly, I am proposing that the dichotomy of the nonreasoning, conforming child and the reasoning, principled adult is a false dichotomy. Children possess both distinctively moral and distinctively social-conventional concepts that each follow a developmental course.

The failure of moral development theories to distinguish social convention from morality has an important implication for educational applications. Namely, since our knowledge is still tentative, there is need for much caution in any application of theories in practical educational settings. It appears, however, that there has been a recent proliferation of moral education programs that are primarily aimed at moving students through stages of moral judgment. As it was stated a few years ago in an issue of *Newsweek*, the efforts in the 1950s to upgrade the teaching of science and math stemming from Sputnik are paralleled in the 1970s by increased efforts at teaching morality in the schools as an aftermath to Watergate and revelations of illegal corporate payoffs.

> Most parents seem willing to allow the schools to pick up the moral slack. According to the Gallup poll's latest annual report on American education, 79 per cent of the people surveyed favor "instruction in the schools that would deal with morals and moral behavior."
>
> In their search for such a curriculum, many educators are turning to the theories of Dr. Lawrence Kohlberg . . . who claims that moral development—like intellectual development—is a natural process that teachers can nurture in children. . . . Kohlberg's theories are now being introduced into a variety of U.S. classrooms . . . . Last month, the public school district of Tacoma inaugurated a program that over the next three years will expose every student from kindergarten through grade 12 to Kohlberg's method of moral education . . . . In addition, more than 6,000 public-school districts are now using sophisticated audio-visual aids that are based on Kohlberg's six stages. *

In my view, moral education should proceed with an awareness of the limitations of our understanding of the sequence of moral development and of the processes of developmental change. Furthermore, as much as possible, moral education should be coupled with educational research. The research on social convention discussed here, I believe, shows that much still needs to be done before moral development is fully understood.

REFERENCES

Aronfreed, J. The effects of experimental socialization paradigms upon two moral responses to transgression. *Journal of Abnormal and Social Psychology*, 1963, *66*, 437–448.

Aronfreed, J. *The internalization of social control through punishment: Experimental studies of the role of conditioning and the second signal system in the development of conscience.* Proceedings of the XVIIIth International Congress of Psychology, Moscow, USSR, August, 1966.

* Reprinted with permission from *Newsweek*, March 1, 1976, pp. 74–75.

Aronfreed, J. *Conduct and conscience: The socialization of internalized control over behavior.* New York: Academic Press, Inc., 1968.

Aronfreed, J. Moral development from the standpoint of a general psychological theory. In T. Lickona (Ed.), *Moral development and behavior: Theory, research and social issues.* New York: Holt, Rinehart and Winston, 1976.

Aronfreed, J., Cutick, R. & Fagen, S. Cognitive structure, punishment, and nurturance in the experimental induction of self-criticism. *Child Development,* 1963, *34,* 281-294.

Aronfreed, J., & Reber, A. Internalized behavioral suppression and the timing of social punishment. *Journal of Personality and Social Psychology,* 1965, *1,* 3-16.

Brandt, R. B. *Ethical theory.* Englewood Cliffs, N. J.: Prentice-Hall, Inc., 1959.

Broughton, J. *The cognitive-developmental approach to morality: A reply to Kurtines and Greif.* Unpublished manuscript, Wayne State University, 1975.

Brown, R., & Ford, M. Address in American English. *Journal of Abnormal and Social Psychology,* 1961, *62,* 375-385.

Brown, R. & Gilman, A. The pronouns of power and solidarity. In T. A. Sebeok (Ed.), *Style in Language.* New York: John Wiley & Sons, Inc., 1960.

Cheyne, J. A. Some parameters of punishment affecting resistance to deviation and generalization of a prohibition. *Child Development,* 1971, *42,* 1249-1261.

Cheyne, J. A., Goyeche, J. R. M., & Walters, R. H. Attention, anxiety and rules in resistance to deviation in children. *Journal of Experimental Child Psychology,* 1969, *8,* 127-139.

Cheyne, J. A. & Walters, R. H. Intensity of punishment, timing of punishment and cognitive structure as determinants of response inhibition. *Journal of Experimental Child Psychology,* 1969, *7,* 231-244.

Damon, W. *The social world of the child.* San Francisco: Jossey-Bass, Inc., Publishers, 1977.

Dewey, J. *Experience and education.* New York: The Macmillan Company, 1963. (Originally published, 1938.)

Durkheim, E. *Sociology and philosophy.* New York: The Free Press, 1974. (Originally published, 1924.)

Durkheim, E. *Moral education.* Glencoe, Ill.: The Free Press, 1961. (Originally published, 1925.)

Foster, G. M. Speech forms and perceptions of social distance in a Spanish-speaking Mexican village. *Southwestern Journal of Anthropology,* 1964, *20,* 107-122.

Freud, S. Some psychological consequences of the anatomical distinction between the sexes. In S. Freud, *Collected Papers* (Vol. 5). New York: Basic Books, 1959. (Originally published, 1925.)

Freud, S. *The ego and the id.* New York: W. W. Norton & Company, Inc., 1960. (Originally published, 1923.)

Freud, S. *Civilization and its discontents.* New York: W. W. Norton & Company, Inc., 1961. (Originally published, 1930.)

Goody, E. "Greeting," "begging," and the presentation of respect. In J. S. LaFontaine (Ed.), *The interpretation of ritual.* London: Tavistock Publications, 1972.

Grinder, R. Parental child-rearing practices, conscience, and resistance to temptation of sixth-grade children. *Child Development,* 1962, *33,* 803-820.

Hartshorne, H., & May, M. S. *Studies in the nature of character* (Vol. I, *Studies
in deceit;* Vol. II, *Studies in self-control;* Vol. III, *Studies in the organization of
character).* New York: Macmillan, Inc., 1928-1930.

Inhelder, B., Sinclair, H., & Bovet, M. *Learning and the development of cognition.* Cambridge, Mass.: Harvard University Press, 1974.

Jones, V. *Character and citizenship training in the public schools.* Chicago: University of Chicago Press, 1936.

Kaplan, B. The study of language in psychiatry. In S. Ariete (Ed.), *American
handbook of psychiatry* (Vol. 3). New York: Basic Books, 1966.

Kohlberg, L. *The development of modes of moral thinking and choice in the years
10 to 16.* Unpublished doctoral dissertation, University of Chicago, 1958.

Kohlberg, L. Stage and sequence: The cognitive-developmental approach to
socialization. In D. A. Goslin (Ed.), *Handbook of socialization theory and research.* Chicago: Rand McNally & Company, 1969.

Kohlberg, L. Moral stages and moralization: The cognitive-developmental approach. In T. Lickona (Ed.), *Moral development and behavior: Theory, research and social issues.* New York: Holt, Rinehart and Winston, 1976.

Kurtines, W., & Greif, E. B. The development of moral thought: Review and
evaluation of Kohlberg's approach. *Psychological Bulletin,* 1974, *81,*
453-470.

Langer, J. *Theories of development.* New York: Holt, Rinehart and Winston,
1969. (a)

Langer, J. Disequilibrium as a source of development. In P. H. Mussen, J. Langer,
& M. Covington (Eds.), *Trends and issues in developmental psychology.* New
York: Holt, Rinehart and Winston, 1969. (b)

Lickona, T. (Ed.). *Moral development and behavior: Theory, research and social
issues.* New York: Holt, Rinehart and Winston, 1976.

Malinowski, B. *Crime and custom in savage society.* Totowa, N. J.: Littlefield,
Adams and Co., 1962. (Originally published, 1926.)

Mischel, W., & Mischel, H. N. A cognitive social learning approach to morality
and self-regulation. In T. Lickona (Ed.), *Moral development and behavior:
Theory, research and social issues.* New York: Holt, Rinehart and Winston,
1976.

Nucci, L. P. *Social development: Personal, conventional and moral concepts.* Unpublished doctoral dissertation, University of California, Santa Cruz, 1977.

Nucci, L. P., & Turiel, E. Social interactions and the development of social concepts in preschool children. *Child Development,* 1978, *49,* 400-407.

Parke, R. Nurturance, nurturance withdrawal and resistance to deviation. *Child
Development,* 1967, *38,* 1101-1110.

Parke, R., & Walters, R. Some factors influencing the efficacy of punishment
training for inducing response inhibition. *Monographs of the Society for Research in Child Development,* 1967, *32,* 1.

Piaget, J. *The moral judgment of the child.* Glencoe, Ill.: The Free Press, 1948.
(Originally published, 1932.)

Piaget, J. *The psychology of intelligence.* New York: Harcourt, Brace, 1950.
(Originally published, 1947.)

Piaget, J. First discussion. In J. M. Tanner & B. Inhelder (Eds.), *Discussions on child development IV*. New York: Basic Books, 1958. (Originally published, 1954.)

Piaget, J. *The child's conception of the world*. Patterson, N. J.: Littlefield, Adams and Co., 1960. (Originally published, 1928.)

Piaget, J. Piaget's theory. In P. H. Mussen (Ed.), *Carmichael's manual of child psychology*. New York: John Wiley & Sons, Inc., 1970.

Piaget, J., & Inhelder, B. *The psychology of the child*. New York: Basic Books, 1969.

Rest, J. R. New approaches in the assessment of moral judgment. In T. Lickona (Ed.), *Moral development and behavior: Theory, research and social issues*. New York: Holt, Rinehart and Winston, 1976.

Sears, R. R., Maccoby, E. E., & Levin, H. *Patterns of child rearing*. Evanston, Ill.: Row, Peterson, 1957.

Slaby, R. E., & Parke, R. D. Effect on resistance to deviation of observing a model's affective reactions to response consequences. *Developmental Psychology*, 1971, *5*, 40-47.

Slobin, D., Miller, S., & Porter, L. Forms of address and social organization in a business organization. *Journal of Personality and Social Psychology*, 1968, *8*, 289-293.

Snyder, S. S., & Feldman, D. Internal and external influences on cognitive developmental change. *Child Development*, 1977, *48*, 937-943.

Stein, A. Imitation of resistance to temptation. *Child Development*, 1967, *38*, 157-169.

Stouwie, R. J. Inconsistent verbal instructions and children's resistance to temptation. *Child Development*, 1971, *42*, 1517-1531.

Strauss, S. Inducing cognitive development and learning: A review of short-term training experiments. I. The organismic-developmental approach. *Cognition*, 1972, *1*, 329-357.

Turiel, E. Developmental processes in the child's moral thinking. In P. H. Mussen, J. Langer, & M. Covington (Eds.), *Trends and issues in developmental psychology*. New York: Holt, Rinehart and Winston, 1969.

Turiel, E. Stage transition in moral development. In R. M. Travers (Ed.), *Second handbook of research on teaching*. Chicago: Rand McNally & Company, 1973.

Turiel, E. Conflict and transition in adolescent moral development. *Child Development*, 1974, *45*, 14-29.

Turiel, E. The development of social concepts: Mores, customs and conventions. In D. J. De Palma & J. M. Foley (Eds.), *Moral development: Current theory and research*. Hillsdale, N.J.: Lawrence Erlbaum Associates, 1975.

Turiel, E. Conflict and transition in adolescent moral development: II. The resolution of disequilibrium through structural reorganization. *Child Development*, 1977, *48*, 634-637.

Turiel, E. The development of concepts of social structure. In J. Glick & A. Clarke-Stewart (Eds.), *The development of social understanding*. New York: Gardner Press, 1978. (a)

Turiel, E. Social regulation and domains of social concepts. In W. Damon (Ed.), *New directions for child development* (Vol. 1). San Francisco: Jossey-Bass, Inc., Publishers, 1978. (b)

Turiel, E. Distinct conceptual and developmental domains: Social convention and morality. In C. B. Keasey (Ed.), *Nebraska symposium on motivation, 1977.* Lincoln, Nebraska: University of Nebraska Press, 1979.

Walters, R., Parke, R. & Cane, V. Timing of punishment and the observation of consequences to others as determinants of response inhibition. *Journal of Experimental Child Psychology*, 1965, *2*, 10-30.

Weber, M. *The theory of social and economic organization.* Glencoe, Ill.: The Free Press, 1947. (Originally published, 1922.)

Werner, H. *Comparative psychology of mental development.* New York: International Universities Press, Inc. 1948.

Whiting, J. W. M. Resource mediation and learning by identification. In I. Iscoe & H. W. Stevenson (Eds.), *Personality development in children.* Austin, Texas: University of Texas Press, 1960.

4

The Relationship Between Moral Judgment and Moral Behavior

GOLDA R. ROTHMAN

As indicated in previous chapters, the structural-developmental approach primarily focuses on moral judgment and the qualitative transformations of one's thought in the resolution of moral conflicts. Generally, stage of moral reasoning is assessed by examining the way an individual resolves conflicting claims in hypothetical situations of right and wrong (*see* Kohlberg, 1963a, 1969b; Piaget, 1932/1965). The information most relevant to assessments of developmental stage is the *reasoning* that leads to a particular choice—not the choice itself. The emphasis on reasoning and hypothetical situations often prompts the questions: "So what?" and "What does all this have to do with the 'real' world and the actual behavior of individuals confronted with a moral dilemma?" For instance, when someone is presented with a hypothetical dilemma and asked whether a man should steal a drug to save his wife's life, he or she is being asked about the actor in the story, not about himself or herself. Even if the respondent were asked what he or she would do in a hypothetical situation, we would not necessarily know what he or she would do if actually confronted. Thus, choices made within the context of hypothetical dilemmas may tell us little about actual behavior.

Considering these difficulties, can the development of moral behavior (which can only be measured as a choice) be related to the development of moral reasoning? Or is it as Grinder (1964) concluded in a study of children's resistance to temptation, that behavioral and cognitive dimensions of conscience develop independently? That is, behavior reflects social learning experiences more than changes in the child's cognitive structure.

The structural-developmental approach does provide one means for examining the development of moral behavior in relation to moral reasoning. This is through its focus on the *correspondence* of maturity of moral thought to maturity of moral action (Kohlberg, 1969a, 1971). In the study of moral behavior, the concern of structuralists has not been with the correspondence of what a person will do (e.g., steal or not steal) to what he or she says he or she should do. Rather, it has been with the correspondence of maturity of moral thought to maturity of moral action (Kohlberg, 1969a, 1971). Does the person who reasons at a higher level of moral judgment in fact behave in accordance with that reasoning? In order to study such correspondence, the individual's behavior must be compared to his or her judgments of right and wrong about the situation. Whether or not a person chooses to steal in a real-life situation will then depend upon the way the situation and one's rights and duties in that situation are defined. Moral reasoning influences moral behavior by providing the individual with concrete definitions of those rights and duties in the behavioral situation (Kohlberg, 1969a).

The structural-developmental approach (*see* Kohlberg, 1965, 1969a) has thus focused on an examination of moral behavior within the context of the individual's moral judgments. Rather than focusing on the particular behavior as viewed by an outside observer, the ways in which the individual defines the behavioral situation and his or her choice in that situation are concentrated on. Moral behavior, then, can be studied as a developmental dimension which parallels moral reasoning, since particular behavioral choices are examined in terms of the structural-developmental processes which they reflect (Kohlberg, 1965, 1969a, 1969b, 1971; Rothman, 1971, 1976; Turiel, 1973; Turiel & Rothman, 1972). Consider cheating behavior, for example. Rather than examining a behavior such as cheating in and of itself, the judgmental processes underlying the behavioral decision to cheat or not to cheat would be explored and related to the behavioral choice. It may be that one person avoids cheating so as not to get caught, whereas another avoids cheating so as not to break a bond of mutual trust. When the situation is one of no surveillance, presumably only the latter would avoid cheating. Situational influences would thus be seen as interacting with structural processes, and the development of moral reasoning would be reflected in behavior.

THE RELATIONSHIP BETWEEN BEHAVIOR AND MORAL REASONING

In attempting to examine the relationships between moral behavior and moral reasoning, it is important to determine whether understanding a person's moral reasoning enables a better prediction of that person's moral behavior in a given situation. If so, this would imply a close correspondence between particular stages of reasoning and particular behavioral choices, as well as a consistent way of dealing with moral conflict situations. An alternative view is that understanding a person's moral reasoning clarifies the meaning which a situation has for the individual, thereby enabling the researcher to relate behavioral choice to that meaning. If so, discrepancies and a lack of perfect predictability between moral reasoning and moral behavior may be expected. Nevertheless, behavioral choices hold more meaning if the process by which people decide to do what they do is understood.

Several avenues of exploration are possible. If individuals at different stages of moral reasoning define right and wrong in a situation differently, and if that definition influences their behavior, there should be a correspondence between stage of moral reasoning and behavioral choices. One approach is to study this empirical correspondence and see whether particular behavioral choices are associated with particular stages of reasoning in concrete behavioral situations.

Or if there are discrepancies in the relationship between moral reasoning and moral behavior, it could be that the hypothetical moral dilemmas used to assess the stage of moral reasoning are too remote from real-life moral conflicts. To address this problem, the moral reasoning used to arrive at choices in both hypothetical and concrete situations can be compared. Discrepancies between reasoning and behavior can then be examined in terms of the distinctions between hypothetical and concrete moral conflict situations. These studies investigate the relationship between hypothetical and concrete situations.

Or if there is some relationship between moral reasoning and moral behavior such that people at certain stages are more or less likely to demonstrate particular behaviors, we might further ask how moral reasoning and moral behavior are related at particular stages. That is, how is the development of moral reasoning related to and coordinated with the development of moral behavior?

We will now consider these ways of examining the relationship between moral reasoning and moral behavior.

Stage of Moral Reasoning and Concrete Behavioral Choice

In real-life situations of moral conflict, we usually observe the behavioral choices people make without having the opportunity to examine their behavior in relation to their moral reasoning. Within the context of research studies, however, both stages of moral reasoning and actual behavior choices can be examined. The correspondence between the two can then be measured.

The general conclusion that has emerged from such research is that there *is* a relationship between an individual's stage of moral reasoning in response to hypothetical moral dilemmas and his or her behavioral choices in concrete situations of moral conflict. People at certain stages are more likely to make certain behavioral choices in particular moral conflict situations. For example, studies of sixth-graders (Krebs, 1967, as reported by Grim, Kohlberg, & White, 1968) and of college students (Schwartz, Feldman, Brown, & Heingartner, 1969) have shown that those at the principled stages (Stages 5 and 6) are less likely to cheat then those at the conventional stages (Stages 3 and 4). Thus, maturity of moral reasoning corresponds to maturity of moral behavior in this situation.

The ways in which people at different stages define the experimental cheating situation appear to be important in understanding the relationship between stage and behavioral choice. Kohlberg (1965, 1969a, 1969b) suggests that because there is no supervision within an experimental cheating situation, the conventional reasons for not cheating are not present. The principled subjects, however, define the situation as involving the maintenance of a trust and the inequality of opportunity which arises from cheating. Kohlberg thus concludes that because these subjects are sensitive to the justice aspects of the situation which are ignored by the conventional subjects, they are less likely to cheat.

The relationship between stage of moral reasoning and behavioral choice is not as clear-cut as it would seem from such studies of cheating. Although consistent non-cheating seems to emerge from the principled thinking of Stages 5 and 6, in other situations behavioral choice does not reflect stage of reasoning so directly. The relationship between stage and behavior is not one to one; it is complex and often ambiguous.

The complexity and ambiguity may in part be attributed to the fact that people at different stages may arrive at the same behavioral choice by using different ways of reasoning. This is illustrated by research which did not show a clear increase in "mature" moral behavior with developmental stage. For example, in one of the earliest attempts at relating stage of moral reasoning to behavioral choice, thirty-two of the subjects involved in Milgram's studies of obedience to authority (Milgram, 1963, 1974) were administered a moral judgment interview (cf. Kohlberg, 1965, 1969a, 1969b). Milgram found that when instructed to "shock" a confederate victim under the guise of a learning experiment, most subjects continued to administer "electrical shocks." Kohlberg has reported, however, that the mean moral reasoning score for those who refused to shock was significantly higher than for those who continued "shocking" the confederate victim. Stage 6 principled subjects were more likely to refuse than were lower stage subjects. Stage 6 subjects felt that they themselves had to make a choice in the situation and had to decide on the legitimacy of the experimenter's demands. Although Stage 5 subjects thought similarly, and most said they had wanted to stop the experiment, those at Stage 5 focused on the fact that both they and the "learner" had agreed to the situation beforehand (Kohlberg, 1965, 1969a, 1969b). Thus, they were less likely to stop the experiment than were Stage 6 subjects, and their behavior was similar to that of Stage 3 and 4 subjects.

The behavioral choices of subjects at Stage 5 to obey and continue "shocking," however, had a qualitatively different meaning from that of Stage 3 and 4 subjects in this situation. Stage 3 and Stage 4 subjects readily accepted the external authority definition of the situation, which Stage 5 subjects did not (Kohlberg, 1965, 1969a, 1969b). Stage 5 subjects did, however, emphasize the agreement made by themselves and the confederate victim with the experimenter. At different stages, therefore, different reasons for the same behavior could be offered.

The relationship between stage of moral reasoning and moral behavior is, of course, also apparent in the finding that Stage 6 subjects were the most likely to refuse to administer "shocks." They resisted the pressure of authority to act in violation of their beliefs. Other studies corroborate the relationship between stage of moral reasoning and behavior. Kohlberg (1963b, 1965) has reported a moderate correlation between level of moral reasoning and measures of resistance to various types of adult interviewer and peer group pressure to change one's opinion in response to hypothetical moral dilemmas. Fodor (1971, 1972) has also found that individuals at higher stages are more likely to resist an experimenter's attempts at influencing their moral decisions. However, Saltzstein, Diamond, and Belenky (1972) have reported that Stage 3 subjects are more likely than those at higher or lower stages to conform to peer pressure (in an Asch [1956] type of social influence situation).

The choices of people at higher stages might resemble those of people at lower stages, but they arrive at their choices through different reasoning. This is further illustrated in a study of the original Free Speech sit-in of Berkeley students, conducted by Haan, Smith, and Block (1968). The study found that individuals at Stage 6 were the least likely to comply with the requirements of authority which to them seemed indefensible, in this case regarding student-administration relationships. They were therefore the most likely to participate in the sit-in. However, there were participants at lower stages as well who offered different arguments for civil disobedience. For example, whereas principled participants were concerned with the issues of civil liberties and rights and the relationship of students within the university, those at Stage 2 were concerned with individual rights in a conflict of power. Stage 3 participants focused on the failure of the administration in their role of good authorities, whereas those at Stage 4 were concerned with the administration as violators of legal understandings. Thus, the same behavior had different meanings at different stages and reflected different structural processes.

This still implies a relationship between moral reasoning and behavior, as does the finding that the proportion of Stage 6 participants was the greatest. In addition, in a later examination of all students by Haan and Block (1969, as reported by Haan, 1975), a majority of the activists used principled reasoning as a major or minor way of resolving hypothetical dilemmas, whereas only a smaller percentage of the nonactivists did. Similarly, in a study of activism resulting from the bombing of Cambodia,

Fishkin, Keniston, and MacKinnon (1973) found that stage of moral reasoning related to the content of political ideology.

This body of research shows that there is a relationship between stage of moral reasoning and behavioral choice in actual situations of moral conflict. Furthermore, although people at different stages may make the same choice, they do so for different reasons.

The bases for behavioral choices.   In order to understand the basis for people's behavioral choices, interview questions may be devised to tap the decision-making process. For example, people can be asked to justify their behavioral choices. The justifications that people give for their actual choices can then be examined in relation to their behavior so as to further our understanding of the qualitative meaning of this behavior. These justifications can also be examined in terms of the stage of reasoning they reflect. Finally, a standard moral judgment interview can be administered to relate this reasoning to a more general stage assessment.

A study of McNamee (1977) provides a clear illustration of how such an approach leads to the conclusion that one's definition of the situation, as provided by stage of moral reasoning, significantly influences one's behavioral choice. McNamee's research has interrelated actual behavior, moral stage assessment, and the assessment of "level of motivation" of one's behavior (i.e., the reasons for choosing a particular course of action).

In McNamee's experimental situation, the subject could perform either a "helping" response, by intervening and helping a confederate drug user, or an "obedient" response by failing to intervene and instead complying with the researcher's expectations to participate in the experiment. A clear, linear relationship between stage of moral reasoning and behavioral choice emerged: at each successive stage more subjects intervened and helped—but only at Stage 6 did every subject help. Furthermore, the only personal assistance offered, rather than merely stating sympathy or offering information about assistance, was offered by subjects at Stages 5 and 6. There was also a clear relationship between people's justifications for their choices and their overall stage. A postexperimental interview that asked subjects about their decisions showed that the "level of motivation" was similar to the level on the moral judgment interview.

Thus, not only did behavioral choice differ for higher and lower stage subjects, but so, too, did the qualitative meanings they assigned to the situation. Again, different meanings could be attributed to similar choices made by subjects at different stages.

Several studies of children's altruism have found a correspondence between children's generosity and the development of moral reasoning as measured by Piaget's (1932/1965) stories (Dreman, 1976; Elmer & Rushton, 1974; Olejnik, 1975). Other studies have found such correspondence using Lee's (1971) adaptation of Kohlberg's (1958) moral judgment interview and stages (Rubin & Schneider, 1973), and Baldwin &

Baldwin's (1970) measure of the meaning of kindness (Dlugokinski & Firestone, 1973). Such studies of correspondence, however, do not necessarily provide a clear understanding of how children perceive and define the situation in which they find themselves. For this, one must examine children's justifications for their generosity or selfishness in a particular situation (*see* Dreman, 1976; Dreman & Greenbaum, 1973; Rothman & Cusworth, in preparation; Rothman & Sussman, 1976; Ugural-Semin, 1952). Once again, similar choices may have different meanings. For example, "I gave so he'll be happy" as compared with "I gave to him so he'll play with me" (Dreman, 1976; Dreman & Greenbaum, 1973); "It's nice to share because you feel that you've got a friend and you're helping them and being nice and making them happy" as compared with "I don't want anybody mad at me" (Rothman & Cusworth, in preparation). These contrasting definitions also provide insight into the salience of cues within the situation from the children's point of view. This permits a better understanding of children's behavior in other situations in which the cues differ somewhat. For example, whether or not anonymity in giving will influence generosity depends upon the extent to which the giver deems it significant that the recipient be aware of his or her identity.

One can also further investigate how such perceptions and definitions reflect the children's ways of reasoning about moral conflict situations, and how these are integrated with their behavior in the situation. Lickona (1974) has in fact suggested that altruistic motivation may be defined in terms of six forms of altruism, each of which corresponds to one of the six stages of moral reasoning (Kohlberg, 1958, 1963a, 1969b). In terms of such an approach, the form of altruistic concern would change as a function of the individual's level of moral reasoning.

Examination of the way people reason about their behavioral choices in a particular behavioral situation thus enables us to understand how they define the situation for themselves. We can then better understand how that definition influences the content of a person's ultimate choice. Different people may arrive at similar decisions using different reasoning and, conversely, the same stage of reasoning may result in different decisions. This is no longer as problematic as it may have initially seemed. Using altruistic behavior as an illustration, giving to charity in one situation yet not helping a person in distress in another, may both emerge from within the context of an individual's focus on "approval" in defining those situations.

This examination of moral reasoning in relation to behavioral choices in particular moral conflict situations leads to the conclusion that moral reasoning influences moral behavior. Understanding a person's reasoning enhances our understanding of his or her behavior. Nevertheless, a strong and clear-cut relationship between moral reasoning and moral behavior is lacking. As has been pointed out, the complexity in the relationship may be attributed in part to the relationship between meanings and choices.

Next to be considered are other factors affecting the influence of moral reasoning on moral behavior.

Ego-strength, affect, and role-taking.   The earlier discussion of the relationship between stage of reasoning and behavioral choice established a correspondence between maturity of moral thought and action, particularly at Stage 6. This corroborates Kohlberg's claim that "the man who understands justice is more likely to practice it" (1968, p. 30). However, the distinction between the behavior of Stage 5 and 6 subjects in some studies and the complexity of real-life situations may suggest that "even the highest levels of moral reasoning do not alone guarantee truly virtuous behavior" (Keniston, 1970, p. 591). What interacts with moral reasoning in such instances to modify its effect on behavior?

The studies of cheating referred to earlier have shown that the relationship between stage of reasoning and cheating behavior is mediated by nonmoral "attentional-will" factors or attentiveness to a task (Grim, Kohlberg, & White, 1968). These attentional processes were assessed by measures of reaction time which correlated significantly with cheating. Those children who were more distractible on ordinary task performance were also more likely to be distracted on the "cheating" task. This was particularly true for those at the conventional level of moral reasoning (Krebs, 1967 as cited by Grim et al., 1968). Grim, Kohlberg, and White concluded that such "attentional-will" factors which influence cheating may be situationally general and stable. They thus act as "ego-strength" factors (Kohlberg, 1964). For example, greater ego-strength might lead to the control of impulses and the ability to delay gratification. These ego-strength factors mediate the effects of moral reasoning on moral behavior and may lead people "to differentially follow the moral judgments that they themselves make in the situation" (Kohlberg, in Beck, Crittenden, & Sullivan, 1971, p. 381). In other words, behavior may be unpredictable and perplexing unless we examine mediating factors.

Examination of ego-strength factors, then, may somewhat resolve the complexity and ambiguity in the reasoning-behavior relationship. Other factors may also mediate this relationship. Affect, for example, probably plays a role, but we do not as yet know enough about the role of affective reactions such as guilt nor about the way these interact with moral reasoning in influencing behavior. In a study of delinquents, Ruma and Mosher (1967) found a positive relationship between level of moral reasoning and guilt regarding one's transgressions. Delinquents have also been found to be lower in their moral reasoning than nondelinquents (Campagna & Harter, 1975; Fodor, 1972; Kohlberg, 1963b). Further analysis is needed about the relationship among guilt, moral reasoning, and delinquent behavior. Such research could have significant implications for the role of affect in the reasoning-behavior relationship.

Other affective reactions such as sympathy may also play a role in the reasoning-behavior relationship. Kohlberg (1969b) has reported that Stage 6 principled subjects in Milgram's (1963) study were not necessarily higher on a measure of sympathy, although they were more likely to refuse to "shock" than were lower stage subjects. Similarly, Emler and Rushton (1974) have concluded that increases in children's generosity with age were attributable to changes in concepts of distributive justice rather than to a changing capacity to experience sympathy. Nevertheless, because the basis for sympathy, as well as for guilt, may differ at different stages, an examination is needed of the role of such affective reactions in relation to moral reasoning as well as to moral behavior. An interaction among these may mediate the reasoning behavior relationship.

The relationship among role-taking (seeing things from the perspective of another), moral reasoning, and behavior, as examined in studies of children's altruism (Olejnik, 1975; Rothman & Cusworth, in preparation), may provide yet another dimension at work in the reasoning-behavior relationship. The developmental capacity for role-taking may be another link in this relationship.

But even a close examination of the interaction of ego-strength, affect, and role-taking in the reasoning-behavior relationship may still leave a gap between moral reasoning and moral behavior. A correspondence between the two in one situation does not necessarily mean a similar correspondence in a different situation. What role does the situation itself play in the reasoning-behavior relationship?

Situational variables. The examination of the behavior of different stage subjects in Milgram's (1963) research did not reveal the consistent increase in moral behavior with stage that we found in McNamee's research (1977). The different findings may have resulted from the larger number of subjects and the less formidable authority conditions in McNamee's research. The different findings may also reflect a distinction between a positive helping response and a helping response in the form of ceasing the administration of "shocks." That is, the elements of the situation and the particular choices involved may mediate the effects of moral reasoning on moral behavior.

A comparison of two other studies also illustrates the role of situational variables. In one set of studies (Rothman, 1971, 1976; Turiel & Rothman, 1972), the presentation of moral reasoning statements for particular behavioral alternatives very clearly had different effects on the behavioral choices of different stage subjects. In another study (Rothman & Sussman, 1976) such clear-cut differences were not found. The choices in the former studies were to continue with an experiment which involved taking someone's prize money, or to stop the experiment. In the latter study, the subjects could give a prize coupon to charity or keep it for themselves. The possible mediating effects of situations and choices imply that the process by which moral reasoning influences moral behavior is complex.

The complexity is further highlighted by the example of a person making what appears to be inconsistent behavioral choices when the elements of the situation are changed. Just as two people using the same stage of reasoning may arrive at different behavioral decisions in a particular situation, so, also, may one person make different choices across two situations using similar reasoning. The person focuses on issues which his or her stage defines as salient and reasons about the issues in each situation accordingly. For example, Kohlberg (1969a) refers to the person at law-and-order Stage 4 who decides to participate or not participate in acts of civil disobedience depending on the definition of the situation by the authorities. When the social order is against civil disobedience, the person probably will not participate; if the authority is on the side of civil disobedience, it is unclear what the person will do. A further example, an individual reasoning at stage 3 may offer to help someone in distress in one situation, but not in another because approval considerations may work in opposite directions in the two situations. From the individual's point of view, however, there is consistency in behavior in terms of his or her moral reasoning (Lickona, 1974).

We can see that the various elements of a situation that interact with moral reasoning must be taken into account. This will provide a better understanding of why people choose to do what they do and enable observers to bridge the gap between situational influences and moral reasoning in their relationship to moral behavior.

From this discussion we can conclude that (1) behavioral choice can be related to the meaning that a situation has for the individual, and (2) nonmoral factors interact with moral reasoning in influencing behavior, and inconsistencies may emerge within the context of this interaction. Inconsistencies may also result from the distinctions between hypothetical situations used to assess moral reasoning and concrete situations of behavioral conflict.

Reasoning in Hypothetical Situations Versus Concrete Situations

As already discussed, a person's stage of reasoning is determined by assessing the process used to resolve conflicting claims in hypothetical situations. This stage bears a complex relationship to the person's actual behavioral choice in various concrete situations. But, does a person reason about hypothetical situations in the same way that he or she reasons about concrete behavioral situations in which he or she is directly involved? Does a person confront real-life moral conflict situations in the same way that he or she confronts hypothetical dilemmas or even concrete dilemmas designed by researchers to promote moral conflict?

When we earlier explored the relationship between stage of reasoning and actual behavioral choices, we found a relationship marked by correspondences and discrepancies. As we examine the relationship between reasoning used in hypothetical and concrete moral conflict situations, we also find a relationship which includes correspondences as well as discrepancies. One way to study this relationship is to ask people to reason about their behavioral choices and about the concrete situation in which they find themselves. Their reasoning about a concrete situation can then be compared with the reasoning used in response to standard hypothetical dilemmas. Using such an approach, McNamee (1977) found that the stage of reasoning underlying one's choice to help or not help the confederate victim of a drug reaction was similar to one's level on a standard moral judgment interview. Similarly, Gerson and Damon (1975) found a strong relationship between four to ten year olds' reasoning about distributive justice in both hypothetical and analogous concrete situations.

But discrepancies between reasoning in response to hypothetical and concrete situations can be expected. In real-life situations, the outcome of one's choice actually affects the individual. Certain issues may then become more or less salient in the decision-making process and similar issues may be defined differently. Furthermore, the role of dimensions such as affective processes, interpersonal relations, and self-interest might emerge somewhat differently in hypothetical and concrete situations.

In the Gerson and Damon (1975) study, for example, the relationship between reasoning in the two kinds of situations was marked by a tendency to use lower levels of reasoning in response to the concrete situation (which involved the actual distribution of candy bars after making bracelets for hospital children) than in response to the hypothetical dilemma (which involved the hypothetical distribution of money after children made drawings sold at a fair). Only in the practical context were the children directly involved in the outcome of their reasoning—by having real candy bars. Gerson and Damon therefore attributed the discrepancy between the two kinds of reasoning to self-interest.

A factor such as self-interest, then, seems to affect the relationship between reasoning in hypothetical versus concrete situations. If such is the case within the relatively controlled context of research, even stronger effects might be expected for such factors in real-life moral conflict situations. Within such situations, the feature of immediacy may play a crucial role (Straughan, 1975), that is, situations of an immediate, compelling nature may arise in real life that require solution. The individual's environment also may play a significant role. Is the concrete environment about which the individual reasons structured in such a way so as to encourage or discourage optimal reasoning? Research conducted in prisons, for example, has shown that inmates use lower stages of reasoning in response to prison dilemmas than in response to standard hypothetical dilemmas (Kohlberg, Kauffman, Scharf, & Hickey, 1975; Scharf & Kohlberg, 1974). The inmates were capable of using higher stage reasoning about their concrete prison environment, but this environment was operating at a lower level (Kohlberg et al., 1975). Since individuals do function at several levels of reasoning, "the total constellation of forces operating in the situation" (Lickona, 1974, p. 14) may play a role in determining one's reasoning.

Explaining the discrepancies. Some discrepancy between reasoning in hypothetical situations and reasoning in concrete situations can be expected. Individuals do not only function at their dominant stage, but display a certain amount of stage mixture even in their reasoning about one dilemma. When standard hypothetical dilemmas are examined (Kohlberg, 1958), they show that different dilemmas tap different sets of issues, specifically those involving the "informal" morality of empathic, personal considerations and the "formal" morality of social rules and structures. They also show that there is situational variation in reasoning (McGeorge, 1974). Therefore, variation in the specific issues tapped in the dilemmas used to assess stage of moral reasoning can affect the relationship between hypothetical reasoning and concrete behavior.

Schwarz (1975) found, for example, that although adolescents' reasoning in response to sexual dilemmas was related to sexual behavior, their reasoning in response to standard moral dilemmas was not. The content of the issues tapped in the sexual dilemmas and in the behavioral measure were more similar to each other than to those in the standard dilemmas. Behavior, thus, more closely reflected the structure of one's reasoning about the sexual dilemmas than about the more general moral dilemmas. Similarly, in a study of children's altruism (Rothman & Cusworth, in preparation), it was found that (actual) generosity related more closely to the reasoning used in dealing with questions of altruism than to responses to standard dilemmas.

Although such studies have found a closer relationship between stage of hypothetical reasoning and behavior when the issues are analogous, the discussion earlier in this chapter suggests that reasoning on standard dilemmas does relate to behavioral choice even though the issues differ. In fact, it seems that parallel thought processes are involved in hypothetical and concrete contexts, and that "both reasoning in response to hypothetical dilemmas and behavior in concrete situations seem to reflect structural processes" (Rothman, 1976, p. 405).

This point is clearly illustrated in research on the effects of the presentation of moral reasoning statements on children's own subsequent behavioral choices (Rothman, 1971, 1976; Turiel & Rothman, 1972). In that research, the subjects' predominant stage in response to hypothetical moral dilemmas (i.e., Stage 3 or Stage 4) affected the way the presentation of higher stage reasoning influenced subsequent behavioral choice. Children at Stage 4 used the higher stage of reasoning presented to them in making their own subsequent behavioral choice; those at Stage 3 did not. Only the behavioral choice of Stage 4 subjects was that advocated at a higher stage, regardless of the particular choice. In this research there was both a concrete behavioral situation, in which subjects acted on their choices, as well as a hypothetical situation, in which subjects were asked what they would do. Concrete and hypothetical choices were similar. This implies that when reasoning was presented in support of the concrete or hypothetical choices, the processes involved in reaching a behavioral decision were similar (Rothman, 1976).

We may thus conclude that parallel processes were involved in hypothetical and concrete choices when reasoning was presented in support of the choices. However, these processes differed somewhat for Stage 3 and 4 subjects. We may therefore direct our examination of the reasoning-behavior relationship toward yet another issue: if there is a relationship between reasoning and behavior, how may we define this relationship at the different stages? And if the development of reasoning is related to the development of behavior, how are the two coordinated with each other in developmental change?

Specific Relationships Between Stages of Reasoning and Behavior

Although the relationship between stage of moral reasoning and behavioral choice is not necessarily linear with respect to developmental stage, it seems most consistent for those at Stage 6. Stage 6 individuals are less likely to cheat (Grim, Kohlberg, & White, 1968; Schwartz, Feldman, Brown, & Heingartner, 1969) or to continue the administration of shocks (Kohlberg, 1969b; Milgram, 1963), and are more likely to help a "victim" (McNamee, 1977) and to engage in civil disobedience (Haan, Smith, & Block, 1968). This lends validity to Kohlberg and Kramer's contention that "adult age change is not only toward greater consistency of moral judgment, but toward greater consistency between moral judgment and moral behavior" (1969, p. 107). In fact, McNamee (1977) concludes that at higher stages there is greater consistency between feelings of responsibility and actual helping behavior, so that perhaps at Stage 6 people do what they think they should do.

Other studies have also shown a relationship between stage and resistance to pressure (Fodor, 1971, 1972; Kohlberg, 1965; Saltzstein,

Diamond, & Belenky, 1972), political ideology (Fishkin, Keniston, & McKinnon, 1973; Fontana & Noel, 1973), delinquency (Fodor, 1972; Kohlberg, 1963b), resistance to temptation (LaVoie, 1974), and altruism (Dreman, 1976; Emler & Rushton, 1974; Olejnik, 1975; Rubin & Schneider, 1973). Does this relationship also reflect increased consistency at progressively higher stages? It may, at least in terms of the way certain kinds of verbalized judgments relate to certain behaviors. For example, Saltzstein, Diamond, and Belenky (1972) found that boys at higher stages (Stages 3 and 4-5) showed greater consistency between conformity to peer pressure and their stated beliefs about the rights of the group than did those at lower stages (Stages 1-2). Research has also shown greater con- sistency at Stage 4 than at Stage 3 between verbal preferences for partic- ular pieces of advice and actual behavior subsequent to the presentation of that advice (Rothman, 1971, 1976; Turiel & Rothman, 1972).

The possible developmental trend implied in the consistency between behavior and judgments also takes us back to our examination of the relationship between hypothetical and concrete situations. Do hypo- thetical judgments correspond to concrete behavior? Do judgments in hypothetical situations correspond to judgments in concrete situations?

From a developmental perspective, an increased correspondence between judgment and behavior might be expected as one moves from one developmental stage to the next. If each successive stage is more dif- ferentiated and equilibrated than the previous stages (Kohlberg, 1969b; Turiel, 1973), and each represents a more balanced interaction between the individual and the environment in resolving conflicting claims, increased coordination of judgments and behavior might be found. Illustra- tive of this developmental premise is Piaget's contention that it is only among older children that one finds a correspondence between the "con- sciousness of rules and a genuine observation of the rules" (1932/1965, p. 70). That is, the behavior of older children (at higher stages) is more likely than that of younger children to correspond to their moral judgments.

Recent research has also lent support to the increased coordination of judgment and behavior with developmental stage. Studies of the influence of the presentation of moral reasoning statements on children's subsequent behavior (Rothman, 1971, 1976; Turiel & Rothman, 1972) have shown that whereas Stage 3 subjects chose a particular behavioral alternative regardless of the level of reasoning at which that alternative was advocated (either one stage above or below their own), Stage 4 subjects chose the alternative presented at the higher stage. Stage 4 subjects related and coordinated their behavioral choice with the reasoning presented for that choice, whereas Stage 3 subjects did not. It is, thus, possible to hy- pothesize a developmental progression in the way behavioral choices and reasoning presented for these choices are coordinated at successive stages.

**The correspondence between hypothetical and concrete judg-
ments.** The relation of stage and behavior thus reflects developmental
progression. How does the relation of hypothetical and concrete judgments reflect developmental change? If, as Piaget proposed, the developing correspondence between judgment and behavior is marked by a "time-
lag" such that "the idea of autonomy appears in the child about a year later
than cooperative behavior and the practical consciousness of autonomy"
(1932/1965, p. 119), is there a similar lag between hypothetical and concrete judgments? That is, how do children's "verbal" thoughts when presented with a hypothetical dilemma correspond to their "active" thoughts
when actually confronted with a concrete situation similar to that depicted
in the dilemma? Here, too, Piaget proposes a "time-lag." He illustrates this
lag with instances where children do not yet take intentions into account
when judging the actions of hypothetical others, but do so when asked for
personal experiences (i.e., when they are asked to judge their own
behavior).

More recently, Gerson and Damon's (1975) research has shown that
where receipt of candy bars rather than culpability was the issue, children
used lower reasoning for the concrete situation than for the analogous
hypothetical dilemma. In addition, a study by Keasey (1977) has shown
that even within the realm of hypothetical judgments, children are more
likely to judge themselves than another on the basis of intent. Are we then
to conclude that discrepancies between hypothetical and concrete reasoning may tell us only about, for example, the direction of self-interest or self-
other distinctions, but nothing about developmental change? Perhaps if we
examine the relationship between reasoning about hypothetical dilemmas
and reasoning about concrete situations in conjunction with actual behavior, correspondences and discrepancies between hypothetical and concrete reasoning can have implications for developmental change.

Hypothetical reasoning, concrete reasoning, and behavior. In a study
of Berkeley students enrolled during the Free Speech Movement crisis in
1964, Haan (1975) found some discrepancies between reasoning used for
actual situations of civil disobedience and for standard hypothetical
dilemmas. In dealing with these discrepancies, Haan pointed to a distinction between hypothetical and concrete moral conflict situations such that
"the interaction of moral and nonmoral features within actual moral situations may have different sequelae than they do in hypothetical situations"
(1975, p. 268). Ideology and personal-social constructions were the nonmoral features Haan referred to. In conjunction with action choice, these
nonmoral features enabled Haan more clearly to relate stage of hypothetical reasoning to reasoning about the Free Speech Movement.

By doing so, the direction of discrepancy between the two kinds of
situations emerged as significant. Gains in the reasoning of lower stage stu-

dents in the actual situation were especially prevalent among those who had taken a clear position on the crisis. That is, action consistent with ideology may have stimulated their use of higher stage reasoning, particularly if they were "developmentally ready" and had shown minor use of higher stage reasoning on the hypothetical dilemmas. Conversely, inconsistency between action and ideology, particularly among those who had difficulty in dealing with authority conflict and disobedience, may have resulted in the use of lower stage reasoning in response to the concrete situation. This "dysfunctioning" may have been specific to the stressful Free Speech Movement situation (cf. Haan, 1975).

The "gains" may have been similarly specific—or may, in fact, have later been reflected in developmental change in response to hypothetical dilemmas. How does studying the reasoning-behavior relationship guide us to a more general conceptualization of developmental change? My own research (Rothman, 1971, 1976; Turiel & Rothman, 1972) has led to the conclusion that the coordination of reasoning with behavior may stimulate developmental change.

The coordination of reasoning with behavior. Studies of the influence of the presentation of reasoning on subsequent behavior (Rothman, 1971, 1976; Turiel & Rothman, 1972) point to the significant role of behavior in interaction with reasoning in the process of stage progression. Stage 4 subjects were found to coordinate their own behavior choices with the higher stage reasoning communicated to them. This ability may represent a process by which the subjects' reasoning may be subsequently transformed. That is, the presentation of reasoning affected the behavior of children at a particular stage of moral reasoning. Their behavior in accordance with higher stage reasoning may, in turn, affect their own subsequent reasoning. If so, this would highlight the mutual influence of reasoning and behavior on each other in the process of developmental change.

Furthermore, just as behaving in accordance with higher stage reasoning may mediate stage transition, so, too, might the conflict of certain Stage 3 subjects represent a transitional mechanism from Stage 3 to Stage 4. In this research, two behavioral choices were presented—either to continue with an experiment involving taking someone's prize money, in accordance with the instructions, or to stop. Stage 3 subjects chose to continue regardless of whether that choice was presented at the stage above or below their own. However, Stage 3 subjects who chose to continue when arguments in support of continuing were presented at the lower stage, and arguments for stopping were presented at the higher stage, vacillated in their behavior decision and displayed other inconsistencies as well (Rothman, 1971, 1976; Turiel & Rothman, 1972). Their conflict and "behavioral ambivalence" may reflect an intermediate transitional phase between the initial separation and later successful relation of behavior and

higher stage reasoning. In what may have been an attempt at relating behavioral choice and the higher stage reasoning presented to them, they
may have become aware of the discrepancy between this level of reasoning and their own. Structural conflict and disequilibrium may thus have
been precipitated.

This implies that study of the coordination of reasoning and behavior
may help us delineate the transitional mechanisms from stage to stage.
Although periods of transition have been said to involve conflict and disequilibrium which stimulate developmental change (Langer, 1969; Piaget,
1947/1968, 1964/1968; Turiel, 1973), the characteristics of such transitions at each stage have not been precisely defined. Turiel (1969) has
claimed that research on particular transitional mechanisms may provide a
more formalistic definition of the stages of moral development. Turiel's
recent research (1974, 1977) on the characteristics of the structural transformation and conflict in the process of transition from Stage 4 to Stage 5
shows that the transitional state itself has characteristics which differ from
those of either stage.

Examination of the coordination of behavior and reasoning at particular stages may similarly have implications for the mechanism of particular
stage transitions. This may, in turn, clarify the stages of moral reasoning
and the way they relate to behavior.

CONCLUSIONS AND APPLICATION

Several conclusions emerge from our examination of the relationship
between moral reasoning and moral behavior. First, it appears that there is
a relationship between the two, but that relationship is complex. Moral reasoning seems to influence moral behavior, but in interaction with other
situational and personal dimensions. Second, by examining a person's
moral reasoning in a behavioral situation, we seem to have a better picture
of that person's point of view as he or she defines the situation. We can
then better understand how that definition, perhaps in interaction with
other factors, influences an individual's ultimate choice. Although two
people may make the same choice for different reasons, or use similar reasoning and arrive at two different choices, our understanding of their different bases for choosing or their focus on different issues within a similar
context may advance our understanding of moral reasoning in relation to
moral behavior. Third, although there may be discrepancies between
hypothetical and real-life moral conflict situations, as reflected both in
terms of the reasoning used to arrive at behavioral choices as well as in the
particular choices themselves, particular choices seem to emerge as more
meaningful within the context of our understanding the process by which

people decide to do what they do. Our understanding of the framework within which people make the many complexly interrelated choices of daily life may thus be enhanced.

   As parents and as educators, we must thus try to see things through the child's eyes. We must ask ourselves how the child perceives and defines the situation and how he or she reasons about the available behavioral alternatives. We can then try to relate the child's behavioral choice to its meaning for the child. This would enable us to communicate and reason more effectively with the child about his or her behavior. We must also ask ourselves how the child defines and reasons about our behavior, and, ultimately, how our reasoning and our behavior, in interaction with the child's reasoning influence the child's subsequent reasoning and behavior.

   Finally, by examining the development of reasoning in relation to the development of behavior, we find a mutual influence of each on the other in the process of developmental change. By studying the interaction between reasoning and behavior at each stage, we may clarify how reasoning and behavior are integrated and related at particular stages and how behavior in interaction with reasoning may stimulate stage change. We may thus achieve a more complete understanding of the process of moral development.

REFERENCES

Asch, S. E. Studies of independence and submission to group pressure. I. A minority of one against a unanimous majority. *Psychological Monographs,* 1956, *70.*

Baldwin, C. P., & Baldwin, A. L. Children's judgments of kindness. *Child Development,* 1970, *41,* 29-47.

Beck, C. M., Crittenden, B. S., & Sullivan, E. V. (Eds.). *Moral education: Interdisciplinary approaches.* Toronto, Canada: University of Toronto Press, 1971.

Campagna, A. F., & Harter, S. Moral judgment in sociopathic and normal children. *Journal of Personality and Social Psychology,* 1975, *31,* 199-205.

Dlugokinski, E. L., & Firestone, I. J. Congruence among four methods of measuring other-centeredness. *Child Development,* 1973, *44,* 304-308.

Dreman, S. B. Sharing behavior in Israeli schoolchildren: Cognitive and social learning factors. *Child Development,* 1976, *47,* 186-194.

Dreman, S. B., & Greenbaum, C. W. Altruism or reciprocity: Sharing behavior in Israeli kindergarten children. *Child Development,* 1973, *44,* 61-68.

Emler, N. P., & Rushton, J. P. Cognitive-developmental factors in children's generosity. *British Journal of Social and Clinical Psychology,* 1974, *13,* 277-281.

Fishkin, J., Keniston, K., & MacKinnon, C. Moral reasoning and political ideology. *Journal of Personality and Social Psychology,* 1973, *27,* 109-119.

Fodor, E. M. Resistance to social influence among adolescents as a function of level of moral development. *Journal of Social Psychology*, 1971, *85*, 121-126.

Fodor, E. M. Delinquency and susceptibility to social influence among adolescents as a function of level of moral development. *Journal of Social Psychology*, 1972, *86*, 257-260.

Fontana, A. F., & Noel, B. Moral reasoning in the university. *Journal of Personality and Social Psychology*, 1973, *27*, 419-429.

Gerson, R., & Damon, W. *Relations between moral behavior in a hypothetical-verbal context and in a practical, "real-life" setting.* Paper presented at Eastern Psychological Association, New York City, April 1975.

Grim, P. F., Kohlberg, L., & White, S. H. Some relationships between conscience and attentional processes. *Journal of Personality and Social Psychology*, 1968, *8*, 239-252.

Grinder, R. E. Relations between behavioral and cognitive dimensions of conscience in middle childhood. *Child Development*, 1964, *35*, 881-891.

Haan, N. Hypothetical and actual moral reasoning in a situation of civil disobedience. *Journal of Personality and Social Psychology*, 1975, *32*, 255-270.

Haan, N., Smith, M. B., & Block, J. Moral reasoning of young adults: Political-social behavior, family background, and personality correlates. *Journal of Personality and Social Psychology*, 1968, *10*, 183-201.

Keasey, C. B. Young children's attribution of intentionality to themselves and others. *Child Development*, 1977, *48*, 261-264.

Keniston, K. Student activism, moral development, and morality. *American Journal of Orthopsychiatry*, 1970, *40*, 577-592.

Kohlberg, L. *The development of modes of moral thinking and choice in the years ten to sixteen.* Unpublished doctoral dissertation, University of Chicago, 1958.

Kohlberg, L. The development of children's orientations toward a moral order. I. Sequence in the development of moral thought. *Vita Humana*, 1963, *6*, 11-33.(a)

Kohlberg, L. Moral development and identification. In H. W. Stevenson (Ed.), *The 62nd yearbook of the National Society for the Study of Education: Part I. Child psychology.* Chicago: University of Chicago Press, 1963.(b)

Kohlberg, L. Development of moral character and moral ideology. In M. L. Hoffman & L. W. Hoffman (Eds.), *Review of child development research* (Vol. I). New York: Russell Sage Foundation, 1964.

Kohlberg, L. *Relationships between the development of moral judgment and moral conduct.* Paper presented at the Society for Research in Child Development, Minneapolis, Minnesota, March 1965.

Kohlberg, L. The child as a moral philosopher. *Psychology Today*, Sept. 1968, 25-30.

Kohlberg, L. *The relations between moral judgment and moral action: A developmental view.* Paper presented at the Institute of Human Development, University of California, Berkeley, March 1969.(a)

Kohlberg, L. Stage and sequence: The cognitive-developmental approach to socialization. In D. A. Goslin (Ed.), *Handbook of socialization theory and research.* Chicago: Rand McNally, 1969.(b)

Kohlberg, L. From is to ought: How to commit the naturalistic fallacy and get away with it in the study of moral development. In T. Mischel (Ed.), *Cognitive development and epistemology.* New York: Academic Press, Inc., 1971.

Kohlberg, L., Kauffman, K., Scharf, P., & Hickey, J. The just community approach to corrections: A theory. *Journal of Moral Education,* 1975, *4,* 243-260.

Kohlberg, L., & Kramer, R. Continuities and discontinuities in childhood and adult moral development. *Human Development,* 1969, *12,* 93-120.

Langer, J. Disequilibrium as a source of development. In P. Mussen, J. Langer, & M. Covington (Eds.), *Trends and issues in developmental psychology.* New York: Holt, Rinehart and Winston, 1969.

LaVoie, J. C. Cognitive determinants of resistance to deviation in seven-, nine-, and eleven-year-old children of low and high maturity of moral judgment. *Developmental Psychology,* 1974, *10,* 393-403.

Lee, L. C. The concomitant development of cognitive and moral modes of thought: A test of selected deductions from Piaget's theory. *Genetic Psychology Monographs,* 1971, *83,* 93-146.

Lickona, T. *A cognitive-developmental approach to altruism.* Paper presented at the American Psychological Association, New Orleans, Louisiana, September 1974.

McGeorge, C. Situational variation in level of moral judgment. *British Journal of Educational Psychology,* 1974, *44,* 116-122.

McNamee, S. Moral Behaviour, moral development and motivation. *Journal of Moral Education,* 1977, *7,* 27-31.

Milgram, S. Behavioral study of obedience. *Journal of Abnormal and Social Psychology,* 1963, *67,* 371-378.

Milgram, S. *Obedience to authority.* New York: Harper & Row, Publishers, 1974.

Olejnik, A. B. *Developmental changes and interrelationships among role-taking, moral judgments and children's sharing.* Paper presented at the Society for Research in Child Development, Denver, Colorado, April 1975.

Piaget, J. *The moral judgment of the child.* New York: The Free Press, 1965. (Originally published, 1932.)

Piaget, J. *The psychology of intelligence.* Totowa, N.J.: Littlefield, Adams, and Co., 1968. (Originally published, 1947.)

Piaget, J. *Six psychological studies.* New York: Vintage Books, 1968. (Originally published, 1964.)

Rothman, G. R. *An experimental analysis of the relationship between level of moral judgment and behavioral choice.* Unpublished doctoral dissertation, Teachers College, Columbia University, 1971.

Rothman, G. R. The influence of moral reasoning on behavioral choices. *Child Development,* 1976, *47,* 397-406.

Rothman, G. R., & Cusworth, R. Cognitive dimensions of children's altruism. Manuscript in preparation.

Rothman, G. R., & Sussman, R. *The influence of moral reasoning on children's charitable behavior.* Unpublished manuscript, Teachers College, Columbia University, 1976.

Rubin, K. H., & Schneider, F. W. The relationship between moral judgment, egocentrism, and altruistic behavior. *Child Development,* 1973, *44,* 661-665.

Ruma, E. H., & Mosher, D. L. Relationship between moral judgment and guilt in delinquent boys. *Journal of Abnormal Psychology,* 1967, *72,* 122-127.

Saltzstein, H. D., Diamond, R. M., & Belenky, M. Moral judgment level and conformity behavior. *Developmental Psychology,* 1972, *7,* 327-336.

Scharf, P., & Kohlberg, L. *Inmate perceptions of institutional and legal norms: A cognitive-developmental perspective.* Paper presented at the American Psychological Association, New Orleans, Louisiana, September, 1974.

Schwarz, D. A. *The relationships among sexual behavior, moral reasoning, and sex guilt in late adolescence.* Unpublished doctoral dissertation, Columbia University, 1975.

Schwartz, S. H., Feldman, K. A., Brown, M. E., & Heingartner, A. Some personality correlates of conduct in two situations of moral conflict. *Journal of Personality,* 1969, *37,* 41-57.

Straughan, R. R. Hypothetical moral situations. *Journal of Moral Education,* 1975, *4,* 183-189.

Turiel, E. *Progressive and regressive aspects of moral development.* Unpublished manuscript, Harvard University, 1969.

Turiel, E. Stage transition in moral development. In R. M. Travers (Ed.), *Second handbook of research on teaching.* Chicago: Rand McNally & Company, 1973.

Turiel, E. Conflict and transition in adolescent moral development. *Child Development,* 1974, *45,* 14-29.

Turiel, E. Conflict and transition in adolescent moral development. II. The resolution of disequilibrium through structural reorganization. *Child Development,* 1977, *48,* 634-637.

Turiel, E., & Rothman, G. R. The influence of reasoning on behavioral choices at different stages of moral development. *Child Development,* 1972, *43,* 741-756.

Ugurel-Semin, R. Moral behavior and moral judgment of children. *Journal of Abnormal and Social Psychology, 1952,* 47, 463-475.

5

A Social Learning Theory Approach to Morality

JOAN E. SIEBER

How does a person learn to act in ways that are moral? Why are some people more moral than others? What can parents, teachers, and other responsible people do to help the members of human society learn to behave morally?

Some tentative answers to these questions can be found by drawing on social learning theory to show how people *learn* the beliefs and actions that have to do with morality, and how situational and personal factors affect the *performance* of moral acts. To give coherent answers to these questions, we must also draw somewhat on the literature of human development and philosophy. From developmental psychology we can obtain information about the timing of learning experiences: At what stage in the sequence of human development is a given learning experience optimal from the point of view of producing morality? From philosophy we can obtain concepts and definitions of morality which provide the framework for determining what behaviors we will consider as moral.

To lay the groundwork for this discussion, I will: (1) state very briefly what social learning theory is about, (2) introduce the concepts of developmental psychology that are needed to understand the role of learning in the development of moral behavior, and (3) show why and how certain concepts from moral philosophy are needed to define our inquiry. Social learning theory will then be used to describe the acquisition of moral behavior, drawing on developmental and philosophical concepts as required to make the explanation complete.

SOCIAL LEARNING THEORY

Social learning theory has provided the conceptual framework for much of
the recent research on the socialization of morality. It is a product of learning theory which, in turn, developed out of the behavioristic movement in
psychology begun by J. B. Watson about 1920.

Learning theory consists of empirical laws that relate the properties of
observable events (stimuli) to those of subsequent observable behavioral
responses. Clark Hull, of Yale, was one of the leaders in the development
of learning theory. Some of Hull's students, including Robert Sears and
Neal Miller, have attempted to build a theory of human development that
is an extension of learning theory. This extension, which has sought to
explain in learning theory terms some of the developmental phenomena
observed by Freud and others, is called *social learning theory*. It employs
the basic explanatory concepts of learning theory: operant and classical
conditioning, negative and positive reinforcement, punishment, extinction, suppression, generalization, discrimination, and others. In addition,
to explain the phenomena of human development and socialization, social
learning theory has borrowed or invented concepts such as modeling,
vicarious reinforcement, nurturance, and a host of others which will be
introduced as needed in this discussion. Some of these major concepts of
learning theory and social learning theory are defined in the glossary at the
end of this chapter.

In the last two decades, social learning theory has grown away from
traditional learning theory and has come to include whatever concepts
necessary to predict and explain how people learn new ways of behaving
in social settings. Social learning theory has retained its emphasis on the
development of empirical laws that relate the properties of observable
events to those of subsequent observable behavioral responses. However,
in the process of creating a useful theory about the socialization of human
beings, it has had to take into account many of the qualities of the organism that mediate the stimuli and produce the responses. These qualities
include symbolic and verbal activity; personality characteristics; physical,
biological, and temperament qualities; stages of physical and psychological
development; and so on. But, primarily social learning theory deals with
the phenomena of learning—the learning of response tendencies that
become manifest in behavior.

When applied to the acquisition of morality, social learning theory is
useful in explaining how particular response tendencies are acquired and
how they are orchestrated into a somewhat consistent approach to moral
dilemmas. Consistency of moral behavior is notoriously difficult to demonstrate (Hartshorne & May, 1928). People are not very consistent at doing
such things as resisting particular temptations (as operationally defined by
a researcher-observer), although even in contrived research settings, some

individual consistency in degree of morality is observed (Burton, 1976). It has become apparent that a more subjective approach needs to be taken. Consistency of moral behavior must be sought within the framework of the individual's values, behavioral repertoire, and understanding of the particular moral context. Social learning theory explains in part the learned variability between individuals in degree and kind of moral behavior, and the apparent variability of moral behavior within individuals. Another essential part of the explanation is provided by developmental theories.

DEVELOPMENTAL PSYCHOLOGY

This branch of psychology studies the order of development of specific structures or functions (such as locomotor abilities or the capacity for moral reasoning) that characterize a particular species. It is concerned with the sequences of behavior that are found at various ages or stages of development. As such, developmental psychology is concerned with the genetic *constants* of human psychology—the basic psychological structures within which learning and learned variability occur. Developmental theorists are quick to point out that meaningful learning occurs only when the individual is at the stage of development at which he or she is ready for the given learning experience. This notion of readiness for meaningful learning experiences applies both to physical development (e.g., crawling, walking, dancing) and to the various facets of intellectual and emotional development. Piaget (1970) has demonstrated that the capacity to think logically develops in stages. The processes of thinking in one stage are qualitatively different from those in other stages. As we shall see, meaningful moral learning depends primarily on the prior development of appropriate logical concepts and emotional characteristics.

In 1932, Piaget (1932/1965) first published *The Moral Judgment of the Child*. Here he described how the development of moral concepts was related to the overall sequence of conceptual development. Later, Kohlberg (1958, 1964, 1971) elaborated extensively on these ideas, as has his colleague Turiel (1969). An extremely brief summary of some of Kohlberg's main ideas is given here since they provide a basis for understanding *when* in the sequence of development certain kinds of learning experiences are meaningful or appropriate for the individual.

According to Colby and Kohlberg (*see* Lickona, 1976), the development of logical thinking along the lines described by Piaget is a necessary but not sufficient condition for the development of moral reasoning. That is, an individual can be functioning at a higher logical stage than moral stage, but not vice versa. It is important to note that Kohlberg's concern is with stages of moral reasoning, not with actual behavior. Kohlberg points out that one needs to have developed a high stage of moral reasoning to be able to act consistently in terms of those advanced moral principles. However, there are a variety of reasons why one might reason in terms of such principles but fail to live up to them. Kohlberg (1976) has developed and empirically validated six moral stages, which are grouped into three major levels. (*See* Chapter 8 for a review of Kohlberg's stages and levels.)

The role of learning is evident in moral development in two major respects: (1) The individual advances to higher stages of moral development only after mastering the prior stage, *and* when he or she is faced with the need and opportunity to learn a developmentally more advanced way of responding to a specific moral dilemma. (2) The particular moral values and moral behaviors of the individual are acquired through social learning. One learns how to behave and when it is appropriate to do so. Other learned qualities such as leadership or shyness affect the kinds of moral acts that are performed.

As mentioned earlier, emotional development also plays an important role in the way learned behavior is ultimately used—or not used—when the individual is confronted with moral dilemmas. Unfortunately, psychological theories of emotional development are not as elegantly developed as those of conceptual development. A few major principles of emotional development, however, are well established and will be outlined here.

Some Principles of Emotional Development

Bridges (1930) found that the emotions of the newborn seem to vary along just one dimension, from calm to excited. It is not until about the age of six months that fear begins to develop. Gibson (1969) found that at about that time, the infant is also becoming sensitive to the emotional state of other people, for example, to the difference between smiles and frowns. By about the age of nine months, the baby becomes very aware of who his or her parents or guardians are and begins to fear strangers. The child's awareness of and responsiveness to parents and others depends on the amount of caring and attention he or she receives. At the unfortunate extreme of this continuum is the abused and the institutionalized child who does not have an adult devoted to his or her care. Spitz and Wolf (1946) observed that such children, in about the middle of their first year, ceased to cry for care and attention and became expressionless and passive. Subsequent research (Provence & Lipton, 1962) has added to our knowledge of the development of such children. They do not show recognition of people nor do they fear strangers; they respond to frustration without anger, but with passive crying or turning away; their language development is delayed. By contrast, the child who has a loving adult caretaker develops a powerful emotional attachment to that person. The child seems to know that food, comfort, and other forms of kindness and nurturance are associated with that person, and shows every obvious distress when that person is out of sight. The loved child learns effective ways to demand that needs be met, and the responsible parent is one who finds reasonable and reliable ways to meet these demands. The child is not abandoned or punished for expressing needs. Awareness of the feelings and emotions of others and the opportunity to observe and imitate loving and considerate adults are basic to the development of morality. Also essential is the kind of gentle firmness a loving and self-assured parent extends to his or her child, causing the child to want to stay in the parent's good graces. This makes it easy for the repentant misbehaver to return fully to those good graces without trauma or long delay.

Emotional attachment develops into a broader form of need and behavior called *dependency*. Dependency is the desire to be nurtured, aided, protected, comforted, or loved by others in addition to the primary caretaker. In the second year, the child begins to reach out to others. The parent who gives the child a moderate amount of freedom to investigate other people and new situations, at the same time letting the child know that the parent is there to meet needs as they arise, establishes in the child the emotional foundations of self-confidence, spontaneity, and autonomy.

The healthy two-year-old child seeks attention, help, approval, reassurance, and affection from the adults in the environment. Separation from adults is resisted, and adult attention is sought in ways that may be destructive or inconvenient from the point of view of the adult. At this point, reasonable limits on behavior are desirable, but punishment of emotional dependency per se seems to be harmful. If dependency is punished or ignored (e.g., if the child is admonished not to act like a baby), the dependency behavior tends to become suppressed and in its place the child experiences unusually great amounts of anxiety. To be prone to anxiety may continue throughout life, and it may be especially salient in situations where the person feels expected to achieve (e.g., in school, work, or social settings or wherever achievement is deemed desirable). Children who are first punished for their dependency and then ultimately given the attention or help requested also develop in undesirable ways, maintaining a high level of overt dependency coupled with anxiety (Sears, Maccoby, & Levin, 1957). On the other hand, the child whose dependency is responded to positively tends to resolve that need as follows. Up until about the age of three or four, the child seeks affection and attention (*emotional dependency*) as well as assistance in order to perform tasks (*instrumental dependency*). Then, after about the age of four, the child begins to use instrumental dependency (help-seeking) as a way of becoming an autonomous, goal-directed problem-solver. He or she ceases to show many signs of emotional dependency. In other words, the need for emotional dependency is largely resolved, and goal-directed help-seeking continues only as needed for continued development of competence and independence (Emmerich, 1966).

As implied in the discussion of Kohlberg's stages of moral development, the later stages call for a strong sense of self—self-assurance, self-knowledge, and a sense of being strong and able to deal with life's problems on one's own. Accordingly, there are a few other comments that are appropriate here about the antecedents of emotional maturity. Children tend to learn their parent's fears: timid parents tend to have timid children; parents who harp on the fact that the father is unable to pass exams that would qualify him for a better job tend to have children who fear failure; and so on (Sarason, 1972). The parent who is secure, loving, and competent has many of the qualities the child wants to acquire and which are pleasant for the child to observe. Children very readily identify with parents who are warm, competent, and loving. They observe and imitate them and derive much security from that affiliation and imitation. Later, they derive security and self-assurance from their independent use of the skills acquired in this process.

More needs to be said about the development of emotional qualities enhancing moral development than can be dealt with in this chapter. A few additional aspects of emotional development will be discussed again in relation to moral learning.

PHILOSOPHICAL CONCEPTIONS OF MORALITY

Can an objective definition of moral behavior be given? Doesn't the morality of an act depend not just on the overt act, but also on the intentions of the person who performs the act? There are no clear-cut rules for deciding which acts, per se, are moral. There are some acts that under most circumstances most persons would consider moral, such as respecting the property of others, obeying rules of competition, or suppressing behavior that would cause physical or psychological harm to others. Psychologists interested in moral behavior have studied the acquisition of these kinds of behavior. The results of such investigations will be discussed in this chapter. However, a review of research on the development of moral behavior should examine the results of scientific effort in relation to a clear definition of moral behavior.

Morality is not a behavioral concept, it is a philosophical concept.* At

---

*Behavioral concepts deal with overt behavior, such as hitting someone or saying "Thank you." This is opposed to subjective processes, such as deciding what is the right thing to do. Of course, morality has a behavioral component; people may *act* on their moral decisions. The morality of an act, however, depends on whether the individual intended to do good. Thus, the major component of morality is the intention and reasoning that underlies the act. The development and examination of ideas about what is right and wrong is a philosophical activity.

its more mature levels, morality is a matter of interpreting very general principles and applying them in action. Depending on the particular moral code to which one subscribes, morality has to do with respecting certain of the rights or claims of others. The domain of others to which morality extends tends to expand with the society's level of civilization. In primitive societies, one tends to consider the rights of only certain others—older people in one's family or one's entire village. As the level of civilization advances, moral concern spreads to the people at one's own level of culture and education, to all the people in one's nation, and finally to all the people in the world. As our world shrinks and our understanding of possible futures increases, many are beginning to talk about mankind's moral obligation to animals (Singer, 1976), to certain species of plants, and to members of advanced cultures which may inhabit other planets. How do we respect these rights? How do we resolve competing claims among them? Clearly we have, at present, no clear set of rules or habits to guide us in these new forms of morality. Established norms and behaviors do not necessarily make for a moral society when other conditions change. As examples, American settlers, for the most part, did not create norms having to do with fair treatment of American Indians. German physicians in the 1930s lacked the appropriate moral code to go with their new programs of biomedical research, and consequently performed harmful and fatal research on people whom they deemed unfit to live.

Morality, then, is not just another pattern of behavior—at least not of the kind that behaviorists typically study. As the examples given here were intended to show, morality may actually consist of a change in behavior, feelings, attitudes or ideas of right and wrong. One's morality depends on one's stage of moral development, as Kohlberg's stage theory of moral development indicates. This applies whether one's morality consists of obeying externally enforced rules, cooperating within an internalized framework of socially acceptable rules, or behaving in accord with principles which may conflict with the laws of one's society. At each stage, most individuals have *some* moral code. What we need to define, then, is what it means to have a moral code. Moral philosophers have provided subtle and contradictory views of what it means to have a moral code. About all that most modern moral philosophers will agree to is:

1. Moral codes have to do primarily with what is good or bad for people, with what promotes or detracts from human happiness, well-being or satisfaction.
2. Moral discourse (i.e., moral principles, codes, judgments, admonitions) has some bearing on behavior. What is done may be in harmony with or in conflict with what is actually said.
3. The individual may experience motivation to behave in accord with his or her moral beliefs and may feel guilty or uncomfortable for behaving otherwise. This guilt or discomfort may arise from social disapproval or from conflict with one's own ideals.

Beyond this, the definition of morality varies from theory to theory. I turn, therefore, to a brief review of three major theses in moral philosophy that attempt to say what it means to have a moral code.*

Intuitionism

The intuitionist theory of morality holds that people know intuitively what is moral and good. The moral and the good are properties independent of all other properties; consequently, they cannot be further defined. The intuitionist view is in accord with our sense of knowing the difference between right and wrong, hence it corresponds quite well with naive views on morality and guilt. However, intuitionism provides no rational basis for determining what is moral, and it leaves us wondering whose intuition to believe, given the great differences between societies and even between individuals. For example, in contemporary American society, individuals differ greatly in their opinions as to the morality of such practices as premarital sex, interracial marriage, affirmative action, abortion, and eating meat, to name just a few of today's controversial issues.

Despite the intellectually barren character of intuitionism, it demonstrates that philosophers of the most distinguished ability (e.g. Sidgwick, Ross, and perhaps even Plato) have been capable of believing that intuition is infallible in matters of morality. Consequently, it is all the more interesting to inquire into the psychological factors that predispose persons to intuit that they should act in such and such a way, and to have difficulty seeing that other moral codes and levels of moral reasoning can exist.

Emotivism

In response to the problems created by the intuitionist theory of morality, the logical positivist school proposed a radically different explanation which has come to be known as the emotivist theory of morality. The logical positivist doctrine holds that there are just two species of significant propositions: tautologies and empirically verifiable assertions of fact. This would suggest that moral judgments or assertions are not genuine assertions at all. The logical positivists hold, rather, that a moral judgment conveys an attitude. It is an attempt to influence someone (possibly oneself) to behave in a certain way. A moral judgment may or may not state reasons

---

*These three views of what it means to have a moral code were chosen to indicate the wide variety of processes a psychologist might study in an attempt to determine how people learn moral codes. No attempt is made here to summarize the major positions in moral philosophy, since that would take us far beyond the scope of this chapter. It should be noted, however, that there is an entire field, known as *normative ethical theory*, devoted to the discussion and evaluation of possible bases for deciding what actions are right and wrong. The reader who is interested in pursuing this topic is referred to Frankena (1963) for an introductory discussion of normative ethical theories.

or deal in facts. It is a kind of command and produces a predisposition to feel and behave in a certain way. Moral behavior, then, would be behavior that demonstrates obedience to a moral command.

The doctrine of emotivism thus takes into account an important aspect of morals that is neglected by the intuitionist doctrine—the position that morality has a practical point. It is for the promotion of certain kinds of behavior and states of affairs, and for a decrease in the occurrence of others. Much of what we call moral behavior in children fits this definition quite well. If an adult commands a child to do such and so and the child obeys without direct supervision, we tend to consider his or her behavior to be moral. For that matter, it also coincides with conventional morality (in Kohlberg's terms) and probably describes quite well the dynamics of most adults' morality.

It is not hard to find problems with the emotivist definition of morality. Any propaganda, advertising, repressive law, or misguided supervision becomes moral discourse. Shouldn't a definition of morality enable us to distinguish between that which is only convincing or intended to be convincing and that which is a valid moral principle? Likewise, should we not have a rational basis for distinguishing between moral behavior and behavior that is gullible, thoughtless, or blindly obedient? For these reasons many moral philosophers find the emotivist theory of morality untenable. Nevertheless, it is of psychological interest since it provides a natural link between judgment and behavior, and it is in accord with many of the kinds of behavior that have been called moral. Not only are children taught that it is "good" to obey requests of adults without examining the moral status of the requests, adults have throughout history engaged in holy and patriotic wars that were carried out as moral acts by both sides—supposedly for the ultimate good of mankind.

Prescriptivism

Because it troubled many philosophers that a theory of morality could embrace any command, no matter how unreasonable, incomprehensible, or intuitively immoral, the emotivist theory of morality led to the creation of a definition that had more to do with reasoning and consistency of behavior, and less to do with emotion and persuasion. Hare (1972), in his prescriptive theory of morality, suggested that moral statements are meant to guide or prescribe rather than to influence behavior. According to the prescriptivist theory, a moral code is understandable. That is, it has a rational content, even if that content is false. The code may be buttressed with reasonable explanations. It is also universal. That is, the same judgment would be made in any other comparable situation. For example, "Don't steal" is in many circumstances accepted as a valid moral principle, and the behavior of not stealing is moral behavior under those circumstances. By contrast, a command such as "Don't go" is usually understood to be based on momentary desires, and it would not necessarily be inconsistent to say later, "Go away."

According to the prescriptivist view, morality consists of agreeing to certain basic principles about how to treat others, and in the consistent application of these principles. However, this does not necessarily result in agreement as to what is moral behavior. My application of principles may be consistent, but quite different from yours. For example, I may hold that everyone has a right to what he or she earns and consequently vote against "socialistic laws." You may basically agree with this principle. Nevertheless you may vote for socialistic laws because you oppose taxation policies that result in some persons lacking even the health, education, or opportunity to earn a decent wage.

In summary, moral philosophy does not offer concrete definitions of moral behavior. Rather, it offers a wide range of psychological phenomena (beliefs, attitudes, emotions, behaviors, and so on) as evidence for the existence of a moral code within an individual or a society. Moreover, moral philosophers' own definitions of morality are undergoing considerable change. Bearing in mind that we must continue to be somewhat vague about what is meant by moral behavior, let's try to define moral behavior in psychological terms from a learning theory perspective.

THE ACQUISITION OF MORAL BEHAVIOR

To behave morally is to have internalized the controls on behavior that inhibit harmful acts and facilitate beneficent acts (acts that promote the well-being of others). The behavioral evidence of internalized control is the repeated demonstration of that control in the absence of a reinforcer. The young child who repeatedly shares cookies with a younger sibling even when the parent is absent is demonstrating internalization of control.

As the individual grows older, moral dilemmas arise in which sets of internalized controls are pitted against one another. Should one hurt another's feelings or tell a white lie? Should one participate in civil disobedience to protest an unjust law? What becomes internalized as the individual develops is not just a set of controls, but also a set of principles or meta-controls that set priorities among the controls, thus dictating the most moral solution to moral dilemmas.

Conceptually, there is no sharp distinction, but rather a continuum, between internal and external control of behavior. This point is well illustrated by the research of Hartshorne, May, and Shuttleworth (1930) which shows that children's scores on tests of moral knowledge and opinion varied widely depending on where the test was taken—at home, in Sunday school, at a children's club, or in the classroom. The researchers concluded that "a child does not have a uniform generalized code of morals, but varies his opinions to suit the situations in which he finds himself" (pp. 107-108). Even among adults who are well socialized with respect to morality, it is not uncommon for an individual to reflect on the way in which important others would evaluate his or her acts, or to reflect on the embarrassment of being judged immoral or irresponsible. What characterizes the internalization of behavior control is not whether one has fantasies about his or her socializing agents, but the character of these thoughts. Is the individual concerned with avoiding actual punishment, with supporting the moral code of society, or with avoiding commission of acts that are not in the best interests of others? Clearly, this question relates to the individual's stage of moral development as described by Kohlberg. Other questions also need to be asked to establish how completely a control has been internalized: Does it call for behavior that is easy or difficult to execute? Is demonstration of the particular moral control in conflict with other nonmoral controls such as internalized norms of conformity or courtesy? Accepting the fact that internalization is a matter of degree and is not always easy to demonstrate, we move on to the most basic question concerning the acquisition of moral behavior: How does internalization of moral controls come about?

Social learning theory assumes that most of an individual's behavior is controlled by the patterns of stimuli and reinforcement that are experienced, and that in the child's early years, most of these events are under the control of the parents. Human infants become emotionally attached to any person who consistently treats them in a nurturant way. Consequently, infants who receive normal parenting develop a very strong emotional attachment to the parents by the age of six to eight months. The parent's presence and nurturance is highly rewarding and satisfying, while their absence is aversive. In other words, a mechanism has been developed by which the parent can reward and punish the child. Not only does the parent's presence or absence serve as positive or negative reinforcement, but the words, smiles, and gestures that are associated with the parent's presence and nurturance take on positive value for the baby and the scolding, frowning, and tenseness that precede withdrawal and absence acquire aversive value.

Much of the earliest socialization of behavior occurs through operant and classical conditioning. Desired forms of behavior are rewarded by attention and nurturance and undesired forms are suppressed by withdrawal of attention. However, most of the kinds of behavior that we would consider to be moral or immoral do not exist in any form in the very young child's behavioral repertoire. What is occurring at the early stage of learning described here is establishing only the groundwork for later learning of rules and of obedience to these rules in order to avoid unpleasant consequences.

In the actual learning of rules and rule-abiding behavior, other learning mechanisms are required in addition to reinforcement of existing responses. Among these other mechanisms are: observational learning (modeling), shaping, and the development of substitute behaviors. Observational learning is said to occur when an individual imitates the behavior of another. Shaping refers to rewarding of behavior that approximates desired performance. As the child learns to talk, the process of shaping is speeded up by a discussion and suggestion as to the kinds of behavior that are expected. The development of substitute behavior refers to punishing an undesirable behavior, teaching the child to substitute some acceptable behavior for it, and reinforcing the substitute behavior. This is an important technique, since the suppression of behavior by punishment alone has a temporary effect and is quite different from extinction of behavior. Before discussing exactly how these aspects of learning are employed in the socialization of moral behavior, let's examine the broad general characteristics of parent-child relations that are thought to influence moral learning.

Parent-Child Relations and Moral Learning

What is the relationship between the kind of early socialization a child receives and his or her response to discipline and internalization of controls over behavior? Internalization appears to be unrelated to any specific practices of care, feeding, weaning, or toilet training that have been studied to date (Allinsmith, 1960). However, there is much evidence indicating that internalization is affected by the nurturance the child receives in his or her early years. In this sense, there is a critical period in moral development. If a satisfactory emotional attachment is not formed with an adult during the first year, or if that attachment is not continued through the first few years of life, the internalization of moral values is unlikely to occur at all. As we will discuss subsequently, McCord and McCord (1956) have found that many psychopathic individuals have a history of parental neglect and brutality. Simpson (1976) summarized anecdotal accounts of immoral, brutal events that have played a salient role in human history and concluded that those who committed the immoral acts seemed convinced that the world is a rejecting, unsafe, and hateful place over which the individual has little control. While it is difficult to establish a causal connection between nurturance and attachment in early childhood and the development of moral behavior, the connection is empirically and intuitively quite compelling.

There has been some disagreement about *how* nurturance leads to internalization and *how much* nurturance is required to produce a high degree of internalization of moral values. According to the psychoanalytic (Freudian) tradition, the nurturant adult is loved by the child because he or she is associated with care, affection, and approval. The more nurturance the child receives, the more the adult becomes a love object whose presence gives pleasure. To create pleasurable feelings in the absence of the adult, the child imitates the adult's nurturant values and behaviors. Studies have shown that adult nurturance does indeed increase the child's tendency to imitate the adult's expressive behavior. For example, children prefer to play the sex-typed role of their more nurturant parent (P. Sears, 1953). Nurturance also seems to be related to the learning of specific prosocial behaviors. Cross-cultural research has shown that a high incidence of theft and lack of guilt feelings are prevalent in societies that use severe socialization practices on young children (Bacon, Child, & Barry, 1963).

The psychoanalytic view is too restricted, however, to take into account presently known facts about the effects of punishment, about children's tendencies to be self-critical, and about the kinds of cues that evoke in children internalized reactions to transgressions. Some nurturance is necessary if internalization is to occur, but nurturance isn't the whole story. To begin with, the view that *the more* nurturant the parent, *the more* the child internalizes the parent's moral values is not supported by empirical evidence. There is, for example, evidence that while the children of rejecting or extremely punitive parents tend to be socially irresponsible and unable to control their aggressive behavior, the children of highly nurturant parents show less responsibility and cheat more readily than do those of parents who are moderately nurturant (Burton, Maccoby, & Allinsmith, 1961). This is not surprising; parents who are highly indulgent and who impose few demands or constraints may create in their children little or no anxiety about transgression. The children of highly nurturant parents may have as much of an internal control orientation as other children in the areas of conduct where they have been taught to apply controls, but they may not gain as early or as comprehensive an understanding of the conventional constraints on social behavior. That is, there is no reason to believe that excessive nurturance is, in and of itself, inhibitory to internalization of control where restriction or punishment have been introduced into the child-rearing process. Nurturance apparently is one crucial ingredient of moral development; specific learning of moral rules is another. It would appear that nurturance must come first and that specific behavior controls need to be introduced gradually as the child becomes ready to learn and understand them.

Why is nurturance necessary? What else is required for internalization to occur? Most social learning theorists take the position that a strong emotional attachment to a nurturant adult is essential for the following reasons:

1. Children imitate nurturant persons to whom they have formed a strong attachment. Nurturant behavior is defined as care and consideration for another. As such, it is usually moral behavior. The nurturant adult caretaker provides a model of moral behavior and is imitated.

2. The nurturant adult provides the child with an opportunity to become empathic. We cannot take into account the needs, feelings, and general welfare of others without being sensitive to social cues conveying the pleasurable or distressing consequences of our actions for others. The child's earliest sense of the consequences of his or her actions occurs when the parent becomes distressed and withdraws affection or expresses pleasure and gives affection. If the parent is rarely or never nurturant, however, the absence of affection is the normal state of affairs. It is not punishing, and the expression of affection may not have reward value.

3. The nurturant adult is in a position to offer the most powerful of rewards and punishments—the engagement or withdrawal of affection.

4. The love-oriented or nurturant adult offers a strong incentive for close interaction; this parent is an object to be sought, rather than avoided.

In addition to nurturance, a "psychological" or love-oriented style of disciplining children is required for extensive internalization of moral controls (Allinsmith, 1960; Aronfreed, 1961; Burton, Maccoby, & Allinsmith, 1961; Hoffman & Saltzstein, 1967; Sears, Maccoby, & Levin, 1957). The love-oriented style of discipline involves day-to-day verbal transmission of values through reasoning, explanation, discussion, and verbal disapproval of the child's behavior, as well as inquiry into the child's motives, and suggestions for and reinforcement of corrective actions. The kinds of punishment that are used in love-oriented discipline include withdrawal of affection, ignoring, and short-term isolation. There is an absence of attack, such as physical punishment, "bawling out," ridicule, and public shaming.

The severe and love-oriented discipline styles have differing psychological implications. The severe style creates a high level of emotionality in the child, making it unlikely that he or she will think reflectively about his or her actions or absorb new information about moral principles. Under the calm regimen of the love orientation, however, the parent's detailed verbal evaluation is transmitted to the child and understood, giving the child new concepts to internalize and use in controlling subsequent behavior.

A second important difference between the two orientations has to do with the locus of anxiety. In love-oriented discipline, the parent warns the child extensively about the kinds of behavior that are to be avoided, the reasons for avoiding them, and the circumstances under which they are especially undesirable. As these discussions ensue, the child gains a clearer and more abstract conception of the moral principle that is involved, and begins to exercise moral judgment rather than mere obedience. He or she also understands that the parent's affection will be withdrawn if he or she transgresses. As a consequence, when the child contemplates committing a transgression, the loss of parental affection is anticipated and anxiety is experienced.

Since this is a major mechanism of moral socialization, let's review it in detail. First, consider the classical conditioning paradigm of Pavlov:

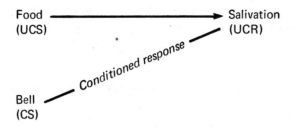

The dog sees the food and salivates. The ringing of a bell is paired with the food which is the conditioned stimulus. Then only the bell is rung and the dog salivates—the conditioned response.

Now consider how symbolically mediated classical conditioning works:

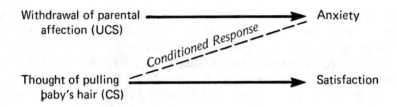

An unconditioned stimulus occurs (e.g., the parent expresses dismay and withdraws affection). As a result, the child feels anxious and unpleasant. A to-be-conditioned stimulus occurs (e.g., the child thinks about pulling baby brother's hair), a thought that makes the child feel rather satisfied. If the idea of pulling the baby brother's hair and proceeding to do so is regularly followed by parental punishment (which leads to anxiety), the thought of hair-pulling alone will begin to arouse anxiety. Ideas about hair-pulling will become a conditioned stimulus that evokes the conditioned response of anxiety. Let's assume that the love-oriented parent has previously conveyed that the little brother is not to be harmed. The child can readily imagine that if he or she pulls brother's hair, he or she will be punished. There is strong evidence, from studies in which involuntary emotional responses are continuously recorded, that imagined punishing events can produce emotional responses that are very similar to those produced by the actual punishment itself (Barber & Hahn, 1964; Clark, 1963; Mackay & Laverty, 1963). To the extent that the child anticipates punishment when he or she begins to plan transgression, the child will acquire conditioned fear responses in the absence of an actual unconditioned stimulus (e.g., punishment).

Let's compare, diagrammatically, the sequences of events under the two different child-rearing techniques:

Love-oriented

Thought of transgression ⟶ *Anxiety* ⟶ Anxiety is reduced by avoiding contemplation of or commission of the transgression

Severe

Thought of transgression ⟶ *Transgression* ⟶ Parent (the source of anxiety) approaches ⟶ Anxiety is reduced by avoiding parent under these circumstances

Thus far, we have focused primarily on mechanisms for suppression or inhibition of behavior. Suppression is not the same as extinction. Suppression is what the word implies—the behavior is simply not committed under certain controlling circumstances, otherwise it occurs. The lasting effect of suppression is inversely related to the reward provided by the prohibited behavior. For example, it has been found that cheating at a task is directly related to the child's need for achievement (Mischel & Gilligan, 1964). Similarly, cheating on tests is greatest in children whose parents reward them highly for success (Pearlin, Yarrow, & Scarr, 1967). This doesn't mean that rewarded behaviors cannot be suppressed effectively. If the socializing agent (1) punishes an act, (2) works out with the child an acceptable substitute behavior, and (3) rewards the substitute behavior, then the substitute behavior will have two sources of reward value. It is directly rewarded, and it is also a way of reducing the anxiety that is aroused when the child contemplates committing the forbidden act.

The shaping of substitute behaviors is an important part of love-oriented discipline. The parent prolongs his or her withdrawal of affection while giving the child options of ways to reinstate parental affection. The parent verbally focuses on the problem and how the child can resolve it. He or she helps the child to work out approved solutions. If a sufficiently satisfying substitute behavior is learned, extinction rather than suppression of the undesirable behavior will occur. Research has indicated that withdrawal of affection accompanied by giving the child options of ways to reinstate the affection is more effective in producing internalization than just the withdrawal of affection alone (Hoffman & Saltzstein, 1967). This pattern of problem-solving and behavior substitution does not occur in the severe-discipline pattern.

Three major characteristics of love-oriented discipline have been mentioned so far:

1. Anxiety occurs *before* the transgression.
2. A lot of information about values and the consequences of behavior is conveyed verbally.
3. The child learns to solve moral problems by finding satisfactory substitute behaviors that do not violate his or her moral principles.

Another major characteristic may be deduced from what has already been described. Since anxiety is conditioned to the contemplation or commission of a transgression, it is not contingent on the parent's presence. In the pattern of severe discipline, anxiety is dependent on the parent's presence. The love-oriented parent teaches his or her child, in effect, to control anxiety by suppressing or substituting behaviors. The severe parent teaches his or her child, inadvertently, to control anxiety by avoiding the parent or any other external monitor—a habit delinquents practice.

Resistance to temptation is not the only characteristic of moral persons. We also consider a person to be moral if, after he or she commits a transgression, he or she engages in self-criticism, reparation, or confession. How does social learning theory explain the acquisition of these kinds of behaviors?

These behaviors follow directly from the fact that love-oriented discipline results in anxiety that is elicited by the transgression rather than by the external monitor. The punishment that is received is usually verbal criticism and is usually quite brief, marking the end of the anxiety and the return to the good graces of the parent. When the child transgresses in the absence of the parent, a way to reduce anxiety is to engage in behavior that has previously marked the termination of his or her anxiety—criticism of himself or herself. That is, self-criticism. It has been found that children are far more likely to engage in self-criticism in instances of transgression for which an adult has previously verbalized an explicit criticism of the child's act (Aronfreed, Cutick, & Fagan, 1963).

Confession is explained in a similar fashion. Three related mechanisms have been proposed: (1) A child who experiences anxiety following a transgression may terminate the anxiety by bringing about parental punishment. (2) Confession is rewarded. (3) Children learn that they usually receive less punishment if they confess than if they are found out. Since young children are under rather careful surveillance, the likelihood of being found out is quite high.

Reparation—an act of restoring or correcting what was destroyed by the transgression or somehow benefiting the person against whom the act was committed—is also explained in terms of anxiety reduction. When a child transgresses, the parent's affection is often withheld until the child makes some form of reparation. Consequently, through operant conditioning, reparation becomes a means of terminating anxiety.

What are some of the conditions under which love-oriented discipline is likely to occur? This regimen requires that a reasoning and concerned adult be present a large portion of the time the young child is awake. The adult should be one to whom the child is emotionally attached. It is not surprising, therefore, that the development of guilt feelings and resistance to temptation is minimal in societies where children are raised in extended families in which they do not develop strong emotional ties with any one adult (Whiting, 1959). Similarly, studies of control of aggression have shown that institutionalized children who have had a variety of parent figures have poorer control over their aggression than do children who have had a consistent individual parent figure (Goldfarb, 1945). The love-oriented approach requires not only a consistent parent figure, but a consistent parent figure who is present and closely supervising the child's activities. To the extent that the parent is actually restrictive, socially prohibited forms of aggression are suppressed (Davis & Havighurst, 1946).

There are marked social-class differences with respect to discipline orientations. Middle-class parents are more verbally oriented than their lower-class counterparts. They are available to give close supervision. They are concerned with developing the child's ability to reason about his or her behavior and intentions. The lower-class parent is often too occupied with the basic demands of life, such as working and keeping some semblance of order at home, to provide close supervision and extensive discussion. He or she is concerned primarily with visible manifestations of transgressions. Punishment is likely to be severe, physical, and without explanation. However, it is probably not the severity of the punishment per se that makes this style ineffective. Rather the ineffectiveness of the severe style is probably due to the fact that the child lacks the framework for reasoning about his or her own behavior (Aronfreed, 1968). As one might expect, lower-class children show less concern than middle-class children about matters of intention and principle in their reasoning about their acts. They are oriented towards authority more as a source of possible punishment than as a source of information (Boehm, 1962; Tuma & Livson, 1960).

There is some evidence that the love-oriented approach to discipline produces the most extensive internalization of moral values in children of relatively high intelligence. Much of the learning that is presumed to occur in the love-oriented style is due to observational learning and to reasoning, skills that are related to intelligence (Terman & Merrill, 1937). Intellectually gifted children have been found to be more mature in their moral judgments than children of average intelligence (Boehm, 1962).

Most of the preceding discussion has been concerned with moral behavior in general. It would be useful to focus briefly on a specific aspect of moral socialization, namely the socialization of aggression. Aggression is defined as behavior that is intended to hurt someone. Sears, Maccoby, and Levin (1957) have pointed out that two important dimensions of the socialization of aggression are permissiveness of aggression (the extent to which the parent is willing to let the child be aggressive), and severity of punishment for aggression (the extent to which the parent punishes the child after he or she has behaved aggressively). These are distinctly different dimensions. Permissiveness refers to the parent's actions before a transgression. Does he or she expect it? Does he or she give many or few advance warnings that would lead the child to fear being aggressive? Punishment refers to the parent's actions after a transgression. How severely does he or she deal with a child who has transgressed?

Given that permissiveness provides no signals that create anxiety about transgressions (planned or committed), we would expect children with permissive mothers to be more aggressive than children with nonpermissive mothers. Similarly, since punishment suppresses behavior, we would expect that the more punitive the mother is for acts of aggression, the more the child would avoid being aggressive. As we shall see, however, this prediction is partly incorrect. Sears, Maccoby, and Levin (1957) obtained mothers' reports on their child-rearing practices and on the extent of aggression of their children. A summary of their findings appears in the following table.

It is amusing to note that the parents who are most lenient (Group C) tend to have children who differ very little in level of aggressiveness from those of the parents who are the least lenient (Group B). The parents who produce the least aggression (Group A) are those who are neither permissive nor punitive. These parents take the attitude that aggression is wrong and will not be tolerated. They subtly express to the child that this is so, but, they do not punish aggression severely. This is, of course, the love-oriented, nurturant style of child-rearing. The parents who produce the most aggression (Group D) are those who do not convey such an expectancy; rather they act as though any form of behavior is acceptable, giving few signals in advance that warn the child not to be aggressive. However, when the child does act aggressively, he or she is punished severely.

Table 5-1. Percentage of high aggressive children in subgroups divided according to whether mother was in the upper or lower half of the distribution on permissiveness and severity of punishment for aggression toward parents.

| | **Highly Aggressive** | | | |
| | **Boys** | | **Girls** | |
Group	Percent	N*	Percent	N*
A. Low permissive and low punitive	3.7	27	13.3	30
B. Low permissive and high punitive	20.4	51	19.1	47
C. High permissive and low punitive	25.3	81	20.6	63
D. High permissive and high punitive	41.7	36	38.1	22

*N stands for number of subjects.
SOURCE: Reprinted with permission from *Patterns of Child Rearing* by R. R. Sears, E. E. Maccoby, & H. Levin. Evanston, Ill.: Row, Peterson & Co., 1957.

From the previous discussion, it is not difficult to understand the importance of the low-permissive attitude. Warning and reasoning about aggression produces the internalized anxiety that precedes and suppresses transgressions. But why is punishment so ineffective? Social learning theorists offer two related explanations in the case of the socialization of aggression. (1) Punishment, if it is severe, probably generates hostility in the child and leads to further aggression. (2) The punitive parent is a model of aggression. The child learns from the parent that aggression is a standard way of coping with frustrations. It has been found that in twenty-minute sessions of doll play, the children of high-punitive parents display far more fantasy aggression than the children of low-punitive parents (Levin & Sears, 1956). This relationship between parental aggression and aggressive tendencies in children may not be readily apparent to the aggressive parents, however. Parental aggression, if it is consistent and severe enough, may suppress most of the child's aggression in the presence of parents. Children who are punished severely for fighting tend to be less aggressive at home, but *more* aggressive out of the home than children who are not punished severely for fighting (Sears, Whiting, Nowlis, & Sears, 1953).

SOME FAILURES TO SOCIALIZE MORALITY

In the course of this discussion of the acquisition of moral behavior, we have been increasingly concerned with the acquisition of specific behaviors that a parent demands. However, unless we are willing to accept an emotivist definition of morality, we would wish to regard the acquisition of moral behavior as something more than learning to live according to any set of rules that a parent insists upon. Since the prescriptivist definition of morality is perhaps the most satisfactory definition of morality we have at present, let's examine society and socialization from that framework. In what way does "morality," as it is taught and practiced, fall short of the prescriptivist concept of morality? How would a social learning theorist explain these "failures" of socialization? What changes in patterns of socialization would be recommended?

To review briefly, the prescriptivist view holds that moral statements are meant to guide or prescribe rather than to persuade or influence. Moral concepts that are internalized in moral socialization have rational content and are understandable. They can also be made universal and to apply to all relevant situations. They consist of certain reasonable basic principles about how to treat others. Moral behavior is the consistent application of these principles.

What are some examples of contemporary moral beliefs, exhortations, and acts that seem to fall short of this definition? There are a variety of taboos and matters of conscience that fall into this category:

1. There is the view that premarital sex is immoral. On the other hand, the "love" generation holds that sex is a natural act of love that should be free of all controls. At their extremes, both views are held without accompanying rational argument concerning human welfare.

2. There is the view that people who belong to the counter-culture cause all the ills of society. The counter argument is that traditional society spreads the seed of its own destruction. Again, there is little rational argument. One suspects that there is an element of scapegoating in many of these cases in which one segment of society points a moralizing finger at another. Scapegoating is a form of aggression; when the source of one's frustrations and hostilities is diffuse and difficult to identify or when it lies within oneself, one tends to look for a scapegoat onto whom the blame may be laid. Typically, the scapegoat is someone very different from oneself, thus differentiating oneself sharply from the "troublemakers."

3. Another taboo has to do with interracial relations, including interracial marriage. "It is wrong." "That simply isn't the way man was meant to live." Some individuals intuitively feel that interracial relations are wrong. The arguments that are given in support of such beliefs often seem more intended to persuade or coerce than to create understanding and open exploration of the issue. How does one come to hold intuitive "moral" beliefs that have serious, undesirable implications for the welfare of many human beings?

Another form of dubious morality involves the ignoring of moral issues. Some of the major moral problems that adults face involve moral dilemmas, situations in which moral principles are in conflict. Kohlberg has invented some clear examples of moral dilemmas. For example, is it moral to steal in order possibly to save a human life? Life offers many more subtle examples of problems without obvious solutions. For example, what should be done to protect society from crime? Clearly, it is moral to consider the welfare of noncriminal members of society. But what of the welfare of criminals? What constitutes the most effective and humane rehabilitation of criminals? How should such rehabilitation be carried out? At what point does a rehabilitation program become a crushing tax burden on the rest of society? What is the best measure of the adequacy of a rehabilitation program? How long a trial run is required to decide upon the adequacy of an experimental rehabilitation program? In some sense, all of these questions are moral questions—at least all of them have moral implications. They also represent moral dilemmas. The course of action that seems best to serve the immediate interests of one constituency is not in the best interests of another. Rational consideration, experimentation and compromise are called for. Viscount Morley has put it nicely, "Those who would treat politics and morality apart will never understand the one or the other." Responsible management of social problems (i.e., moral government) involves the recognition of conflicting moral issues, and the search for new solutions. Much of the process of government does not measure up to this standard.

What explanation can social learning theory give to account for these failures of moral socialization? Moral socialization involves being exposed to a moral code and internalizing the controls and meta-controls that the code dictates. Modern society does not yet have satisfactory moral codes to accompany some of its problems. The alternative solutions to some problems are not sufficiently understood to indicate what solutions produce the most good for society at large. The problem is not a failure of moral socialization; it is a failure to explore problems openly and to evaluate potential solutions honestly and responsibly. I will discuss this further in the upcoming section entitled "Failure to Explore Problematic Issues."

Classical Conditioning of Emotions

Most of the examples given in this chapter have involved "moral" views that are held with considerable emotionality. Emotional responses may be classically conditioned. Thus, they remain an irrational basis for beliefs and attitudes. Supposedly moral beliefs may be concocted to rationalize feelings of right and wrong. One explanation for some intuitively held moral beliefs is as follows: If a neutral stimulus event is regularly accompanied by some action on the part of the parent that arouses anxiety in the child, then after a few such pairings, the previously neutral stimulus event becomes classically conditioned—it alone elicits the anxious response on the part of the child. Moreover, by semantic generalization, words that are associated with the object will also elicit anxiety. By the time the child is old enough to wonder about his or her reactions to certain kinds of persons and ideas, he or she may find many irrational, nonverbal "intuitions" about them. Some of these intuitions may be so widely held among his or her peers that there is no need to discuss them. They are obvious. To question these intuitive notions of right and wrong would be to question the obvious.

The emotional components of negative attitudes have been detected physiologically. For example, Porier and Lott (1967) studied the galvanic skin responses of white persons who were known to be either prejudiced or unprejudiced against blacks. The subjects were led to believe that they were participating in a routine experiment requiring them to be connected to physiological measuring equipment measuring galvanic skin responses, a common index of emotionality. During the experiment, a black research assistant adjusted the electrodes and "inadvertently" touched the subject as he did so. Prejudiced subjects showed greater galvanic skin responses to being touched than did the unprejudiced subjects.

Socially Reinforced
Compartmentalization of Beliefs

Most of the examples discussed here have also involved instances of beliefs that were mentally disassociated from related moral principles. For example, while many persons who hold prejudicial and irrational moral beliefs probably believe in some form of the golden rule, they are not aware of the contradiction between the two belief structures. It is a fairly safe bet that the contradiction is not obvious to the holder's close friends either. Studies of changes in racial prejudice indicate that prejudice is sustained primarily by conformity to prevailing local social norms (Pettigrew, 1959). The dynamics of conformity to immoral social norms are complex and discussion of these phenomena is beyond the scope of this chapter. For an excellent analysis of various forms of prejudicial behavior, including lynchings, *see* Brown (1965).

Social changes may occur that bring about moral changes. Esteemed or charismatic leaders may serve as models of change and reinforce change in their constituents (much as a mother molds the morals of her child). Exposure to new peers who hold differing moral beliefs may result in reexamination of the old beliefs. Discussion of conflicts between beliefs may result in the development of more integrated and universal principles. New modes of behavior may be learned which make it easy to act in accord with the new morals. New laws may be introduced that enforce the new morals.

For example, in the early 1960s the dehumanizing aspects of science and technology began to be recognized. This resulted in various social and moral changes. One branch of society—the "youth culture"—sought a more egalitarian, peaceful, cooperative, tolerant, and aesthetically attractive society. Folk singers, political activists, and other public figures modeled new slogans and life-styles. People of all ages followed their example, creating much social conflict and reexamination of prevailing morals. From the youth culture there emerged a new breed of lawyers, politicians, teachers, and parents. Not all were young; some had been resocialized in adulthood. The new culture had a powerful effect on all levels of society. A host of contemporary legislative innovations reflect the general acceptance of the new morality. These include equal rights legislation, arms control legislation, and environmental protection legislation.

Another branch of society—the scientific community—began to comprehend that science was ruling mankind rather than serving it. In the behavioral and biomedical sciences, for example, there was a growing awareness of inequities in science such as: research done on the underprivileged to benefit the privileged; the use of subjects without their knowledge or consent; and harm without compensation. Trivial or harmful research was being done for commercial profit or professional advancement, with no concern for society at large. Society, the youth culture, and scientists themselves prevailed on the scientific establishment to adopt more ethical practices. Many formal programs of resocialization were undertaken. For example, the American Psychological Association appointed a committee of respected and concerned individuals to revise the APA Ethical Guidelines for Research. Congress established a National

Commission for Protection of the Human Subjects of Biomedical and Behavioral Research. These and similar groups worked in close consultation with their constituents to arrive at more satisfactory ethical guidelines. Much debate raged among scientists as to the kinds of controls scientists should accept and put into effect. Much attention was focused on the recommendations of these groups. New formal mechanisms were created for enforcement of the recommendations. And thus a process of moral re-socialization, which is still occurring in science, began. Now scientists are devoting considerable energy to devising new research procedures that promote the well-being of subjects as well as scientific validity.

Failure to Explore Problematic Issues

Earlier, we discussed an example of dubious morality in which complex moral issues were ignored. Are we socialized to ignore complex and problematic issues about which we cannot produce simple solutions? There is evidence that we are. Although many would agree that it is good pedagogy to create warranted uncertainty about some matter and then to help students obtain and organize the information they need in order to gain understanding (e.g., Bruner, 1965; Dewey, 1916), there is well-documented evidence that few teachers provide such experience. Bellack, Kliebard, Hyman, and Smith (1966) observed that there is little questioning or expression of uncertainty by pupils or teachers in the classroom. The most common communication pattern is one in which teachers ask questions to which students give simple, factual answers. Bellack et al. observed that teachers asked 80 percent of all questions, and of all teachers' questions, only 19 percent required students to give explanations. The effects of this kind of regimen on students are as one might expect. It has been observed that when questioned about problematic matters, children usually give simple, dogmatic answers, rather than raise relevant questions or otherwise express their uncertainty (Sieber, Epstein, & Petty, 1970; Sieber, Clark, Smith, & Sanders, 1978). Classroom research has shown that this norm can be changed, however. Field experiments, in which class leaders served as models of the expression of warranted uncertainty and in which students were explicitly taught to distinguish between problematic and nonproblematic statements, have resulted in radical changes, both in students' ability to recognize when it is warranted to be uncertain, and in the character of students' attitudes about complex problems (Bezanson, 1972; Sieber, Clark, Smith, & Sanders, 1978).

MORAL EDUCATION

In this discussion of failures in the socialization of morality, a number of educational implications have been touched upon. We have seen that some of the morality that exists in society is moral in the emotivist sense only; it consists of belief structures that are not based on any serious examination of the consequences of acts for the welfare of others. Social pressures are brought to bear to produce conformity to these beliefs. It is perhaps unavoidable that pressures for conformity to social norms should exist. However, it is disturbing that norms are mistaken for moral structures with the results that nonconformists are sometimes persecuted on grounds of immorality. Religious wars, racial conflict, the destruction of relationships between parents and their children are perpetrated in defense of these "morals" that are only norms. An important question for educators to ask is how can we reduce this confusion of norms or attitudes with morals.

It should be apparent by now that just as there is no easy way of deciding which acts are moral and which are not, there is no easy answer to this question. However, a tentative suggestion seems in order. In middle childhood, children begin to internalize the moral reasoning of their parents. Therefore, certain kinds of moral discourse on the part of parents and other socializing agents might move society toward the resolution of this confusion of norms with morals. The kind of moral reasoning to which I am referring include the following:

1. Examination of the consequences of one's acts for others
2. Examination of instances in which different people have different information at their disposal and reach different conclusions when reasoning about the same moral question
3. Examination of instances in which moral and nonmoral norms are confused with one another

If these conjectures are correct, a number of changes in existing socialization patterns are in order. These changes involve education of parents and teachers in the ways of love-oriented socialization as well as in moral discourse. They require educators to be sufficiently accepting of morally deviant children to create emotional attachment and to permit the transmission of moral values. This form of "therapy" has been used effectively with delinquent children (McCord & McCord, 1956).

A curriculum is needed that will both facilitate the generalization of moral principles over all cases to which they relate and teach individuals not to overlook or oversimplify complex and problematic moral issues. Role playing, simulated political decision-making activities, and honest, detailed inquiries into the life-styles of others would be useful instructional activities. These activities would need to be carefully planned to produce an understanding of the relationship between social acts and social consequences. Visits to a jail, an Indian reservation, or a home for the aged could be outstanding opportunities for moral growth, depending on the level of moral discourse and debate that preceded and followed them.

What I have proposed here are some rudiments of an experiment in moral education, not a tried and true solution. Social learning theory explains a lot, but we cannot be certain of the adequacy of its explanations. The concept of moral behavior is an elusive one. The experiments I have cited concern children and a rather constrained set of behaviors. The antecedents of innovative and responsible social leadership have not been dealt with, for example, nor have the problems of preserving our ecology or of behaving responsibly and morally in an intercultural setting. Social learning theory has given us enough new knowledge to enable us to try out some promising ideas in moral education. Until we have more clearly defined the domain of moral behavior, however, and until more longitudinal research is conducted concerning the socialization of moral behavior, the behavioral foundations of moral education remain in the early stages of development.

CONCLUSIONS AND APPLICATION

Social learning theory provides a framework for predicting and understanding the behavioral consequences of various styles of socialization or child-rearing. With a basic grasp of learning theory and stages of human development, one can reason intelligently about the kinds of moral learning that individuals are likely to acquire from their parents, teachers, peers, and others in their social environment.

This section is intended to focus attention on ways of asking what is *actually* being learned about morality in a given situation—as opposed to what parents or teachers may think is being taught. For example, what are the roles of reasoning and punishment in moral socialization? Should children be punished for doing harmful things? Should parents and teachers be permissive (i.e., not punish, scold, or insist on serious reasoning) of harmful behavior? What about the parent or teacher who essentially requests: Do as I say and not as I do? Let's examine what is *learned* under each of these conditions.

Punishment, if it is quite harsh and not accompanied by reasoning, may teach children to be more hurtful and aggressive, rather than less so. It demonstrates that punishment, leading to counter-aggression, is a major part of interpersonal relations. The adult who does the punishing is actually setting an example of aggressive behavior for the child to follow. Severe punishment can also teach children the importance of *avoiding* the consequences of their harmful behavior—of lying, running off as soon as they hurt someone else, and otherwise failing to take responsibility for doing harm. And, severe punishment is likely to teach the importance of siding with powerful people, as opposed to the importance of developing sound moral principles and sticking with them even when the opposition is powerful.

Permissiveness avoids the problems caused by severe punishment, but it raises certain other problems. Failure to correct children at all when they do harmful things allows them to go on being insensitive to the feelings and needs of others and to the importance of keeping promises and agreements. While permissiveness sets an example of nonpunitiveness, it also sets an example of lack of concern for justice and lack of empathy for those who are hurt. By a different process, the permissively socialized child learns to be about as aggressive as the child who is punished a lot.

What is learned from teachers or parents who scold or reason with children about harmful behavior, but who obviously fail to follow their own rules? Probably, hypocrisy. Research shows that a great deal is learned through modeling the actual behavior of others.

Thus, moral, nurturant adults who establish and discuss clear and understandable rules which they enforce firmly and consistently provide the most effective environment for learning to behave morally.

Should emotional independence and mature moral behavior be required of children from the very beginning? No. Insistence on mature behavior, before meeting children's needs for dependency and for the learning of basic components of moral behavior, does not produce a strong, moral, independent person. The basis for learning emotional independence seems to be confidence in the love and nurturance of one's parents and other caretakers. The basis for learning mature moral reasoning and behavior is years of experience with nurturant parents who explain and enforce the basic principles of moral living. The reasoning and decision processes that underlie mature morality are filled with subtlety and conflicting ground rules. It takes a lot of experience with moral and reasonable parents before a child can learn how to take into account the many factors that enter into deciding how to act morally in a wide range of social situations. Thus, too early insistence on moral and independent behavior is likely to result in anxiety, confusion, and a general inability to be a strong, effective, moral person in crisis situations. Independence and mature moral behavior should be encouraged and expected as the child becomes able to engage in them, but instances of regression to earlier forms of behavior are to be expected in the course of coping with life's problems.

GLOSSARY OF TERMS

Classical conditioning. The procedure or set of psychological events that occur when one stimulus which is originally ineffective in eliciting a given response becomes capable of eliciting that response through pairing with an effective stimulus. The classical conditioning procedure is as follows. Two stimuli are presented in close temporal proximity. One of them has the capacity to elicit a certain response (due to prior learning or reflex reaction) and the other does not. If the two stimuli are both made to occur together several times, the second stimulus eventually acquires the capacity to evoke a response that is very similar to the response evoked by the first stimulus. For example, when a mother spanks her child, the child feels anxiety and remorse. If the mother usually raises her eyebrows and purses her lips as she decides to do the spanking, that facial expression will become a conditioned stimulus that evokes in the child anxiety and remorse similar to that experience during the spanking. That is, feelings of anxiety and remorse become classically conditioned to pursed lips and raised eyebrows.

Extinction. The process whereby a conditioned response is progressively reduced. If the conditioned stimulus to which a classically conditioned response has transferred is never again paired with the unconditioned stimulus that naturally elicits that response, then the conditioned response will finally cease to occur. For example, lifted brows and pursed lips that are never again paired with spanking will finally cease to arouse fear. Similarly, behavior acquired through operant conditioning will extinguish (stop occurring) if it is not reinforced. Complete extinction, expecially of fear responses, may take a long time. Even after the individual has ceased responding to the conditioned stimulus, the extinguished response often spontaneously recovers, or reappears, on another day or in a slightly different stimulus situation. But, eventually, after continued nonreinforcement, it will finally disappear completely.

Inhibition. *See* suppression.

Nurturance. Qualities of warmth, responsiveness to a person's needs, and frequent giving of praise and approval. Nurturance does not mean permissiveness; the nurturant parent may apply strong pressures for social conformity. However, nurturance is the opposite of severe socialization—lack of affection, neglect of the child's needs, imposition of demands that the child cannot yet meet, or frequent punishment (Sears, Maccoby & Levin, 1957).

Operant conditioning. The psychological processes involved in a procedure wherein a stimulus, having evoked a response that results in a reward, is more likely to evoke that response again. For example, a child sees another child drop money and picks it up and returns it to that child. He is praised and rewarded, hence he or she tends to return lost items to their rightful owners on subsequent occasions.

Socialization. The process, beginning at birth, by which an individual learns the expectations of society, acquires sensitivity to the pressures and obligations of group life, and learns to get along with others.

Suppression. A variety of processes whereby impulses or tendencies to action are kept from overt expression. For example, responses that are extremely satisfying, but that are punished under certain circumstances, will be suppressed under those certain circumstances but will otherwise occur. For example, among students who have a great deal to gain by cheating, cheating will be suppressed by the presence of a vigilant proctor, but will occur otherwise.

REFERENCES

Allinsmith, W. The learning of moral standards. In D. R. Miller & G. E. Swanson et. al. (Eds.), *Inner conflict and defense.* New York: Holt, Rinehart and Winston, 1960.

Aronfreed, J. The nature, variety and social patterning of moral responses to transgression. *Journal of Abnormal and Social Psychology,* 1961, *63,* 223-240.

Aronfreed, J. *Conduct and conscience.* New York: Academic Press, Inc., 1968.

Aronfreed, J., Cutick, R. A., & Fagan, S. A. Cognitive structure, punishment, and nurturance in the experimental induction of self-criticism. *Child Development,* 1963, *34,* 281-294.

Bacon, M. K., Child, I. L., & Barry, III, H. A cross-cultural study of correlates of crime. *Journal of Abnormal and Social Psychology,* 1963, *66,* 291-300.

Barber, T. X., & Hahn, Jr., K. W. Experimental studies in "hypnotic" behavior: Physiologic and subjective effects of imagined pain. *Journal of Nervous and Mental Disease,* 1964, *139,* 416-425.

Bellack, A. A., Kliebard, H. M., Hyman, R. T., & Smith, F. L. *The language of the classroom.* New York: Teachers College Press, 1966.

Bezanson, K. *The expression of warranted uncertainty in Ghanaian classrooms.* Unpublished dissertation, Stanford University, 1972.

Boehm, L. The development of conscience: A comparison of American children of different mental and socioeconomic levels. *Child Development,* 1962, *33,* 575-590.

Bridges, K. M. B. A genetic theory of emotions. *Journal of Genetic Psychology,* 1930, *37,* 514-527.

Brown, R. W. *Social psychology.* New York: The Free Press, 1965.

Bruner, J. S. The growth of mind. *American Psychologist,* 1965, *20,* 1007-1017.

Burton, R. V. Honesty and dishonesty. In T. Lickona (Ed.), *Moral development and behavior.* New York: Holt, Rinehart and Winston, 1976.

Burton, R. V., Maccoby, E. E., & Allinsmith, W. Antecedents of resistance to temptation in four-year-old children. *Child Development,* 1961, *32,* 689-710.

Clark, D. F. The treatment of monosymptomatic phobia by systematic desensitization. *Behavior Research and Therapy,* 1963, *1,* 63-68.

Colby, A., & Kohlberg, L. The relation between the development of formal operations and moral judgment. In D. Bush & S. Feldman (Eds.), *Cognitive development and social development: Relationships and implications.* Hillsdale, N.J.: Lawrence Erlbaum Associates, 1977.

Davis A., & Havighurst, R. J. Social class and color differences in child rearing. *American Sociological Review,* 1946, *11,* 698 -710.

Dewey, J. *Democracy and education.* New York: Macmillan, Inc., 1916.

Emmerich, W. Continuity and stability in early social development. II. Teacher ratings. *Child Development,* 1966, *37,* 17-28.

Frankena, W. *Ethics.* Englewood Cliffs, N.J.: Prentice-Hall, Inc., 1963.

Gibson, E. *Principles of perceptual learning and development.* New York: Appleton-Century-Crofts, 1969.

Goldfarb, W. Psychological privation in infancy and subsequent adjustment. *American Journal of Orthopsychiatry,* 1945, *15,* 247-255.

Hare, R. M. *Essays on the moral concepts.* London: Macmillan, 1972.

Hartshorne, H., & May, M. A. *Studies in the nature of character* (Vol. I: *Studies in deceit*). New York: Macmillan, Inc., 1928.

Hartshorne, H., May, M. A., & Shuttleworth, F. K. *Studies in the nature of character* (Vol. III: *Studies in the organization of character*). New York: Macmillan, Inc., 1930.

Hoffman, M. L., & Saltzstein, H. D. Parent discipline and the child's moral development. *Journal of Personality and Social Psychology,* 1967, *5,* 45-57.

Kohlberg, L. *The development of modes of moral thinking and choice in the years ten to sixteen.* Unpublished doctoral dissertation, University of Chicago, 1958.

Kohlberg, L. Development of moral character and moral ideology. In M. L. Hoffman & L. W. Hoffman (Eds.), *Review of child development research* (Vol. I). New York: Russell Sage Foundation, 1964.

Kohlberg, L. Stages of moral development as a basis for moral education. In C. M. Beck, B. S. Crittenden, & E. V. Sullivan (Eds.), *Moral education: Interdisciplinary approaches.* Toronto: University of Toronto Press, 1971.

Kohlberg, L. Moral stages and moralization: The cognitive-developmental approach. In T. Lickona (Ed.), *Moral development and behavior.* New York: Holt, Rinehart and Winston, 1976.

Levin, H., & Sears, R. R. Identification with parents as a determinant of doll play aggression. *Child Development,* 1956, *27,* 135-153.

Lickona, T. (Ed.). *Moral development and behavior: Theory, research and social issues.* New York: Holt, Rinehart and Winston, 1976.

Mackay, H. A., & Laverty, S. G. *GSR changes during therapy of phobic behavior.* Unpublished manuscript, Queen's University, Ontario, Canada, 1963.

McCord, W., & McCord, J. *Psychopathy and delinquency.* New York: Grune & Stratton, Inc., 1956.

Mischel, W., & Gilligan, C. Delay of gratification, motivation for the prohibited gratification and responses to temptation. *Journal of Abnormal and Social Psychology,* 1964, *69,* 411-417.

Pearlin, L. I., Yarrow, M. R., & Scarr, H. A. Unintended effects of parental aspirations: The case of children's cheating. *American Journal of Sociology,* 1967, *73,* 73-83.

Pettigrew, T. F. Regional differences in anti-Negro prejudice. *Journal of Abnormal and Social Psychology,* 1959, *59,* 28-36.

Piaget, J. *The moral judgment of the child.* New York: The Free Press, 1965. (First published in English in London by Kegan Paul, 1932.)

Piaget, J. Piaget's theory. In P. Mussen (Ed.), *Carmichael's manual of child psychology* (Vol. 1). New York: John Wiley & Sons, Inc., 1970.

Porier, G. W., & Lott, A. J. Galvanic skin responses and prejudice. *Journal of Personality and Social Psychology,* 1967, *5,* 253-259.

Provence, S., & Lipton, R. C. *Infants in institutions.* New York: International Universities Press, 1962.

Sarason, I. G. Experimental approaches to test anxiety: Attention and the uses of information. In C. D. Spielberger (Ed.), *Anxiety: Current trends in theory and research* (Vol. II). New York: Academic Press, Inc., 1972.

Sears, P. S. Child-rearing factors related to playing of sex-typed roles. *American Psychologist,* 1953, *8,* 431. (Abstract)

Sears, R. R., Maccoby, E. E., & Levin, H. *Patterns of child rearing.* Evanston, Ill.: Row, Peterson & Co., 1957.

Sears, R. R., Whiting, J. W. M., Nowlis, V., & Sears, P. S. Some child-rearing antecedents of aggression and dependency in young children. *Genetic Psychology Monographs,* 1953, *47,* 135-234.

Sieber, J. E., Epstein, M. R., & Petty, C. The effectiveness of modeling and con-cept-learning procedures in teaching children to indicate uncertainty. *The Irish Journal of Education*, 1970, *4*, 90-106.

Sieber, J. E., Clark, R. E., Smith, H. H., & Sanders, N. Warranted uncertainty and students' knowledge and use of drugs. *Contemporary Educational Psychology*, 1978, *3*, 246-264.

Simpson, E. L. A holistic approach to moral development and behavior. In T. Lickona (Ed.), *Moral development and behavior*. New York: Holt, Rinehart and Winston, 1976.

Singer, P. *Animal liberation*. London: Jonathan Cape, 1976.

Spitz, R. A., & Wolf, K. M. Anaclitic depression: An inquiry into the genesis of psychiatric conditions in early childhood, II. In A. Freud et al. (Eds.), *The psy-choanalytic study of the child* (Vol. II). New York: International Universities Press, 1946.

Terman, L. M., & Merrill, M. A. *Measuring intelligence*. Boston: Houghton Mifflin Company, 1937.

Tuma, E., & Livson, N. Family socioeconomic status and adolescent attitudes to authority. *Child Development*, 1960, *31*, 387-399.

Turiel, E. Developmental processes in the child's moral thinking. In P. Mussen, J. Langer, & M. Covington (Eds.), *Trends and issues in developmental psychol-ogy*. New York: Holt, Rinehart and Winston, 1969.

Whiting, J. W. M. Sorcery, sin and the superego: A cross-cultural study of some mechanisms of social control. In M. R. Jones (Ed.), *Nebraska symposium on motivation* (Vol. VII). Lincoln, Nebraska: University of Nebraska Press, 1959.

6

A Psychoanalytic Perspective

TERRENCE N. TICE

In one sense, morality is a domain of experience shared by all human beings. Yet it is also among the higher human achievements. It is capable of development to a degree rarely anticipated in scholarly accounts. How do people grow in their ability to be moral? What role does socialization play in this process? What implications can be drawn for educational purposes? Psychoanalysis, both as a clinical method of investigation and as a matrix of scientific theories, presents one distinctive set of approaches to these questions.

Whereas most psychological method today views human life from outside behavior, psychoanalytic approaches chiefly view our experience from inside. One's entire life is seen as the result of intricate patterns of interaction built up, modified, and sustained from infancy onward. The core of these interactions is interpersonal. Usually we cannot see how their continuing influence is carried inside ourselves or others. They remain unconscious. Gaining greater insight into these unconscious processes requires extraordinarily disciplined attention. This is what psychoanalytically oriented therapy and clinically attuned observations of external behavior have been designed to achieve—sharper, deeper ways of seeing. The psychoanalytic perspective is broadly interactionist, taking into account interpersonal, familial, and other sociocultural influences on moral development; but it concentrates, as other methods do not, on intrapsychic structures.

Psychoanalytic method, created by Sigmund Freud (lived 1856-1939) and greatly refined over the past eighty years, has produced a rich body of knowledge and related theory concerning moral development. To unfold the entire story would require a lengthy account, beginning with

161

Freud's unveiling of infantile sexuality. It would feature his painstaking detective work on unconscious processes and his eventual postulation of "the superego" to explain key internal conflicts affecting moral behavior. It would further trace the emergence of character analysis, ego psychology, and other broadening perspectives on the mind as dominant elements in this type of inquiry during and after Freud's lifetime. Finally, it would distinguish the tremendously diverse approaches to understanding personal development that have gone by the name *psychoanalysis* and would show how other psychoanalytic scholars have surveyed the terrain (cf. Flugel, 1945; Hartmann, 1960; Post, 1972).

Despite this long history, the terrain has not been charted as a whole. An initial outline is attempted here, one that centers on the emergence of moral stages. Nevertheless, the exposition should be taken not as an accurate reflection of all that is going on, but as a provisional summary within a still burgeoning and sometimes tangled course of inquiry.

ORIENTATION

Accordingly, I have made several decisions in order to provide a well-focused, manageable, and cohesive account. First, I have made an effort to draw only upon formulations that derive from long-term clinical work or from observations that rely upon the complex set of controls that have emerged in psychoanalytic science.

This treatment also holds to the company of scholar-clinicians that stems directly from Freud and that has increasingly based theory on child analysis and child observation as well as on adult analysis. Anna Freud, Heinz Hartmann, Erik Erikson, Peter Blos, Edith Jacobson, and Margaret Mahler are among the great discoverers and synthesizers within this company whose articles are chiefly published in the periodicals cited here. They have all learned, from Freud's example, the rigorous disciplines of self-analysis, continually open-minded clinical inquiry, and mutual checking and revision. Their knowledge and technique is now, however, far beyond what Freud had available even in his later years.

The psychoanalytic approach taken here assumes that valuable, complementary information can be gained by other methods. It never assumes that what appears on the surface of human behavior is really what it seems to be or that one will derive a full, adequate, accurate description or explanation of behavior from examining surface behavior alone. Where possible, a deeper look is taken.

Attention here is chiefly placed on the development of moral capacities within the several most formative stages of moral development, extending from birth through late adolescence. These capacities are the features of a person's overall development that affect most directly the ability to grow morally and that most clearly represent ways of being moral at each stage. Strictly speaking, as will be shown, the first few years of life can only yield premoral stages, but the way these are formed greatly affects later development. The term *moral capacities* refers chiefly to six overlapping sets of abilities:

1. To be a moral agent, able to take responsibility for one's actions
2. To take a moral point of view concerning the rights and needs of oneself and others
3. To attain moral values, rules, principles, or ideals
4. To gain information relevant to moral decision-making
5. To exercise moral judgment
6. To take a moral course of action once it is chosen

These are conceptual distinctions. In real life, the determinants and expressions of these capacities are often so intertwined, they are inseparable.

In this chapter, morality is defined developmentally, in terms of the six sets of moral capacities. The moral domain is seen to emerge, for the child, only with the formation of superego functioning in early latency (usually in the sixth to eighth year), although there are many other determinants. In our premoral stages as children, almost all of us built up abilities to become moral but we had to achieve the integrating tasks of latency before they could be used morally. Accordingly, in some people, premoral positions persist into adulthood without much alteration. By the same token, the usual philosophical depiction of morality in terms of universalizable prescriptive obligations justified by basic principles of right and wrong refers to a narrow set of rational capacities which are fully achievable only in adolescence at the earliest.

Emphasis here will be placed on the psychoanalytic structural theory of mental functioning. Although many complementary theories have developed through psychoanalytic inquiry and are still valid, the structural theory remains the central paradigm of this science (Arlow, 1975; Modell, 1975). The structural way of comprehensively viewing all mental functioning and behavior was first formulated by Freud in *The Ego and the Id* (1923/1961). In this book, Freud postulated that the id, the ego, and the superego are distinctly though inseparably interactive mental agencies, the latter two having both conscious and unconscious features. This combination of characteristics sharply distinguishes the psychoanalytic structural theory from the Piagetian-type structural-developmental theory, which covers only a portion of mental and behavioral functioning. Many modifications of the theory made since 1923 are reflected in the present account.

The theory of separation-individuation, among the many theories that have emerged through studies of children and adolescents (McDevitt & Settlage, 1971; Mahler, Pine, & Bergman, 1975), is also featured here, both because of its prominence in recent discussion and because it most clearly illuminates the issue of our preparedness for moral interaction.

Finally, this discussion is devoted almost entirely to the ordinary course of development. Thus, it largely omits reference to pathology. The term *ordinary* refers not to average or usual development, as such, but to a normal range within which it is possible for people to move steadily and variously onward, without severe deprivation and without arrest. Thus neurotic or preneurotic elementary school children may continue growth within the ordinary range, and they may be capable of high moral achievement as they grow older, even though they will undoubtedly have serious blocks against efficient use of their moral capacities.

Ordinary moral development chiefly arises out of the child's interaction with supportive parents and parental figures during the premoral stages. Parental influence continues to be important, in varying degrees, as the child's social world expands. Nevertheless, in a real sense the actual integration and restructuring that produces the morally competent person are due to the child himself or herself and to the adult the child becomes. The child is an interactive social being through and through, but in ordinary development he or she becomes increasingly autonomous and creative in his or her own right. Moreover, from the first year on, the child contributes even to the foundations and precursors of moral development, through his or her own disposition, fantasies, and mental structures. The child whose psyche is growing never simply takes in or copies what is presented by the environment.

STAGES AND TURNING POINTS

The psychoanalytic theories of moral development to be reconstructed here contain the following schedule of four-plus stages. Each of these is initially recognizable only through the achievement of certain crucial developmental tasks; here these tasks are called turning points. The turning point in each successive moral stage can be reached only to the degree that the basic developmental tasks of the preceding stage have been achieved. (*See* Table 6-1.)

1. The first stage of moral development is achieved through the formation of superego structures. This achievement rests on important premoral foundations, from birth through experience of the Oedipus complex, which is itself the first turning point into moral development in the strict sense. In particular, results of separation-individuation struggles and an array of superego precursors, formed from infancy onward, provide ingredients for this new mode of functioning.

2. The second stage of moral development is a period of elaboration and consolidation, still in latency, and is brought about by achievement of the structure of latency. This is the second major turning point, and it is usually experienced at about age seven or later.

3. The third stage of moral development appears in early and middle adolescence. It is ushered in by the person's response to puberty, the third major turning point.

4. The fourth stage of moral development is attained upon entering late adolescence, which also has its own distinctive turning points. Then other

Table 6-1. The psychoanalytic stages of moral development.

Stages and Descriptions	Approximate Ages
Premoral stages	Birth-3
Separation-individuation task achievement, Superego precursors	
Turning point: Oedipal task achievement	3-6
Stage 1: Primary morality	5-6
Initial superego formation, Post-Oedipal, Early latency	
Turning point: "Structure of latency" task achievement	6-8
Stage 2: Middle childhood morality	8-12
Latency proper, Prepuberty	
Turning point: Pubertal task achievement—early adolescence	12-14
Stage 3: Adolescent morality	14-16
Second Separation-Individuation phase—middle adolescence	
Turning point: Late adolescent task achievement	16-early 20s
Stage 4: Early adult morality	Late teens on
Turning point: Adult task achievement	
Stage 5+: Later adult morality	ca. 21-25 until death
Facing old age and death—the third Separation-Individuation phase	

turning points and stages may emerge on quite diverse individual time-
tables, extending through adulthood and, notably, including ways of con-
fronting old age and death.

On a very different schedule, Erik Erikson (1964) has postulated the
development of "psychological virtues" (hope, will, purpose, competence,
fidelity, love, care, and wisdom) as resolutions of eight core developmental conflicts, three of which appear in adulthood. The account presented
here also differs from Erikson's in that it does not identify core conflicts or
virtues with particular stages, but indicates the enormous complexity of
individual growth. I agree with Erikson, however, that as a total configura-
tion, the achievements of each stage and turning point depend on those of
preceding stages, and that, at the same time, there is also a new chance for
some moral growth in each period.

FOUNDATIONS: THE PREMORAL STAGES

Virtually everything that happens in the life of an infant contributes to his
or her capacity for social relations and shapes his or her particular way of
entering the moral domain. The way the infant experiences the tasks of
separation-individuation, however, marks his or her progress with special
clarity. Whether a person will eventually enter the moral domain effec-

tively, and what that person's distinctive modes of doing so are, are probably best illuminated by the separation-individuation process that individual goes through.

Separation-Individuation

Ordinarily the first great cycle of separation-individuation, what Margaret Mahler and her associates (1975) have called "the psychological birth of the human infant," will have been achieved by the third birthday. The foundations for moral development are set, sometimes almost inalterably fixed, in this period and in the Oedipal period that immediately follows. The process continues with numerous variations throughout life but rounds the second great cycle in adolescence. The acceptance of death may be considered the third great cycle.

Within the first cycle, if all goes relatively well, we see the formation of a whole personality, of a person possessed of a growing sense of identity and agency, expressing a capacity to relate to other human beings as individuals. The child is on the threshold of being able to internalize, reshape, reject, and augment the moral values and capacities of his or her elders, and to move toward substantial moral autonomy. This is a lifelong task, though distinct markers of achievement can be discerned along the road to be taken over the next twenty years or more.

In *functional* terms we speak of separation-individuation during this foundational period; in *structural* terms we speak of the building of ego capacities and of the precursors of later superego structures and functions. In both respects it is helpful to view all that goes on as a highly complex interactive process in which the total human organism is adapting to the surrounding world and gaining special attachment to parts of it (Hartmann, 1937/1958; Joffe & Sandler, 1968).

In the first three months or so the infant exists in a stage largely undifferentiated from the mothering figure, from that "object" in the environment that satisfies the infant's needs. This is true even though styles of interaction between infant and mother have been important determinants of personality since birth (Fries & Woolf, 1971). In psychoanalytic usage, *object* refers to someone or (by derivation) something at which wishes for gratification of instinctual drives are directed. The mother is thus the first of many objects. There is no implication that the object is perceived as a mere thing.

Through the mothering process, and through fleeting moments of alertness, the initial phase of symbiosis in the first month includes small reachings-out to the environment. Otherwise, the newborn reacts in a diffuse, global fashion to stimuli, relying on reflex equipment as in intra-uterine life. Normally, within the second month the shell that kept external stimuli out and helped maintain equilibrium begins to crack; the infant displays a dim awareness of the mother as the need-satisying object and enters into a more distinct phase of symbiosis with her. That is, to the infant, mother and infant are vaguely two yet exist as one: their boundaries are the same. Although the infant may respond differentially to stimuli from within (e.g., pain) and from without (e.g., a sound), the infant as yet has no definite schema for differentiating the two. The mother's patterns of holding and tending the baby, particularly as these attend special frustrations and gratifications, already begin to be adopted by the infant at this time (e.g., rocking, bouncing, soothing). This prepares the way for what Mahler calls the first subphase of separation-individuation: differentiation.

From birth on, we carry within us remnants of each phase of development—remnants of the state of being, the hallucinations and fantasies, the patterns of motion, the modes of perception, the thoughts, the defenses, the ways of relating. Our development may become fixed in some fashion to a particular phase (in the case of psychotics, to very early ones) because of some trauma not overcome within, some constitutional deficiency, or some lack of external facility for moving on. Particular kinds of pressures, real or imagined, may also lead us to regress toward mental acts or behaviors typical of earlier phases. All these features, at each stage of life, enter decisively into our ways of being moral, or of not being moral, or of preparing to be moral. That is why it is important to understand the infant's experience, even though morality proper emerges only much later.

Differentiation and practicing.   Differentiation, the first subphase of separation-individuation, is overlapped by the second one, called the practicing subphase. Early in the first subphase, the infant is "hatching." That is, at about four to five months, the infant is beginning to show signs of alertly, intentionally, persistently directing attention outward (e.g., exploring mother's face, looking about, playing peekaboo), and at the same time adopting transitional objects and situations apart from the mother—transitional to not being with her at all. From about seven to eight months, the infant is venturing out still further, making comparisons between mother and what belongs to mother (e.g., her hair, a necklace) or is not mother, but checking back to mother all the while, curious about strangers, wondrous, yet occasionally anxious.

The acuteness of anxiety chiefly depends on how trustful the earlier experiences with mother have been. This has led psychoanalytic writers to unanimously lay great emphasis on the early relationship of trust between mother and child as the indispensable foundation for all subsequent relationships between persons, especially moral ones (Erikson, 1964; Ekstein & Motto, 1969).

In the second subphase, practicing, the infant uses his or her abilities to get around both to differentiate bodily from the mother and to form a special bond with her. The first locomotions (crawling, etc.) are performed in close proximity to her (and others, like the father, who are intertwined with that relationship), always coming back for emotional refueling. Then, from about ten or twelve months to sixteen to eighteen months, the child toddles away. "The child seems intoxicated with his own faculties and with the greatness of his own world. Narcissism is at its peak!" (Mahler, Pine, & Bergman, 1975, p. 71).

Rapprochement.   By the middle of the second year, the infant has become a toddler and is entering into use of symbolic language and play. Mahler calls this third subphase rapprochement, because for the next six months or so the child continues to move away. The child does this often with fierce *no's* and dramatic altercations, yet insisting on having mother share every part of life and greatly needing reconciliation with the one who is in normal development so rapidly becoming "the other."

At times, the separateness from mother may bring on acute anxiety. This, in turn, brings on wooing behavior to get her back. Although father has been present in, though never fully part of, the early acts in this drama from birth on (apparently in very special ways not yet well understood), now he (if available) may become the first among additional personal objects to fill the child's expanding world. Difficulty with leavetakings, intolerance of sadness, fits of reaction to strangers, indecision, and ambivalence are all features of this period. Mother is characteristically used as an extension of self. The emotional range broadens considerably, and empathy begins to be expressed in relation to other children. In a great variety of ways, the object world is often split into representations of the "good" and "bad" mother. The child reacts very sensitively to parental expressions of approval or disapproval and is strongly motivated by the fear of losing their love. All these features return to haunt the individual's ways of living in the moral domain later on.

Toward the end of this third subphase, the struggle tends to die down. The child is using language now to name and master and use the environment; portions of the world have now become quite familiar; and the child says "I." Boys and girls, moreover, begin to be decisively aware of their anatomical differences, a key factor in their growing sense of gender identity.

Object constancy and individuality.   Being able to unify representations of good and bad into one object during the third year enables the emergence of an emotional sense of object constancy (to be distinguished from the cognitive sense of "object permanence" which Piaget places at eighteen to twenty months [Mahler, Pine, & Bergman, 1975, p. 111; McDevitt & Settlage, 1971, p. 719]). It further facilitates effective collaboration or fusion between aggressive and libidinal, sexual aspects of the child's instinctual drives. Object constancy occurs in the fourth, open-ended subphase of separation-individuation (McDevitt, 1975, p. 714, sees this as a process probably continuing through adolescence). This subphase emerges interdependently with the child's distinctive consolidation of individuality. These two achievements permit representations of self and object world and their interactions, without all three of which, talk of morality would be meaningless.

By the end of the fourth subphase the child is ordinarily ready to enter the moral domain. The mother is perceived as one who can be basically trusted to satisfy needs, even though this does not happen with complete consistency, and to return to the child after she is away. From about twenty or twenty-two months to thirty to thirty-six months, the child also accrues specific capacities for knowing, reality testing, fantasy, play, and communication that will enable active participation in the moral domain. Behaviorally the child is less self-centered and demanding, is confident and affectionate, shows more regard for the interests and feelings of others, can play cooperatively, and is able to give and take (A. Freud, 1965).

In contrast, the children whose development has been hampered in any way during any of these subphases of separation-individuation, or during their forerunners within the first three months of life, will experience difficulties in understanding moral discourse, in acting morally, or in forming moral judgments later on. Because of inadequacies in early child-rearing or severe disturbances to growth in these crucial years, the foundations for true moral agency may be lacking altogether.

THE OEDIPUS COMPLEX: INTO THE FIRST MORAL STAGE

According to the psychoanalytic perspective, the dissolution of the Oedipus complex, complete or partial, largely determines the major features of the young child's character and constitutes the child's passport into the moral domain.

Culmination of Infantile Sexuality

The existence of the Oedipus complex as the culmination of infantile sexuality was established for Freud in 1897. In *The Interpretation of Dreams* (1900-1901/1953) Freud refers to Oedipus' activities as showing us "the fulfillment of our own childhood wishes," since repressed. This discussion appears in a section on typical dreams, regarding one kind in which there appears the primitive wish to have intercourse with mother and to kill father (pp. 261-264).

Popularly, Freud's concept has often been misunderstood as if it meant only raw fantasy content for boys and something vaguely parallel for girls. This is far from the case, although it is true that the earliest exemplifications of the concept in Freud's writings focused on such content and that anthropological studies have found the specific Oedipal wishes emphasized by early Freud to be the two great crimes prohibited by totemism. Moreover, there has been, especially in recent years, much further alteration of Freud's self-admittedly tentative treatment of female psychology (Schafer, 1974; Jacobson, 1976). This is important for us to notice, because Freud believed that women tend to express morality in very different ways from men.

By 1920 Freud was not only referring to the triadic Oedipal relationship as "the nuclear complex of the neuroses," as he had done for several years, but he was stating that it "constitutes the essential part of their content" (1905/1953, p. 226, *see* footnote from 1920). He held that everyone who reaches that point in development either masters the Oedipus complex or falls victim to a neurosis. It was further clear to him that the whole family constellation, funneled through the primary relationships with the mother and the father figures but significantly including sibling relationships, gave the Oedipus complex its eventual shape.

These views have remained central features of psychoanalytic theory, substantiated in numerous ways through child observation and clinical practice (Brenner, 1976). It should come as no surprise, however, that because by the age of five or six we have repressed almost all that occurred in the earlier years, and also because the infantile sexual roots of our behavior are still bound to be strange and bothersome to us, it is sometimes difficult to hold these things in mind. This can occasionally happen even among those who are engaged in clinical work and who possess the evidence of their own analysis.

Convergence of Developmental Lines

There is not enough space here to even summarize the numerous distinct but interacting "lines" of development in early childhood (A. Freud, 1965; cf. Laufer, 1965; and W. E. Freud, 1967, 1971). Perhaps the most familiar are the partial shift from "the pleasure principle" to "the reality principle" in the regulation of instinctual drives and the dynamic reorganizing of focal interests from "oral" to "anal" to "phallic" and "Oedipal" aspects. The essential point is that all the lines have been seen to converge in the Oedipal period and its aftermath. All deeply affect the way a child enters into the moral domain and acts within it. As the task of resolving the Oedipus complex arises, ego functions of synthesis and integration are first brought into play as a highly organized and deliberate process, functions which continue to serve in each successive stage of development but again take center stage in middle adolescence (Rosner, 1972).

Changes in Modes of Relationship

What happens as a child moves through the Oedipus complex? The Oedipal phase stretches from about two and one-half or three years to about six years of age. The relations of the Oedipal child to parents during this period are characterized by the child's ability, after getting into the fourth separation-individuation subphase already described, to relate to each parent differently. Now, in fantasy or with substitutes if either or both of the original parental figures are not present, the primarily dyadic focus in the pre-Oedipal child's modes of relationship gives way to a triadic focus. The child's constitutional bisexuality enables the boy or girl to take a more masculine or feminine position depending on constitutional dispositions, on the prior determinants of development, on the meanings the child attributes to anatomical discoveries, and on the vicissitudes of relationship in the Oedipal years. Positive and negative attitudes toward each parent contribute to the form of identifications with each parent that will be retained in the next stage of development.

The Oedipal conflicts are shaped by all these factors plus the convergence of all previous lines of development. The core Oedipal conflict for the boy who has truly entered the Oedipal phase is one wishing to have the mother or her substitute exclusively and in the fullest way possible (i.e., as one possessing a penis and having strong sexual urges, as one who now identifies himself as manly) but fearing punishment (ultimately castration or destruction) by the rival father figure, whom he wishes to remove from competition. Anxiety about what the father might do, and attendant guilt over having such strong wishes toward the mother, drives the boy to repress those wishes and to identify more closely with the father. This allows the boy to consolidate his masculinity while sustaining love for the mother in less threatening ways.

Freud once described the character of the "ego" aspect of our psychic structure as "a precipitate of abandoned object-cathexes" (1923/1961, p. 29). Cognitive skills are also ego skills, but here he was speaking of ego aspects of object relations, of abandoned attachments. New ego precipitates form as the Oedipus complex is dissolved and collect into a new structure including earlier messages and identifications relevant to what one wants to be and do. Whereas up to this point these messages and identifications were derived chiefly from the parents, now the sources are expanding. The new structure, called "superego," contains firm directives, criticisms, and prohibitions on the one hand (superego in the narrower sense), and ideals on the other ("ego ideal").

It seems to be superego in the narrower sense that must develop as a virtually new structure if the Oedipus complex is to be dissolved, whereas new ego ideal components are continuous with others that have been forming since the first year. Superego in the narrower sense serves to censor and repress the boy's wishes by, in effect, ordering them as the boy believes, consciously or unconsciously, the father or mother would do.

Sexual Differences

From very early, and not dependent entirely on cultural differences or sex-role typing, girls display a different range of developmental possibilties from boys. Recent psychoanalytic child observation and child analysis show that within these differential ranges of development there need not be any marked difference between boys and girls in their moral capacities. But there may be some differences of emphasis within the range of character traits girls and boys assume and of ideals and concerns to which they direct moral attention within a given culture.

Girls who are able to enter into the Oedipal phase generally display a positive sensuality in approach to objects (people, dolls, etc.) quite different from approaches boys take. Moreover, the wish to have a baby of one's own, earlier shared with boys, now takes on a significantly different drive-derived, heterosexual character. In some instances (contrary to Freud's tentative account), this precedes any concern girls might have about the comparative shape of their genitals. Pre-Oedipal genital exploration and masturbation can be expected to contribute to the Oedipal girl's body image, as to that of boys'. To this may be added maternal identifications formed within the later separation-individuation subphases and growing capacities to be sexually receptive and nurturant. It is these heterosexual trends, not the castration complex postulated by Freud, that many now consider to be the impulse that moves the girl into the Oedipal or first genital phase (the second occurring at puberty). It is nevertheless important to recognize that cultural and child-rearing conditions still make the false sense of deficiency that many girls have, and an accompanying unconscious fantasy that mother made her so, a prominent feature in her turning away from mother to father, and that such conditions are slow to change (Jacobson, 1976).

In any case, the girl has bisexual identifications and problems with those identifications as has the boy. Hence, penis envy is not necessarily out of the picture for girls any more than penis envy and envy of feminine attributes are absent among boys. But the ambivalent attachment to the mother that both girls and boys share early in this period must radically shift for the girl, with the father becoming the object of romantic interest and the mother the rival. In order to achieve this shift, the girl need not relinquish identifications with the mother to the extent necessary for the boy. Both must somehow keep the mother as the primary caretaker on whom they depend. Within the normal range of development, the girl's superego arises out of the same need to avoid punishment and to repress dangerous wishes as does the boy's and draws from whatever directives, criticisms, prohibitions, and ideals she has carried into this period from early childhood identifications. If her experience has been in some measure different from that of boys, as it invariably will have been, she will to that degree be able to bring different contributions into the moral domain. This does not mean (again, contrary to Freud) that her superego is necessarily weaker or that she is more likely to be a masochist.

Attainment of True Morality

> True morality begins when the internalized criticism, now embodied in the standard exacted by the superego, coincides with the ego's perception of its own fault. (A. Freud, 1966, p. 119).

Three developmental observations are presupposed in Anna Freud's statement. First, various ego functions are required, and must be mature enough, to permit superego functioning. "The superego is like a royal personage who can only function through his prime minister" (Beres, 1958, p. 327). Reality testing, memory, perception, conceptualization, and judgment are among the many ego functions that permit action upon superego attitudes.

Second, it is easy to mistake ego responses to external controls (such as shame in its early forms, fear, and need for punishment) where no guilt is present, for superego responses in the narrower sense where a sense of guilt is required. In fact, when the person's psychic structure is well integrated and stabilized, defensive ego reactions and superego functioning may sometimes be impossible to distinguish, because they mesh so well.

Third, there are numerous precursors to superego development which serve directive, prohibitive, self-critical, or ideal-setting functions, but which have very different qualities from superego functioning per se. Sometimes these other processes display "an analogy of function" (Hartmann & Loewenstein, 1962, p. 43), often quite vague and superficial upon closer scrutiny, but nothing more. Any such ego functions can be viewed as forerunners of superego functions.

LATENCY: INTO THE SECOND
MORAL STAGE

Morality, in the sense defined here, presupposes the existence of latency, superego functioning, and guilt. As such, it is a very recent accomplishment in the history of mankind.

The Dawn of Latency

In a recent review of archeological and anthropological evidence, Charles Sarnoff has postulated that the dawn of latency as a social structure capable of being utilized for the transmission and internalization of culture occurred within the fourth millenium B.C. (Sarnoff, 1976, pp. 363, 367). Cultural manifestations of superego functioning, as determined by feelings of guilt, first clearly surfaced with the eighth century prophets in the Hebrew scriptures. The personality and social potentials for this phenomenon, however, no doubt existed some centuries earlier. On the basis of brain size and other indicators, premoral "shame culture" could have existed over 100,000 years before. This type of culture would have been dominant until late in the transition from hunting and food gathering to settled community life in the second and first millennia B.C.

Children in some primitive societies today do not experience latency in the sense to be described. Thus, they cannot experience adolescence in the same way either. Many children in modern society also lack the prerequisite ego skills to achieve latency. Thus, they are developmentally unable to attain a genuine moral position.

The Nature of Latency

As more precise information has been gathered about the middle childhood years, the tendency among psychoanalysts has been to divide this development into two periods, each of which is further subdivided. The first phase covers roughly the ages of five and one half to eight; the second lasts from ages eight to eleven (A. Freud, 1945; Bornstein, 1951). The other way is to divide into three phases: an early phase, latency proper from about ages seven to nine; and late latency, including prepuberty as a transitional phase (Williams, 1972). Some in effect divide the two periods into two phases each (Sarnoff, 1976). The schedule varies greatly among children, but even in modern societies entrance into latency proper before six to eight years of age is extremely rare.

Shapiro and Perry (1976) have suggested that a considerable convergence of evidence from biology, psychology, and other fields may now support, if not wholly confirm, the shift of capacities analysts have observed in children aged seven, plus or minus one year. This evidence seems to show that "processes within the central nervous system and cognitive strategies from maturation [and not lessened drive urgency, as Freud supposed] provide latency with its biological clock" (Shapiro & Perry, 1976, p. 97). These changes permit precisely that growth of autonomous ego functioning, of inhibition and control of drives (notably through repression), of postponement of action, and of superego functioning that we ordinarily see developing at that time. They constitute the second turning point in moral development, the introduction to the second stage.

Many of the cognitive adaptations detailed by Piaget and others were earlier noted by Freud (1911/1958). Nass (1966), like many others before and after him, has noted a further convergence between Piaget's findings on the rapidly changing cognitive capacities that underlie moral development at this age and psychoanalytic findings (e.g., A. Sandler, 1975; Shapiro & Perry, 1976, pp. 98-100). In all, there is now much evidence to suggest that latency is in part a result of brain size, neurological maturation, and cognitive development. Thus, it cannot be attributed simply to particular kinds of socio-cultural influence. Psychoanalytic theory has always incorporated these other factors while centering on vicissitudes of the drives and on the psychic restructuring that takes place with resolution of the Oedipus complex.

When latency is viewed not simply as a time of life, but as a distinct developmental structure, what is it exactly? And how does it come about? For reasons that will become clear, at this stage above all, the answers must rely heavily on child observation and child analysis. Adults tend to give a distorted picture of middle childhood. Relatively little, moreover, is learned about latency from analysis of adults (Bornstein, 1951, p. 282). Here the account relates closely to Charles Sarnoff's (1976) outstanding synthesis of previous psychoanalytic work.

Early Latency

As might well be expected, children who are passing out of the Oedipal stage are unsteady for a time, as if recovering from a blow. The regressive pull to earlier phases is still strong, and they appear restless. Sleeping disturbances and other signs of unquelled anxiety are prominent features of this phase. Sometimes these children "do O.K.," as parents say, in some places like school or in some types of activity, but show discomfort elsewhere. After periods of calm they will suddenly break into excited misbehavior. The old modes of concrete, magical symbolism and association are strongly in conflict with newer ventures into reasoning and reality. They will be for some time.

Early-latency children gradually form a repertoire of fantasies and defenses, built upon their newfound capacities for symbolization. These permit drive discharge in the face of prohibitions against sexual and aggressive activity, and at the same time protect equilibrium. During this early period, fantasy itself becomes a useful defense and is the preferred avenue for drive expression. Direct engagement with real objects and activities is important for the child's growing consolidation of ego skills, but it is frequently tentative and episodical. Just now the child tends to be highly preoccupied with private interests.

Placed in the context of a relatively settled society, latency essentially functions to secure the transmissions of customary social values and practices, to convey cultural meanings among the generations, and to establish skills necessary for future planning and adaptation. States of calm, good behavior, pliability, and educability must be achieved if these aims are to be fulfilled.

If all goes fairly well, such states become regular and natural to the child who is emerging out of the early latency phase. Since what is occurring is a difficult and challenging process of personal growth, and not simply a process of physical maturation or social imitation (Meissner, 1974, p. 518) or modeling, these states exist within an immensely variable matrix of thoughts, feelings, fantasies, defenses, and interactions. Thus, they are interrupted, they take on flexible and changing qualities, and they comprise an elaborately equipped workshop for discovering and trying out new skills. Sarnoff describes the corresponding defense mechanisms used in dealing with breakthroughs of pre-Oedipal and Oedipal conflicts as "the structure of latency" (1976, p. 31).

It is this ego structure that maintains the latency state once it has been reached: through the use of repression above all, but also through other defense mechanisms distinguishable from those used earlier. The nature and developmental uses of these defenses during latency have been systematically explored by Anna Freud (1966), Bornstein (1951), Sarnoff (1976), and many others.

A child is said to be in "a state of latency" when the "structure of latency" is "active, available and effective" (Sarnoff, 1976, p. 8).

The First Stage of Moral Development

These early latency achievements mark a distinct first stage of moral development. Clinically, children who are passing into the state of latency clearly show not only the qualities of action already mentioned, but also the ability to differentiate fantasy events such as dreams and daydreams from reality. They also tend to suppress masturbation, to act more dependably in a variety of different circumstances, and to feel guilt and use it in decision-making (Sarnoff, 1976, p. 87). True autonomy is barely possible, if at all; but earlier identifications, especially with parental figures and with features present in the child's interactions with those figures, are now being "internalized." The earlier directives, criticisms, prohibitions, and ideals are now being heard from inside. Moreover, the child is beginning to modify those earlier identifications with new experience. And it would appear that the child's own earlier criticisms of the parents are among the resources now at the child's command (Hartmann & Loewenstein, 1962, pp. 69-70). Superego functioning has thus begun.

At first the critical, prohibitive functions appear in a sharp outline, in the service of repression. Occasionally, the superego, as we might readily imagine calling this imperative inner voice as Freud did, is quite severe. Then, to the degree that the child does not fix upon neurotic symptom formation, the various other facets of superego functioning—the loving and supportive and ideal-setting facets—gradually consolidate with these functions and a new internal structure, the superego proper, is formed. The child has in this way rounded the first great turning point in moral development and has literally entered a new world.

At this juncture it is important to clarify two matters: (1) the meaning of entering into a new world from the child's perspective, and (2) the movement from earlier identification processes to internalization. After a brief attention to these matters, we will move to a consideration of the dual concepts, superego and ego ideal, which lie at the heart of the psychoanalytic theory of moral development.

The different worlds of childhood.   First we may seek to remind ourselves, as Freud and Piaget have preeminently demonstrated, that the worlds of childhood are very different from the so-called adult world. (The following account is drawn in part from psychoanalyst Anne-Marie Sandler [1975], a former student and co-worker of Piaget.) Piaget has shown, for example, that the world of the "preoperational" child is a world of concrete particulars. The preoperational child is about age eighteen or twenty months to six or seven years, i.e., through early latency. The child is as yet unable to truly consider another person's point of view, a basic prerequisite for moral reasoning. During this period, parental injunctions upon the child's behavior are taken literally and absolutely. The child lives by orders that come from outside. At the same time, the contents of daydreams and play are quite real to the child—no less so, in fact often more so, than reality.

These characteristics prevail, with only slight modification, right through the Oedipal period and into early latency. Moreover, although these childhood perspectives on the world do not remain in our minds unchanged, they do remain. They cannot be extinguished (Meissner, 1973, p. 802; 1974, p. 525). They are never wholly supplanted, but continue to operate among the unconscious determinants of behavior in adult life. Although they may disturb and distort current perspectives, they also serve progressive, creative functions (Loewald, 1973, p. 15). The royal road to the unconscious is the dream, Freud said (1900-1901/1953); but many roads are open everyday, and some of them go back very far.

Using Piaget's perspective, we may well consider, then, what a marked turning point it would have been for us as children to enter Piaget's next cognitive stage at about seven to eleven years of age. Though still tied very much to the concrete, here-and-now experiences, we would have been able during these years to form concepts and modes of thinking that would have enabled us to build a broadening, more cohesive picture of the world. Moreover, we would have been gaining the ability to perceive and act upon the world from our own viewpoint, relying less on fantasy than on actual contact, actual experimentation, actual understanding. Within the moral domain, accruing these cognitive capacities would have enabled us to begin forming and trying out our own values, making decisions, and taking responsibility for their consequences on our own.

According to Sarnoff (1976, p. 91), the "first cognitive organizing period" of early latency involves the capacities to repress, symbolize, and repress one or more of the meanings a symbol comes to represent, the achievement of highly developed conceptual memory organization, and behavioral constancy. The second such period, lasting from about age seven and one half to age eight and one half, involves greatly heightened reality testing, abstract conceptual memory organization, and a shift in fantasy contents from thoughts about fantasy objects to thoughts about reality objects.

The latter set of cognitive achievements facilitates a second stage of moral development, one in which the process of internalization plays a major role. By eight and one half years of age, a child who is developing fairly normally will have discovered a new world theatre, a new stage to act upon.

Identification and internalization.   This leads to the second matter to be clarified. Mid-latency children busily "internalize" values, rules, and the like, that have been known in their interactions with the outside world (Hartmann & Loewenstein, 1962, p. 48). This process, therefore, obviously goes to the heart of cultural processes and cultural differences. Internalization is perhaps best depicted as a late mode of identification. Identification is the process and result of attempting to achieve or restore a state of well-being by being like someone in some fashion. As an "organizing activity" (J. Sandler, 1960, p. 150), it is far more than a mere taking in from outside. Representations of both self and object greatly affect what is taken in. The technique of identification long outlasts childhood and is crucial in adolescent development. Alongside obedience and compliance, it is a primary way of establishing emotional equilibrium from late in the separation-individuation phase through the early latency period.

During latency, a new type of identification is taking place; psychoanalysts call it *internalization*. The difference lies, as Sandler (1960) has explained the process, in its being an identification with a particular introjection of the parents, namely with their authority. If the term *authority* is taken in its root sense, so as to refer to the parents as the previous authors of values, rules, and the like, Sandler's account not only fits other psychoanalytic usage well but helps to clarify the frequent confusion of meanings in this portion of the literature. Now the child acts like that earlier authority, as that authority (quite distorted in some cases) is introjected or taken into the child's own mental schemata. Accordingly, the child's sense of well-being may come to be derived in large part from this new authority rather than directly from the parents.

Whereas repression "tends to keep object representations and object relations on an infantile level" (Loewald, 1973, p. 12), internalization serves a progressive, restructuring function. In the latency period, "Oedipal object relations are renounced as such, destroyed, and the resulting elements enter into the formation of higher psychic structure, leading in turn to the development of object relations of a higher order or organization" (p. 12).

In the process of internalization, or superego identification, the child is becoming a moral agent; he or she is gaining the capacity to "suit oneself," as we say, in moral affairs. Guilt appears as the child's affective response to failing that internalized authority. Pride and other feelings of self-esteem follow from satisfaction of that authority's demands and ideals, if the newly-installed authority is not too demanding or idealistic to allow for harmonious, realistic dealings between that superego agency and ego functioning. Things may go wrong, but the developmental push is progressive. Formed through the internalization process, which is also being directed toward establishing ego functioning, superego functioning serves both in a ruling and in a reconciling fashion, as a means of supporting and consolidating and gaining fulfillment of all the best that ego stands for in human achievement (Hartmann, 1937/1958, p. 52; Hartmann & Loewenstein, 1962, pp. 76-79). As such, it also possesses a future-planning aspect and serves to indicate "the direction of future human evolution" (Loewald, 1962, p. 267).

The Second Stage of Moral Development

The second stage of moral development is brought about by the new ego capacities and internalization processes just detailed. In a more calm and concentrated style than in early latency, children of about seven to nine or ten years are stretching out to express themselves and to gain a broadening sense of competency and self-confidence (Lichtenberg, 1975, p. 481). It is a time to accrue much greater competency in all the six sets of moral capacities mentioned earlier: to be a moral agent, to take a moral point of view, to attain moral values, rules, principles, and ideals, to gain information relevant to moral decision-making, to exercise moral judgment, and to take a moral course of action once it has been chosen.

A fuller account of this period, and of each subsequent period, would require taking each of these sets of moral capacities and examining their growth in three ways: (1) in terms of ego and superego functioning generally, (2) more specifically, in terms of how they represent ways of handling internal conflict characteristic of each person, and (3) in terms of how they help the child to a widening and changing environment. In addition, it would necessitate examining the configurations, both clinically and sociologically defined, of what happens when any of these capacities is not functioning well. Using both kinds of information, we would then need to consider the relation of a person's character structure to his or her developing moral character.

SUPEREGO FUNCTIONING FROM LATENCY ONWARD

Here we'll look more closely at superego functioning, which comprises the primary organizing agency for moral development from this point on. Two matters have to be clarified before we can proceed. First, "conscience" in its usual meanings cannot be identical with superego, chiefly because superego functioning includes self-esteem regulation, self-comfort and protection, internalization of nonmoral values, tastes, rules, and the like, and much more. On the other hand, the term *conscience* also refers to internal regulations of conduct in nonmoral spheres, chiefly social conventions, as well as in the moral domain. Hence these other manifestations of conscience should be treated separately from those that appear in moral development, although they also refer to superego functioning.

Second, from middle latency on, the number of factors and the possible combinations are too great to permit more than an outline of general features and an indication of where the further turning points are within the second decade of life. The general features include: the use of superego precursors, the contribution of separation affects, the formation of ego-ideal structures, the interweaving of regulative and supportive structures, the vicissitudes of aggression, the continuing roles of guilt or shame, and the growing sense of self.

Integration and Advancement of Superego Precursors

From middle latency on, the child is internally hard at work integrating and advancing for new use a disparate set of superego precursors, all of which are essential for healthy moral development. From earlier development, the following superego precursors are particularly important:

1. Parental images derived from the entire range of sensorimotor modalities used in relating to the external world, including smelling and balancing as well as seeing and hearing
2. Imaginative, affect-laden representations of reality, expressed especially through language and gesture, and eventually focused on discriminations of value
3. The abilities to say "No," to criticize oneself, to identify with perceived aspects of aggressors, and to perceive others as "for me" or "against me"
4. Empathy
5. Capacities for dialogue and cooperative play

6. The sense of a "right to life" (Modell, 1965) applied first to oneself and then to others

Separation Affects and Related Feelings

Affective responses to separation look either to the past or to the future. How an individual handles attachment and separation in both respects strongly determines the shape of moral development at each stage.

Learning to experience a loss freely, to leave the past behind, to take into oneself what is of value from the past and go on leads to "an enrichment of the superego" (Loewald, 1962, p. 268). Mourning is, thus, an important ingredient in the latency child's growing ability to select what is of value, to make moral decisions accordingly, and to take responsibility for them. Completed or uncompleted, mourning is often a key factor in creative activity and may be essential to the ability to adapt to change (Pollock, 1977). It is a major task of adolescence and is probably consolidated to a full extent only in young adulthood at the earliest. Much depends on the kinds of losses one has to sustain.

Anticipatory feelings also play an important role in moral contexts. Next to such positive organizing feelings as love and joy, anxiety regarded as a signal of impending danger is perhaps chief among these feelings (S. Freud, 1926/1959; Yorke & Wiseberg, 1976). Guilt is specifically a form of superego anxiety. Both anxiety and depressive affect trigger psychic conflict, which always involves the following components: wishful striving, anticipated danger, defense, and compromise among these three. Depressive affect is a sense of "unpleasure associated with an idea that something bad has happened," while anxiety is "unpleasure associated with the idea that something bad is about to happen" (Brenner, 1975). The developmental issues here are: (1) what does the child come to feel as "bad"; (2) how well does the child learn to discriminate what is morally wrong on principle from what merely feels bad; and (3) how does the child learn to cope with such feelings? One important superego function that may serve such growth is that of scanning one's experience, unconsciously or consciously, in anticipation of internal danger (i.e., recognizing that something is not right inside and protecting against its eruption) (Spiegel, 1966).

On the other hand, as Lowenfeld (1975) has pointed out, many people today feel frustrated even when they are outwardly successful and are not inwardly constrained against seeking satisfaction to any great degree. The key issues in their case often are: (1) what are their ideals, and how well have they learned realistically to tolerate frustration of those ideals; and (2) how do they experience time and the use of time (Hartocollis, 1976)? All these questions are important for the successful moral development of both latency children and adolescents. All relate especially to the formation of ego-ideal functioning and its anticipatory quality.

The first set of issues dealt with in this section were primarily feelings that arise when we face separation from what is past; the second set related primarily to feelings about attachment to what may lie ahead. In this context we have had to treat each all too briefly, but the important thing to note is that in psychoanalytic theory, both sets of issues are central to moral development from latency on. How they will be resolved for each child depends heavily on the nature of influences borne upon the child from societal institutions. After all these years of complicated development, the child cannot be remade. Educationally, however, some deficiencies can be worked on and further growth aided, given the boundaries and potentials each child brings to the learning situation.

Ego Ideal

According to the psychoanalytic structural theory, ego structures emerge from id, superego structures from ego. The continued interconnectedness of all these structures shines through the ego-ideal aspects of superego functioning with special brilliance. This is true because ego ideal structures include narcissistic elements from very early on; these are modified by subsequent object-related experiences, but they are still composed of self-directed aims.

Hans Loewald tells the story in the following way (1962, p. 266): First come hallucinatory wishes to turn back to an imagined original state of perfection, perhaps when id and ego were undifferentiated, when one felt grandly omnipotent and all was one. Then come magical wishes and strivings to achieve some such state in the future by merging with the object. With gradual resolution of the Oedipus complex comes—for some people, not for all—wishes for ego futurity and, we may add, for others' futurity as well, eventually for oneself as a part of all mankind.

To keep in mind the real changes within this continuous development, it is helpful to think both of earlier forms and of later contents as ego ideals (plural), reserving the singular term *ego ideal* for a particular kind of post-Oedipal functioning. In post-Oedipal development, the ego ideal is the bearer of ideal character traits and the site of moral and other high order values and standards. As is true of all other aspects of superego functioning, it originally takes on distinctive structure by means of internalizing one's views of others' traits and ideals, especially those of the parental figures (including grandparents and others in some families). It continues to form as we similarly interact, though hopefully with growing autonomy, with teachers, peers, and others from latency on.

Like the other aspects of superego functioning, ego-ideal aspects may feature greater personal autonomy as the individual grows, but they never gain independence from id and ego structures (Hartmann, 1937/1958, p. 52; Hartmann & Loewenstein, 1962, p. 65). The mere persistence of a psychic activity does not signify autonomy either (Beres, 1971, p. 21).

In the beginning was "the id," the libidinal and aggressive instinctual drives plus a few innate or congenital organizing propensities. Id functioning remains entirely unconscious throughout life. We know "it" only through its derivatives. Development of capacities to perceive and interact with the external world gives rise to ego functions, which gradually become differentiated into a distinct structure. In latency, superego functions develop in the same fashion, only now as an agency turned not only outward but inward as well. These two structures are not simply added on, however; they emerge out of id functioning and maintain a close connection at the unconscious level. As ego controls broaden, id functioning continues to develop and to wield a powerful influence, but one shared and one affected by ego-shaped experiences. Still, because they were not developed all at once or for the same purposes, factors within id and ego, ego and superego, may conflict and often do. As the early years pass by, id functioning comes to be comprised of libidinal and aggressive drives and of attendant need-derived wishes and impulses for mental organizing and action. These conflicts become dramatically evident in dreams and daydreams, slips of the tongue, humor, "weak moments," and episodes of acting out.

In short, many additions are made to the earlier, undifferentiated structures. Some of these additions become relatively autonomous and relatively conflict-free ego functions (e.g., ordinary perception, reasoning). Nevertheless, the overall activity of every human being remains drive-determined. This is so, although the patterns of ego functioning that emerge from early childhood persist throughout life. Why do these patterns persist? Chiefly because of our close dependent ties with early objects, many of which were difficult or impossible to loosen as we grew older. As adults we may occasionally catch a glimmer of insight into the comparatively few options we had as infants-in-arms, toddlers, preschoolers, children of school age, or even teenagers. Hallucinations and fantasies were very real to us, more real the younger we were or the more inclined we were to regress under stress. And if the message of those fantasies was that we might lose the objects important to us, or their love and approval and protection, or that we would not be able to manage by our own devices, we had to adjust somehow. We had to adjust even if this brought on great distress or suffering, even if our modes of adapting were sometimes markedly self-defeating.

Hartmann and Loewenstein have aptly called ego ideal "a rescue operation for narcissism" (1962, p. 61). The sources for this restructuring activity have been variously described. Ritvo and Solnit (1960) have emphasized internalization of the individual's earlier idealizations of the parents and the idealizations of the child by both the parents and the child. These all help the individual "to recognize and follow the limits of socially acceptable behavior" (p. 299). To these should be added the individual's use of reality knowledge, including knowledge not only of the environment but of one's own limitations and potentials. The restructuring is done, however, in such a way that the self-attending, self-esteeming aspects of the narcissistic position are not destroyed but are balanced with other concerns. This feature of the restructuring process has led Edith Jacobson to refer to ego ideal as a "bridging" of the ego system and of other aspects of the superego system (1961, p. 178).

The early narcissistic wishes are, as it were, issued in new editions during each successive stage of development. Eventually they become not only an agency of wish fulfillment, but also a means of coping with frustration and disillusionment. As object relations evolve, they most notably become an instrument of true self-love, as well as of self-esteem, self-interest, and self-aggrandizement. This achievement, in turn, releases one to love others (Bergmann, 1971; Kernberg, 1974, 1977). As the process moves forward, the person's self-representations take on certain ideal shapes, which may later conflict with each other. These become the reference points or, as it were, containers of other ideals.

Two further phenomena are shared among all superego structures and functions. First, because these structures and functions are all parts of a history and have arisen out of different areas of experience, they are in a position to conflict. Further growth may bring further integration, which reduces conflict, but we cannot expect complete cohesiveness to ever be achieved. This perspective implies, in particular, that the ideology by which one lives in a given social domain (e.g., the home, the church, politics), however well-formed and internally consistent it may be, is likely to conflict at some point with ideologies by which one lives in other domains. Second, like ego functions, superego functions are also subject to pathological isolation and distortion, regression, serious weakening, and even suspension in certain situations.

Other important superego functions that have not already been discussed include the following:

1. Self-esteem regulation
2. Capacities for setting, bearing, and proposing ideals
3. Capacities for self-love
4. Self-pity and self-comforting
5. Self-observation and self-criticism
6. A sense of oneself as both loving and being loved (Schafer, 1960)
7. Aspects of aggressiveness that are positively directive, self-assertive, self- and life-preservative, and cooperative, not merely hostile, destructive, or independent.

With the other functions already mentioned, these comprise a continually developing and complex interlocking system from mid-latency onward.

LATE LATENCY AND PUBERTY:
INTO THE THIRD MORAL STAGE

From a psychoanalytic perspective, manifestations of the aggressive, self-assertive drive are essential ingredients of every developmental change. Nevertheless, an explication of why the major turning points in moral development occur rests heavily on what happens with the libidinal drive. Strictly speaking, involvement in the Oedipal complex is a turning point into moral development. This occurs most prominently through a sharp rise in libidinal interest accompanied by greater capacities for object relations. The first turning point within moral development occurs out of the need to dissolve the Oedipal style of relating, coupled with new cognitive structures. The late latency, prepubertal child is moving toward the third major turn in moral development. The onset of puberty, a primary libidinal event, ushers this stage in.

Further Themes in
Late Latency and Adolescence

In ordinary development, formal learning has by late latency strengthened the child's ability to use verbal representation and symbolization to handle conflicts, to work on tasks more abstractly and at a distance, to entertain hypotheses and formulate generalizations, to engage in trial action through thought, and to engage in cooperative efforts. All this is occurring more in relation to real and shared experiences than in relation to the fantasized and idiosyncratic experiences of early latency (cf. Sarnoff, 1976, 136-144). These skills are all important conditions for further moral development in all respects. Their presence leads to greater efforts to give up fantasies of parental omnipotence, to break away from the more passive relations to parents typical in earlier years, and to be more self-assertive. The young person now attaches to peer groups as alternative sources for identification. These efforts will continue through adolescence. Although there are lapses, the general picture until pubertal changes begin is one of much greater psychic balance, effectiveness, and increasingly realistic, expanding awareness of the world. The moral universe enlarges accordingly.

As latency progresses, ego-ideal functioning takes over increasing space as compared with superego functioning in the narrower sense. This process too will continue through adolescence, though with marked setbacks. In many areas, especially in late adolescence, there will be an increasing amount of synthesis between the two sets of superego interests. Ordinary development is not necessarily moving toward a complete integration of the two, however, since it remains worthwhile to distinguish between what one might want of oneself or others and what one may realistically require as an obligation at any given time.

One important feature of ego-ideal development is the use of heroes. The prepubertal child tends to want his or her heroes to be actual people, although these enthusiastically selected heroes are in large part projections of the child's own trial fantasies. By middle adolescence the individual is able to internalize hero images and to make them into more abstract ideals.

Sometimes attachments to heroes display regressive aims and objects. This is also sometimes true of attachments to groups and leaders of groups during late latency through adolescence and, where conditions are ripe, within adulthood as well (Saravay, 1975). Such regression in groups or crowds can go back to a very early merging identification with consequent weakening of reality-testing, impulse control, and superego functioning (*see also* Greenacre, 1972; Peto, 1975; Wolfenstein, 1976). Like other types of regression, these group experiences may serve positive functions for growth and creativity. Adolescents often advance only by first retreating (Blos, 1967, pp. 172-173).

Have notable affective changes occurred by late latency? Yes, and these too are significant for moral development. I have noted that ego-ideal contents grow out of early narcissistic images. For the pre-Oedipal child, success in fulfilling these fancies is met with delight, elation, or pride; motivation is sustained by certain forms of love that arise in this period—notably, erotic need-love and admiration or affection; failure brings on depressive affect, related fear and anxiety, and eventually shame. For the Oedipal child, motivation is also sustained by romance and failure also results in guilt. These affective capacities continue, but in ordinary development they are increasingly redirected in two ways: toward real rather than magically fancied objects, and toward internally held extensions of characteristics once identified with beloved objects, now often in the form of more abstract values, ideals, and principles. In latency, motivation is further sustained by newly forming capacities for caring, benevolence, and filial love, and by friendly bonds between siblings, playmates, and other peers. Self-love, in similar respects, is also a motivating factor, both in the strictly narcissistic sense of regard for one's own self-interest, and in the sense of treating oneself as a person to be loved as others are to be loved.

Shame, which formed in painful, humiliating pre-Oedipal confrontations with parents, becomes between the mid-second and mid-third year a prominent response to failures of ego ideals in their early forms. During latency shame is transformed, so that now the child may feel shame not only when disapproved of but also when he or she fails to measure up to internalized ideals. Insofar as the child adds to the wish that the ideals be fulfilled an internalized sense that they *ought* to be fulfilled, guilt is also felt. Both shame and guilt can thus be realistic, appropriate feelings from this point on. Both can be felt in the same instance. On occasion, both can also be harmfully influenced by unrealistic fantasy. The adult sense of responsibility is fed from both streams.

ADOLESCENCE: FROM THE
THIRD MORAL STAGE TO THE FOURTH

Erik Erikson's work (1968 and earlier) has made *identity crisis* a household word in the United States. To achieve a sense of personal identity is also widely thought of as a special task of adolescence, in contrast to experiences of identity confusion and diffusion also dramatically characteristic of the adolescent period. Erikson would be the first to insist, however, that the task does not begin in adolescence, that such a process presupposes the achievement of latency, and that both latency and adolescence are historically specific, culture-bound phenomena.

In fact, had there been no coalescing of self-representations during latency, there would be no sense of self to diffuse in adolescence. Suppose that there had been no earlier cohesive sense of self (Horner, Whiteside, & Busch, 1976), no images of one's body or of oneself as separated from objects, no earlier narcissistic identifications of grandiosity and omnipotence (Lichtenberg, 1975, p. 459). There would then be no material from which to form a budding sense of self-sameness and continuity through time in latency or a sense of oneself as composed of divergent, conflicting, differently valued parts. From a moral point of view, it is impossible to conceive of one being able to treat other human beings as distinct persons having all these qualities and to treat them fairly in the light of those qualities unless one could perceive oneself in the same way. The achievement of a sense of identity, and a relatively familiar, integrated stable sense of self is the chief end of the adolescent process.

Peter Blos (1967) has appropriately introduced the complementary notion of adolescence as "the second separation-individuation phase" (cf. Furman, 1973). This task begins with the onset of puberty. It includes the specific aim of attaining a clear sense of sexual identity with the achievement of full genitality. It is this task that makes the advent of adolescence the third turning point in moral development and the introduction to the third moral stage. As such, adolescence brings about marked changes in one's relationship both to parents and to peers and in one's attitude to one's own body (Laufer, 1965, p. 115).

Although the old "storm and stress" theory of adolescence need not apply to the outward behavior of all adolescents, Anna Freud has noted that adolescence is "by its nature an interruption of peaceful growth" and that "the upholding of a steady equilibrium during the adolescent process is in itself abnormal" (1958, p. 275). True emancipation from childhood ties cannot occur without such interruption. True understanding of the need of others and society for analogous emancipation cannot form without the experience of this developmental need and freedom in oneself.

At least three phases can be distinguished within this period: early, middle (adolescence proper), and late, each with its own distinct features. Peter Blos appropriately adds a prepubertal, preadolescent phase and a postadolescent phase in young adulthood. In the scheme presented here, the latter phase is an extension of the fourth stage of moral development.

Early Adolescence: Into the Third Stage

Early adolescence is characterized by the outbreak of unsettled, regressive, often inconsistent and vacillating behaviors, too complex to depict here. Suffice it to say that all the old themes of childhood are coming up again. Blos has advanced the thesis that the narcissistically based ego-ideal functioning that becomes prominent in the early adolescent phase points to the ego ideal as "heir to the negative oedipus complex" (1962; 1965; 1972; 1974). For both girls and boys, the negative Oedipus complex is the stage of entry into the Oedipal period in which the child takes a passive homosexual position before advancing into a more active, heterosexual one. This capacity, made possible by the bisexual constitution of human beings, is itself an important, permanent contribution to human development. It is brought into prominence again in late latency and early adolescence. Primitive self-idealizations, Blos has explained, are brought back into play during adolescence. These are "unstable and subject to rapid fluctuations" (1976, p. 46) as the young person ventures out seeking immediate gratification. Only by the end of adolescence does ego ideal, thus conceived, gain some cohesiveness. It becomes an organ of aspiration, delay, anticipation, and striving, rather than a source of immediate gratification.

The Blos thesis, seeing early adolescence as involving many temporary regressive moves, provides a useful interpretation of much early adolescent turmoil and striving. But it is not wholly consistent with the broader view of ego-ideal functioning presented here. In particular, it does not account for the inclusion of object relations within that area of superego functioning (cf. Ritvo, 1971) although Blos does acknowledge that superego functioning undergoes considerable reorganization during adolescence (1967; 1968) as a means toward "the definite consolidation of the self" (1963, p. 127; cf. Laufer, 1964). Nevertheless, it is a valuable reminder of the continuing progressive, as well as regressive, contribution of narcissism in human development. In dynamic terms, moreover, narcissism remains the chief motivating force behind self-interest and its extensions into group interests.

Already in the first phase some synthesizing activity is going on, but this is largely deferred and detached from immediate experience. Henry Rosner has aptly depicted the central task during adolescence proper in this way: it is "the removal of those pathological conflicts that interfere with the spontaneous, transient phase-specific regressions that give adolescence its special flavor and are essential for later synthesis" (1972, p. 397). This enables the teen-ager to resume restructuring, a creative and especially value-producing activity (p. 414).

The adolescent's task, as in the childhood years, is to attain values, not simply to clarify those already internalized. To this task is now added the challenging, and strengthening force of evaluative, comparative reflection. Such creative and reflective activities the child of eleven was only just beginning to perform, if at all. By mid-adolescence, these activities have become essential for further growth, especially in the moral domain. "If the comedy of childhood ends with the discovery of sin—the resolution of the oedipus conflicts—then the tragedy of adolescence creates virtue" (Rosner, 1972, p. 414).

Late Adolescence: Into the Fourth Stage

All the conflicts and features of childhood are brought into play once more in adolescence. In ordinary development, and within the modern cultural settings presupposed here, late adolescence is a time of consolidation and of looking ahead. To get to the heart of the matter, from the viewpoint of moral development, we now focus on the ability to conceive time in an increasingly adaptive way, as a universal standard of reference (Hartocollis, 1974, p. 258). Accordingly, we view the late adolescent's changing sense of time as representing that person's turn toward the fourth stage of moral development.

There have been changes in the individual's sense of time from infancy on, but especially with the establishment of superego functioning. This functioning enables the individual "to endure stressful experiences, to schedule decisions, and to wait, to be punctual, and to synchronize one's activities with those of associates, to procrastinate or to ignore completely the patterning of time, future or past" (Hartocollis, 1974, p. 257). Earlier proclivities for acting out are placed in tension with trends toward consolidation and planned effort (Blos, 1963, p. 127).

In adolescence one is gradually learning to take charge of one's own story rather than depending on the parents to understand and remember one's past. This process leads in time to a more or less ordered sense of one's own history (Blos, 1968, p. 257; Seton, 1974, p. 796). The sense of one's history is ordinarily brought about in middle adolescence by the comparatively diminished influence of narcissism and accompanying fantasies of omnipotence and by the greater tendency to work out problems inwardly rather than by externalizing or acting out.

In late adolescence, the person builds on a developing sense of individual selfhood and identity (Blos, 1965, p. 147), including a sense of total ownership of one's own body (p. 152; cf. Laufer, 1968), to form a personal history, one in which reconstruction of the past and anticipation of the future are both of great importance. It is a time to reform old values, rules, principles, and ideals and to form new ones within freshly ordered structures of meaning, intention, and preliminary action. Paul Seton has called this aspect of late adolescent achievement "psychotemporal adaptation" (1974, p. 796). He holds that in this process superego functioning "becomes the major apparatus and plays the crucial role" (p. 803). Ego and superego combine to form a second essential achievement, the ability to experience duration, in a way quantitatively and qualitatively different from earlier ways of experiencing stretches of time.

Regression to periods of impulsiveness and timelessness are during this late phase necessary temporary reactions to the delaying, prohibiting, closure-making influence of superego structures. Such regression contributes to the reformation of both superego and ego structures. While the earlier structures are essential for cultural transmission, the new ones are essential for cultural reconstruction.

What, in moral terms, are the end results of all this process? In one way, of course, they are not end results at all but a fresh beginning, for they are qualities of life still open to further advancement and expansion as socio-cultural conditions permit. The first major result is the person's disengagement from early objects and, as it were, rebirth by working through the loss (cf. Jacobson, 1961; Laufer, 1966; Blos, 1968). This enables the person to serve within the moral domain as a free and equal agent, having one's own relatively independent or interdependent capacities for forming moral judgments, being able to take full responsibility for one's own actions.

The second result, painted in larger strokes that catch up much that has already been discussed, is character. Blos (1968, pp. 251–259) has emphasized the meeting of four developmental challenges closely related to character formation. The first challenge is the loosening of infantile object ties, just mentioned. The second challenge is the drawing into oneself in a stabilized, ego-syntonic way—a comfortable, steady, familiar, relatively nonconflicted way—of residual traumas from childhood. The third challenge is the overcoming of childish and familial myths about life in establishing a sense of historical continuity and gaining "a subjective sense of wholeness and inviolability" (p. 257). The fourth challenge is the forming of a sexual identity with definitive, irreversible boundaries. These are not all the preconditions, but they are all those of major importance; they all deeply affect the degree of autonomy or defensiveness that each person brings to the task of establishing "the credentials of character" (p. 259) in young adulthood.

The third result of late adolescence, also a springboard into young adulthood, is the beginning of the formation of a personal and autonomous life-style (Blos, 1967, p. 183). One is becoming not only a relatively free moral agent, meeting others on equal terms, but a contributor, one who has unique offerings to make according to one's own style.

For convenience, we have been dealing mostly in singulars. It is therefore necessary to remind ourselves that, strictly speaking, we do not really end up singular. Especially in our day and age, what the person who has gone through the adolescent phases of development with fair success will have achieved is not a monolithic sense of self, not a totally cohesive and final character structure, and not unwavering confidence. It is rather a feeling that the many facets of one's life all really belong to one life, an ability to recognize meaningful connections among a significant number, and, as Schafer has especially emphasized (1973, p. 53), an ability to accept oneself as both variable and changing. "While character structure is of a most durable and irreversible kind, only a degree of openness and flexibility assures its enrichment and modulation during adult life" (Blos, 1968, p. 261).

ADULTHOOD: BROADENING, INTEGRATION, AND FULFILLMENT

For each person, adulthood may present its stages of moral development too. These will be most notably affected by one's entering into intimate and long-term relationships, forming vocational and other commitments, and setting priorities for use of one's time. A mid-life crisis or turning point occurs for many people, not least because they are now at mid-career and must come to terms with what they have and are, sexually and otherwise. As one grows still older, aging and death are bound to take on new significance. One is, in view of old age, whenever one takes that view into account over however long a time, in a position to ask some supremely moral questions, namely: What is of greatest value in human relationships? What is worth keeping? Among the many good investments I might yet make in others, in the world, in myself, which are the right ones? And, finally, how shall I do what I believe?

Optimally, each set of moral capacities noted here will grow at each stage of development: a broadening of moral agency; being able to take a moral point of view more effectively over a wide range of experience; further attainment of moral values, rules, principles, and ideals; an increment of information relevant to moral decision-making; and greater power in exercising moral judgment. In adulthood these are all functions of character and may undergo continuing integration within a person's life.

What are we to say about our capacity to take a moral course of action once chosen? We already know that inhibitions against such autonomous and powerful agency have existed in our lives since childhood, that in certain areas they will always have an effect, especially in unaccustomed moments and in times of stress. Having character means, in part, having whittled these down to size, so that in large areas we are indeed relatively effective at acting on our moral beliefs and decisions, come what may. And there is always room for improvement, for further moral education.

Moral education, in the psychoanalytic perspective, is preeminently a process of sensitive perception and enablement. One element in that process has been lurking behind this entire account of moral development but must now be brought into the open. It is this: our ability to choose and to act morally at any given moment is the product of innumerable perceptions and enablements. It is not the moment of explicit moral choice that is crucial but the gradual forming of moral vision, feeling and intention.

CONCLUSIONS AND APPLICATION

Several important implications are to be drawn from this account of moral development and the accompanying features of socialization.

1. Dewey's definition of education as growth, and of moral education not as indoctrination but as the fostering of moral dispositions and capacities, is enriched by the psychoanalytic understanding of development. Attention to the conditions necessary for growth in the various moral capacities at each stage of development is accordingly the primary task of moral education. The means for doing this must be worked out differently for each age group, person and context, supportive of the relevant developmental tasks.

2. The conception of preconventional, conventional, and postconventional levels of development used by Kohlberg is also roughly corroborated by psychoanalytic investigation, although only the third level strictly warrants the name *morality* as defined in this essay. All four-plus stages of moral development depicted here fall within the last level. Furthermore, Kohlberg's substages are differently defined and are too nearly unidimensional to accord with psychoanalytic thinking, although there is a similar drift with respect to some cognitive functions. It is also possible, on psychoanalytic grounds, to conceive moral thought in non-Kantian, nonrule-oriented terms, and to make room for views of ethical behavior other than the deontological type (oriented to "duty") presupposed by Kohlberg.

3. In psychoanalytic theory, moral development may play a central role in the child's overall socialization—the child's capacities for social relations, variegated perceptions of society, and actual social functioning—but the child's premoral development plays an essential role. The difference between this type of theory and many other current theories lies in its inclusion of internal processes in its explanations, in detail and in depth. In particular, much of what is treated in social learning theory and in cognitive or structural-developmental theory is, in effect, a description of ego functioning and thus offers an important but partial behavioral account of some chief supports of superego functioning. Some aspects of superego functioning are also referred to indirectly.

4. Although the emphasis here has been on ordinary behavior, not on pathology, psychoanalytic study inevitably includes the dark side of human nature—the deep, hobbling conflicts, the irrationality and immorality, the hostile fantasies, the resistances to doing what one may believe to be right. The other two theoretical orientations so far do not do so. Much psychoanalytic theory, in fact, has been drawn from observations of what goes wrong in development. Such material has served to highlight what is effective or adaptive as well as to provide diagnostic tools that properly trained moral educators might use to detect where a child may need special help.

5. There is nothing inherently inconsistent between the three types of theory, to the degree that they are open to consider the phenomena emphasized in each one. Many of the basic explanatory concepts in social learning theory can be seen as referring to ego psychology and could conceivably be integrated with psychoanalytic theory. The affective aspects in recent social learning theory are, in turn, further illuminated in the psychoanalytic literature. The primary interest of Kohlberg and others in moral reasoning is also closely related to ego development and could conceivably be related to psychoanalytic understandings of such ego capacities. It must nevertheless be recognized that these theories also represent different, potentially conflicting ways of seeing behavior, that ego skills in the stricter sense can comprise only a comparatively small portion of psychoanalytic theory, and that the other two types of theory do not so far seem to account either for regression or for incapacities to act on what one believes.

6. Psychoanalytic studies show that neither children nor youths nor adults ordinarily develop morally in all parts of their lives or in a uniform fashion, and that they do not display consistently moral behavior. Furthermore, they show why. Much more work, however, needs to be done in this area.

7. The psychoanalytic literature is far behind cognitive and structural-developmental studies in attempting systematically to specify the stages of development that underlie specific kinds of moral perspective, reasoning, and capacity to act. Some of the framework could probably be teased out of psychoanalytic literature chiefly devoted to other subjects, as has often been done here, but fresh research and thinking are also needed.

8. A general account of moral development is not yet possible. This is the case because such an account would require at least six types of contribution, none of which has been met to any great extent, except perhaps the first, and because the contributions each might make to the others have not been integrated. These needed contributions are as follows:

1. An intensive awareness of human potential and of the problems human beings confront within given domains of experience, such as morality.

2. A well-controlled account of externally observable behaviors from infancy through old age and within a greatly varied array of populations.
3. A rigorously achieved understanding, on small, usually individual scales, of the internal determinants and dynamics of behavior. This understanding should connect biological, psychological, and sociological information wherever possible.
4. A systematic appreciation of differences in behavior among cultural settings.
5. An attentive, carefully reasoned grasp of historical processes over long periods and among many societies.
6. A critical examination of methods, concepts, presuppositions, and modes of communication used for all the above.

What has been offered in this chapter is one small piece of the whole, chiefly reflecting the third type of contribution.

This chapter chiefly presents an introduction to psychoanalytic developmental theory. As such, it cannot always be directly applied to educational settings. It does, however, invite your informed reflection on ways to make applications within your own life situation. Some linking ideas are also provided that will aid such reflection.

Elsewhere I have defined education as any process of learning conducive to human growth that involves the active participation of the learner (Tice, 1973). This is a modification and refinement of John Dewey's definition of education as growth, or "the continuous reconstruction of experience" (Dewey, 1966, p. 80), drawing from psychoanalytic insight. Here, *growth* means, above all, what is developmentally sound and within a broad range of human and cultural variations (cf. Tice, 1976a, 1976b). It is supposed that growth is possible at any age.

Many kinds of learning are not conducive to growth. Among those that are, some (e.g., training in the strict sense) are not educative, although they may have value on other grounds. Psychoanalytic theory helps us understand what may be developmentally sound or harmful in what we do as parents, educators, or colleagues. In particular, it aids our perception both of the stages of moral development and of the conditions underlying each stage. Schooling, as an agency of socialization, inevitably affects people's attitudes toward the moral domain and may contribute to their attaining various moral capacities. According to the psychoanalytic perspective, the greatest and most effective contribution of school to moral development would be directed to the basic conditions in personal development and social interaction without which moral capacities can neither come into being nor thrive. In a school setting we cannot lead or train a person to love, for example, but we can definitely work on the conditions for love.

In this chapter, the chief conditions for growth in moral capacities have been set forth and briefly exemplified. Thus, the reflective reader can readily develop principles of application suitable for an infinite number of settings and for any developmental stage from birth to death. At the same time, a thorough grounding in any of the matters discussed here would require more than the reading of a few paragraphs, and much relevant detail is of necessity left out altogether.

The principal requirements for applying psychoanalytic theory to moral education are these:

1. Sensitivity to the changing worlds of childhood and youth
2. Appreciation both for the continuing role of unconscious processes and for the new structures that form with each stage of development
3. Willingness to sustain critical examination of one's own motivations for action
4. Attention to the whole person—viewing the affective and the cognitive, the individual and the social aspects, the insides and the outsides of behavior

REFERENCES

Arlow, J. A. The structural hypothesis—theoretical considerations. *Psychoanalytic Quarterly,* 1975, *44,* 509-525.

Beres, D. Vicissitudes of superego functions and superego precursors in childhood. *Psychoanalytic Study of the Child,* 1958, *13,* 324-351.

Beres, D. Ego autonomy and ego pathology. *Psychoanalytic Study of the Child,* 1971, *26,* 3-24.

Bergmann, M. Psychoanalytic observations on the capacity to love. In J. McDevitt & C. Settlage (Eds.), *Separation-individuation: Essays in honor of Margaret S. Mahler.* New York: International Universities Press, 1971.

Blos, P. *On adolescence: A psychoanalytic interpretation.* New York: The Free Press, 1962.

Blos, P. The concept of acting out in relation to the adolescent process. *Journal of the American Academy of Child Psychiatry,* 1963, *2,* 118-143.

Blos, P. The initial stage of male adolescence. *Psychoanalytic Study of the Child,* 1965, *20,* 145-164.

Blos, P. The second individuation process of adolescence. *Psychoanalytic Study of the Child,* 1967, *22,* 162-186.

Blos, P. Character formation in adolescence. *Psychoanalytic Study of the Child,* 1968, *23,* 245-263.

Blos, P. The function of the ego ideal in adolescence. *Psychoanalytic Study of the Child,* 1972, *27,* 93-97.

Blos, P. The genealogy of the ego ideal. *Psychoanalytic Study of the Child,* 1974, *29,* 43-88.

Blos, P. The split parental image in adolescent social relations: An inquiry into group psychology. *Psychoanalytic Study of the Child,* 1976, *31,* 7-33.

Bornstein, B. On latency. *Psychoanalytic Study of the Child,* 1951, *6,* 279-285.

Brenner, C. Affects and psychic conflict. *Psychoanalytic Quarterly,* 1975, *44,* 5-28.

Brenner, C. *Psychoanalytic technique and psychic conflict.* New York: International Universities Press, 1976.

Dewey, J. *Democracy and education.* New York: Macmillan, 1916; The Free Press, 1966.

Ekstein, R., & Motto, R. L. *From learning for love to love of learning: Essays on psychoanalysis and education.* New York: Brunner/Mazel, Inc., 1969.

Erikson, E. H. *Insight and responsibility.* New York: W. W. Norton & Company, Inc., 1964.

Erikson, E. H. *Identity: Youth and crisis.* New York: W. W. Norton & Company, Inc., 1968.

Flugel, J. C. *Man, morals and society: A psycho-analytical study.* London: Duckworth, 1945.

Freud, A. Indications for child analysis. *Psychoanalytic Study of the Child,* 1945, *1,* 127-149.

Freud, A. Adolescence. *Psychoanalytic Study of the Child,* 1958, *13,* 255-278.

Freud, A. *Normality and pathology in childhood: Assessments of development.* New York: International Universities Press, 1965.

Freud, A. *The ego and the mechanisms of defense* (rev. ed.). New York: International Universities Press, 1966.

Freud, S. The interpretation of dreams. In *Standard edition of the complete psychological works of Sigmund Freud* (Vol. IV and Vol. V). London: Hogarth Press, 1953, pp. 1-338 (Vol. IV) and pp. 339-630 (Vol. V). (Originally published, 1900-1901.)

Freud, S. Three essays on the theory of sexuality. In *Standard edition of the complete psychological works of Sigmund Freud* (Vol. VII). London: Hogarth Press, 1953, pp. 125-245. (Originally published, 1905.)

Freud, S. Beyond the pleasure principle. In *Standard edition of the complete psychological works of Sigmund Freud* (Vol. XVIII). London: Hogarth Press, 1955, pp. 3-64. (Originally published, 1920.)

Freud, S. Formulations on the two principles of mental functioning. In *Standard edition of the complete psychological works of Sigmund Freud* (Vol. XII). London: Hogarth Press, 1958, pp. 213-226. (Originally published, 1911.)

Freud, S. Inhibitions, symptoms and anxiety. In *Standard edition of the complete psychological works of Sigmund Freud* (Vol. XX). London: Hogarth Press, 1959, pp. 77-175. (Originally published, 1926.)

Freud, S. The ego and the id. In *Standard edition of the complete psychological works of Sigmund Freud* (Vol. XIX). London: Hogarth Press, 1961, pp. 3-66. (Originally published, 1923.)

Freud, W. E. The baby profile: Part II. *Psychoanalytic Study of the Child,* 1971, *26,* 172-194. (Cf. 1967, *22,* 216-238 for the first profile.)

Fries, M. & Woolf, P. Recapitulation of separation-individuation processes when the normal three-year-old enters nursery school. In J. McDevitt & C. Settlage (Eds.), *Separation-individuation: Essays in honor of Margaret S. Mahler.* New York: International Universities Press, 1971, pp. 274-296.

Furman, E. A contribution to assessing the role of infantile separation-individuation in adolescent development. *Psychoanalytic Study of the Child*, 1973, *28*, 193-207.

Greenacre, P. Crowds and crisis: Psychoanalytic considerations. *Psychoanalytic Study of the Child*, 1972, *27*, 136-155.

Hartmann, H. *Ego psychology and the problem of adaptation.* New York: International Universities Press, 1958. (Originally presented, 1937; first German edition, 1939.)

Hartmann, H. *Psychoanalysis and moral values.* New York: International Universities Press, 1960.

Hartmann, H., & Loewenstein, R. M. Notes on the superego. *Psychoanalytic Study of the Child*, 1962, *17*, 42-81.

Hartocollis, P. Origins of time: A reconstruction of the ontogenetic development of the sense of time based on object-relations theory. *Psychoanalytic Quarterly*, 1974, *43*, 243-261.

Hartocollis, P. On the experience of time and its dynamics, with special reference to affects. *Journal of the American Psychoanalytic Association*, 1976, *24*, 363-376.

Horner, T. M., Whiteside, M. F., & Busch, F. The mutual influences of the positive cohesive self, mental representational structures and interactive behavior in the child's involvement with peers. *International Journal of Psychoanalysis*, 1976, *57*, 461-475.

Jacobson, E. Adolescent moods and the remodeling of psychic structure in adolescence. *Psychoanalytic Study of the Child*, 1961, *16*, 164-183.

Jacobson, E. Ways of female superego formation and the female castration conflict. *Psychoanalytic Quarterly*, 1976, *45*, 525-538.

Joffe, W. G., & Sandler, J. Comments on the psychoanalytic psychology of adaptation, with special reference to the role of affects and the representational world. *International Journal of Psychoanalysis*, 1968, *49*, 445-456.

Kernberg, O. F. Mature love: Prerequisites and characteristics. *Journal of the American Psychoanalytic Association*, 1974, *22*, 743-768.

Kernberg, O. F. Boundaries and structure in love relations. *Journal of the American Psychoanalytic Association*, 1977, *25*, 81-114.

Laufer, M. Ego ideal and pseudo ego ideal in adolescence. *Psychoanalytic Study of the Child*, 1964, *19*, 196-221.

Laufer, M. Assessment of adolescent disturbances: The application of Anna Freud's diagnostic profile. *Psychoanalytic Study of the Child*, 1965, *20*, 99-123.

Laufer, M. Object loss and mourning during adolescence. *Psychoanalytic Study of the Child*, 1966, *21*, 269-293.

Laufer, M. The body image, the function of masturbation, and adolescence: Problems of the ownership of the body. *Psychoanalytic Study of the Child*, 1968, *23*, 114-137.

Lichtenberg, J. D. The development of the sense of self. *Journal of the American Psychoanalytic Association*, 1975, *23*, 453-484.

Loewald, H. The superego and the ego-ideal. II. Superego and time. *International Journal of Psychoanalysis*, 1962, *43*, 264-268.

Loewald, H. W. On internalization. *International Journal of Psychoanalysis*, 1973, *54*, 9-17.

Lowenfeld, H. Notes on frustration. *Psychoanalytic Quarterly*, 1975, *44*, 127-138.

Mahler, M. S., Pine, F., & Bergman, A. *The psychological birth of the human infant.* New York: Basic Books, 1975.

McDevitt, J. B. Separation-individuation and object constancy. *Journal of the American Psychoanalytic Association*, 1975, *23*, 713-742.

McDevitt, J. B., & Settlage, C. F. (Eds.). *Separation-individuation: Essays in honor of Margaret S. Mahler.* New York: International Universities Press, 1971.

Meissner, W. W. Identification and learning. *Journal of the American Psychoanalytic Association*, 1973, *21*, 788-816.

Meissner, W. W. The role of imitative social learning in identificatory processes. *Journal of the American Psychoanalytic Association*, 1974, *22*, 512-536.

Modell, A. H. On having the right to a life: An aspect of the superego's development. *International Journal of Psychoanalysis*, 1965, *46*, 323-331.

Modell, A. H. The ego and the id: Fifty years later. *International Journal of Psychoanalysis*, 1975, *56*, 57-68.

Nass, M. L. The superego and moral development in the theories of Freud and Piaget. *Psychoanalytic Study of the Child*, 1966, *21*, 51-68.

Peto, A. On crowd violence: The role of archaic superego and body image. *International Review of Psychoanalysis*, 1975, *2*, 449-466.

Pollock, G. H. The mourning process and creative organizational change. *Journal of the American Psychoanalytic Association*, 1977, *25*, 3-35.

Post, S. C. (Ed.). *Moral values and the superego concept in psychoanalysis.* New York: International Universities Press, 1972.

Ritvo, S. Late adolescence: Developmental and clinical considerations. *Psychoanalytic Study of the Child*, 1971, *26*, 241-263.

Ritvo, S., & Solnit, A. J. The relationship of early ego identifications to superego formation. *International Journal of Psychoanalysis*, 1960, *41*, 295-300.

Rosenfeld, H. The superego and the ego-ideal: A symposium held at the Twenty-Second International Psychoanalytical Congress, Edinburgh, July-August 1961. *International Journal of Psychoanalysis*, 1962, *43*, 258-263.

Rosner, H. "Of Music, Magic and Mystery": Studies in adolescent synthesis. *Journal of the American Psychoanalytic Association.* 1972. *20.* 395-416.

Sandler, A. Comments on the significance of Piaget's work for psychoanalysis. *International Review of Psychoanalysis*, 1975, *2*, 365-378.

Sandler, J. On the concept of superego. *Psychoanalytic Study of the Child*, 1960, *15*, 128-162.

Sandler, J., Holder, A., & Meers, D. The ego ideal and the ideal self. *Psychoanalytic Study of the Child*, 1963, *18*, 139-158.

Saravay, S. M. Group psychology and the structural theory: A revised psychoanalytic model of group psychology. *Journal of the American Psychoanalytic Association*, 1975, *23*, 69-89.

Sarnoff, C. *Latency.* New York: Jason Aronson, 1976.

Schafer, R. The loving and beloved superego in Freud's structural theory. *Psychoanalytic Study of the Child*, 1960, *15*, 163-188.

Schafer, R. Concepts of self and identity and the experience of separation-individuation in adolescence. *Psychoanalytic Quarterly*, 1973, *42*, 42-59.

Schafer, R. Problems in Freud's psychology of women. *Journal of the American Psychoanalytic Association*, 1974, *22*, 459-485.

Seton, P. H. The psychotemporal adaptation of late adolescence. *Journal of the American Psychoanalytic Association*, 1974, *22*, 795-819.

Shapiro, T., & Perry, R. Latency revisited: The age 7 plus or minus 1. *Psychoanalytic Study of the Child*, 1976, *31*, 79-105.

Spiegel, L. A. Superego and the function of anticipation with comments on "anticipatory anxiety." In R. M. Loewenstein (Ed.), *Psychoanalysis: A general psychology*. New York: International Universities Press, 1966, pp. 315-337.

Tice, T. N. Alternatives in education: A framework for inquiry. In C. D. Moody (Ed.), *Alternative education in a pluralistic society*. Ann Arbor, Mich.: Program for Educational Opportunity, School of Education, University of Michigan, 1973, pp. 1-12.

Tice, T. N. *Student rights, decisionmaking, and the law*. Washington, D.C.: American Association for Higher Education, 1976. (a)

Tice, T. N. Setting multi-cultural objectives. In D. E. Cross (Ed.), *Teaching in a multicultural society*. New York: The Free Press, 1976. (b)

Williams, M. Problems of technique during latency. *Psychoanalytic Study of the Child*, 1972, *27*, 598-617.

Wolfenstein, M. Looking backward from *A Clockwork Orange*. *Psychoanalytic Study of the Child*, 1976, *31*, 535-553.

Yorke, C., & Wiseberg, S. A developmental view of anxiety: Some clinical and theoretical considerations. *Psychoanalytic Study of the Child*, 1976, *31*, 107-135.

7

Moral Development
and the Concept of Values

JOHN PAUL McKINNEY

In the layperson's view of the moral order, the concept of "values" plays a major role. Moral judgment and consequent moral behavior are presumed to be based on some interior units of character which must be nurtured in order to grow and develop. Thus, parents are exhorted by their churches to foster correct moral values in their children and the lay press often attributes disruption in the social order to a decline in "values." Democratic values, the value of the family, American ideals, all are perceived as important beliefs to be cherished.

In light of the importance placed on values in the lay view, it is somewhat surprising that this concept has received relatively scant attention, until very recently, in the social science literature. Even in the large volume of recent work on the development of moral judgment, the concept of value is rarely mentioned. A notable exception to this inattention is the work of Milton Rokeach and his students (Rokeach, 1968, 1973.)

What are values and how are they related to morality? Don't the two words mean the same thing? And aren't all researchers who write about moral development talking about values? In answer to the latter question, I'd have to say, "Yes and no." According to my view, moral development always *implies* value development, but not all researchers make that connection explicit. The two words don't really mean the same thing, since not all values are moral values—although all moral behavior presupposes certain values. The harder question to answer is the first: What are values and what is their relationship to morality?

201

WHAT IS MEANT BY VALUES?

Undoubtedly, one of the difficulties with the scientific use of the value concept is the variety of ways in which the term is used and the even larger variety of terms with which it is confused and often used interchangeably. In particular, the term *values* has been confused with such terms as *attitudes, norms, ideals, beliefs, drives,* and *goals.*

> But the increased currency of explicit value concepts among psychologists and social scientists has unfortunately not been accompanied by corresponding gains in conceptual clarity or consensus. We talk about altogether too many probably different things under one rubric when we stretch the same terminology to include the utilities of mathematical decision theory, . . . fundamental assumptions about the nature of the world and man's place in it, . . . ultimate preferences among life styles, . . . and core attitudes or sentiments that set priorities among one's preferences and thus give structure to a life. . . . And, at the same time, we are embarrassed with a proliferation of concepts akin to values: attitudes and sentiments, but also interests, preferences, motives, cathexes, valences. The handful of major attempts to study values empirically have started from different preconceptions and have altogether failed to link together to yield a domain of cumulative knowledge. (Smith, 1969, pp. 97-98).

There have been some attempts to clarify this confusion of terms, however. *See* Kluckhohn (1951) and Thompson (1963).

Let me first approach the meaning of values by considering how it differs from ideals, needs, attitudes, and interests. First of all, values, as the term is generally used, differ from the ideals that people hold. Ideals don't always imply a choice; values do. The culture in which a person grows up may hold certain ideals, but these only become individually held values when a person uses those ideals as a personal *way of making choices.* These choices might be about some desired object or about some behavior which is personally held to be correct, or appropriate, for the individual. Only then do we talk about ideals becoming personally held values; that is, only when the ideals provide some direction for personal behavior. It is this individual or personal aspect of ideals that converts them into values.

Values can also be distinguished from beliefs. A person may hold a belief that something is true or false, correct or incorrect. But the term *value* implies a different sort of judgment, namely that some object or behavior is either good or bad, desirable or undesirable, right or wrong, in the sense of being personally acceptable or unacceptable. In this sense, values are a particular kind of belief having to do with the appropriateness or acceptability of behavior, events or objects, not just whether these behaviors, events, or objects exist.

Needs are also sometimes confused with values. The terms have been used interchangeably by some investigators. Abraham Maslow (1959/1970, 1964) used the term *self actualization* to refer both to a need as well as to a higher-order value. It is a psychological need to strive for self-actualization, but it is also of value to be self-actualized. Robert White (1951) based his list of "values" on an earlier catalogue of "needs," that was developed by Henry Murray (1938).

Although some investigators have stated that the properties of these two terms are similar (e.g., French & Kahn, 1962), others have held that the two concepts are separate. For example, in his book, *The Nature of Human Values*, Milton Rokeach (1973) makes the compelling point that if *needs* and *values* were really two different words for the same concept, even lower animals could be said to possess a value system to the extent that they have needs. He argues that humans are the only animals capable of truly valuing. In fact, the ability of human beings to possess values is held to be one of the primary distinctions between human beings and other animals. Rokeach defines values as "the cognitive representation and transformation of needs" (Rokeach, 1973, p. 20). In this sense, a value implies more than a biological deficit, which would be enough to define a need. Value implies a "complex proposition involving cognition, approval, selection, and affect" (Kluckhohn, 1951, p. 428).

I have already suggested that the element of approval is what distinguishes values from beliefs, and that the element of selection is what distinguishes values from culturally bound ideals. Now we see that cognition is a necessary element in values, distinguishing them from basic needs.

The relationship between these terms is necessarily complex, however. Most would agree that values can emerge out of more primitive needs, and out of social and psychological demands on the individual. Rokeach has made this point and has added that values are sociologically based "because society and its institutions socialize the individual for the common good to internalize shared conceptions of the desirable . . . " (1973, p. 20). Values may also arise out of personal psychological demands, however, since "individual motivations require cognitive expression, justification, and indeed exhortation in socially desirable terms" (p. 20). Sex, for example, can make this point clearer. A biological need for sex, although often repressed in modern society, can be cognitively transformed along culturally approved lines into a value for affection, love, intimacy, spiritual union, etc. Similarly, a child's need for dependency may find cognitive expression in a value of obedience. The need for abasement may be transformed into a respect for elders. It is such cognitive representations and transformations that provide the distinction between needs, which may be shared with infrahuman animals, and values, which are characteristic of human beings alone.

Attitude is another psychological concept which is sometimes confused with value. Attitudes are more specific, while values are more global and may underlie a whole set of attitudes. *Attitude* means a set to respond. *Value* refers to a whole complex of such sets. Another way of saying this is that often there are correlations among particular attitudes. For example, it wouldn't be surprising to find that one's attitudes toward blacks, Chicanos, Jews, the elderly, etc. are all to some extent related. The correlation among such otherwise diverse attitudes might be described as value of equality, or justice, or fairness. In other words, a value that the individual maintains underlies a whole set of more specific attitudes. A value of achievement, as another example, may underlie one's attitude toward tests, books, teachers, or study hall.

Interests also differ from values. Values are more enduring than interests. They are more related to the core of one's definition of oneself. Our personal identity, in other words, is based more on our enduring values than on our interests, which are generally more transitory. Allport (1961) has defined values as "meanings perceived as related to self." His classical study of values with Vernon and Lindzey (1960), however, has been criticized on the grounds that it deals primarily with vocational interests. Others argue that while an interest may be one manifestation of a value, it is more narrow conceptually than value since it cannot be classified as "an idealized mode of behavior or end-state of existence" (Rokeach, 1973, p. 22).

Having made all the foregoing distinctions, what can we say about values? They are personally held, internalized guides in the production of behavior. They are more general than attitudes which they underlie. Values are cognitive units that are used in the assessment of behavior along the dimensions of good/bad, appropriate/inappropriate, and right/wrong. They deal with "what ought to be," rather than simply with "what is."

The Relationship of Values to Moral Development

In my view, moral behavior is based on moral judgment—that is, on a decision that a given behavior would be right or wrong under certain circumstances. Research on morality in developmental psychology has dealt mainly with one of these two issues, moral judgment or moral behavior. Studies of cheating (Hartshorne & May, 1928), resistance to temptation (*see* Hoffman, 1970), etc., have dealt primarily with moral behavior while those based on the cognitive psychology of Jean Piaget (Piaget, 1965; Kohlberg, 1964) have concerned themselves more with moral judgment.

If moral behavior is based on moral judgment, then moral judgment, in turn, is based on some internalized schemata, or cognitive units, whose properties can be delineated and whose development can be studied. These cognitive units are values and it is in this way that values are related to the development of moral behavior. They provide the social framework within which judgments are made, in the same way that perceptual schemata provide the perceptual framework in which meaningful motor behaviors are executed.

CLASSIFICATION OF VALUES

It's obvious that the discussion up to now deals with behavioral values. It should be mentioned, in the interest of clarity, that the term is also used to refer to objects. In an economic sense, objects can be said to possess value. Such value is generally determined via an exchange rate (i.e., what somebody else is willing to exchange for the object in question). Monetary systems are based on this material-value property of objects. While an object may be of more or less value to one individual than to others, because of its relation to his or her needs, the final determination of the value of an object is in terms of its exchangeability.

In this chapter, and in the developmental literature in general, we are concerned with behavioral values, the internalized guides in the production of behavior. We are concerned, that is, with facts, or put another way, with what Allport (1961) has called "matters of importance," or "meanings perceived as related to the self."

The assessment of value raises a further question: Whether the importance of an object or behavior rests in the environment—that is, in the object or behavior in question or in the cognitive organization of the evaluator. Recent analyses (Rescher, 1969; Laszlo, 1973; McKinney, 1975) have suggested that neither alone is the actual locus of value. Rather, values are "indices of subject-environment interactive states in the evaluator" (Laszlo, 1973, p. 253). In other words, evaluators make functionally consistent choices in the face of changing environmental circumstances. This consistency is the demonstration of the existence of values guiding behavior. It has been suggested that "value for an individual is neither entirely objective nor entirely subjective, but, like perception, lies on the interface between external reality and internal commitment" (McKinney, 1975, p. 806).

These behavioral values may refer to the modes of behavior, themselves, or to the result of such behavior. Philosophers (e.g., Rescher, 1969) have thus distinguished between *means* values and *end* values. A useful taxonomy of this distinction has been provided by Rokeach. He uses the terms *instrumental* (means) and *terminal* (end) values. Table 7-1 gives Rokeach's listing of these values along with their definitions.

Until now the discussion has centered mainly on social values. Indeed, traditionally, moral philosophers have concerned themselves with issues arising from interpersonal relations (Aronfreed, 1968, pp. 2-3). Now, however, the term *value* is used to include other "nonsocial" or private values, such as cleanliness, achievement, and independence. Recently this distinction has been supported by factor analytic studies of values (Rokeach, 1973; McKinney, 1973). A group of 774 undergraduates were asked by McKinney (1973) to rate 95 items of behavior on a five-point scale from desirable to undesirable. The items had come from an earlier study in which college students were requested to complete a set of

Table 7-1. Rokeach's list of terminal and instrumental values.

Terminal Values	Instrumental Values
A comfortable life (a prosperous life)	Ambitious (hard-working, aspiring)
An exciting life (a stimulating, active life)	Broadminded (open-minded)
A sense of accomplishment (lasting contribution)	Capable (competent, effective)
A world at peace (free of war and conflict)	Cheerful (lighthearted, joyful)
A world of beauty (beauty of nature and the arts)	Clean (neat, tidy)
Equality (brotherhood, equal opportunity for all)	Courageous (standing up for your beliefs)
Family security (taking care of loved ones)	Forgiving (willing to pardon others)
Freedom (independence, free choice)	Helpful (working for the welfare of others)
Happiness (contentedness)	Honest (sincere, truthful)
Inner harmony (freedom from inner conflict)	Imaginative (daring, creative)
Mature love (sexual and spiritual intimacy)	Independent (self-reliant, self-sufficient)
National security (protection from attack)	Intellectual (intelligent, reflective)
Pleasure (an enjoyable, leisurely life)	Logical (consistent, rational)
Salvation (saved, eternal life)	Loving (affectionate, tender)
Self-respect (self-esteem)	Obedient (dutiful, respectful)
Social recognition (respect, admiration)	Polite (courteous, well-mannered)
True friendship (close companionship)	Responsible (dependable, reliable)
Wisdom (a mature understanding of life)	Self-controlled (restrained, self-disciplined)

SOURCE: Copyright by Milton Rokeach, 1967 and reproduced with permission of Halgren Tests, 873 Persimmon Ave., Sunnydale, CA 94087.

unfinished sentences. Two of the items, "I would be ashamed of myself if . . ." and "I am proud of myself when . . ." yielded statements of behavior which were characteristically perceived as desirable or undesirable by college students, such as "making a good grade," "lying to someone," etc. These statements, 95 in all, were then given to the 774 students for rating. The ratings were then factor analyzed.

Nine factors emerged. The first two are of major interest here. The first factor was an "academic achievement" factor. It was defined on one pole by such items as "making a good grade," "doing well in class," "finishing assignments on time," and on the other by "flunking a test" and "neglecting one's schoolwork." The value here was clearly one of personal achievement of a specific, scholastic sort.

The second factor was comprised of items dealing with interpersonal, rather than private, concerns. Furthermore, each of these items had a moral-ethical connotation: "cutting other people down," "lying to someone," "being jealous of others," "helping someone out," or "helping someone by going out of one's way."

That the structure of college students' values is organized in this way provides empirical support for the philosophical observation that competence values deal with one's private or self-concerns, while moral values deal with social concerns. Another way of stating this personal-versus-social classification of values is in terms of the relationship between the subscriber to the value and the beneficiary. The philosopher, Nicholas Rescher (1969, pp. 17-18), draws this distinction:

> In general, a person subscribes to a value because he sees its realization as beneficial to certain people. Consequently yet another approach to the classification of values takes its departure from this point and classifies values according to the "orientation" of the value, that is, according to the relationship that obtains between the person who holds the value, the subscriber, on the one hand, and on the other, the presumptive beneficiaries who benefit from the realization of the value.
>
> This approach leads to a classification of the following sort:
>
> I. Self-oriented (or egocentric) values . . .
> II. Other-oriented (or distinterested) values . . .

Among the various behaviors guided by values, some, as noted, are prosocial while others are antisocial. It would appear that the conduct of some individuals is guided mainly by values related to prosocial behaviors. These have been called prescriptive, or "Thou shalt," values. Others are guided mainly by proscriptive, or "Thou shalt not" values—those relating to behaviors which are primarily antisocial. Some parents, for example, following a prescriptive child-rearing regime, consistently reward their child's good behavior and punish the child for not doing what is appropriate or expected. Others, using a proscriptive orientation, will tend to punish antisocial behaviors and conversely, and less often, reward the child for not misbehaving. This analysis of values leads to the following four-fold classification:

Reinforcement

Value Orientation	Reward	Punishment
Prescriptive (Thou shalt)	For doing good	For not doing good
Proscriptive (Thou shalt not)	For not doing bad	For doing bad

The reliability of this classification has been measured in a study with 67 university students (McKinney, 1971). They were asked to finish 28 incomplete sentences. Fourteen of these 28 stems involved interpersonal rewards and punishments, seven of each sort. Half dealt with negative reinforcement (e.g., My father gets angry with me when . . . ; I get angry with myself whenever . . .). The other half dealt with positive reinforcement (e.g., I am satisfied with myself when . . . ; My parents would be pleased if . . .). In this way the reinforcement dimension (reward versus punishment) was held constant. One could then observe to what extent the respondents used a prescriptive or a proscriptive value orientation.

The items were scored in the following way:

1. Positive stems
   a) Scored prescriptive—if the subject indicated prescriptive value by stating that he or she would be rewarded for something he or she did, e.g., "My father is pleased with me when . . . I listen to his advice," "I am satisfied with myself when . . . I do well on an exam."
   b) Scored proscriptive—if the subject indicated a proscriptive value by stating that he or she would be rewarded for not doing something, e.g., "My teacher trusts me when . . . I don't cheat."
2. Negative stems
   a) Scored prescriptive—if the subject indicated a prescriptive value by stating that a negative result would occur if he or she failed to do something, e.g., "My father gets angry with me when . . . I don't study."
   b) Scored proscriptive—if the subject indicated a proscriptive value by stating that the negative result would occur because of something he or she did, e.g., "I disappoint my teacher when . . . I come late for class."

The results of this study support the validity of the prescriptive/proscriptive distinction. Scoring each individual's sentence completion test for the number of prescriptive endings, it was possible to arrive at a measure of the individual's internal consistency of the dimension, (that is, the split-half reliability of the prescription scores). This reliability was sufficiently high $(r = .64)$ to provide evidence that the items focused on the same dimension, one requirement of an acceptable scale. In other words, people tend to answer consistently on one or the other of these dimensions.

THE ACQUISITION OF VALUES

Evolution must certainly have contributed to our maintaining certain spe-cies-sustaining values such as the importance of progeny or the desire to reproduce, and the nurturance of children. Furthermore, as the geneticist, Theodosius Dobzhansky, has observed, "Since man is a social animal, he usually profits more from amicable than from pugnacious disposition and behavior" (1970, p. 79). In other words, the human being's sociability is disrupted by fighting and enhanced by sharing and caring. It would be rea-sonable, therefore, to assume that there has been some genetic control over these human values which are basic to the continuance of individual life and the life of the species. The specific mechanisms for the inheritance of values is still an open question, however. Some (e.g., Pugh, 1977) have postulated that the theory of "survival of the fittest" has operated to increase in succeeding generations those values which will promote the likelihood of the survival of one's progeny. He uses altruism as an exam-ple, suggesting that the prototype for this value is found in the nurturance of a mother for her young. If a certain amount of self-sacrifice is required for the continued existence of the young, the process of genetic selection will favor the increase of this value. The offspring of those in whom this value is high will live to produce further offspring, presumably passing onto the next generation those genetic components which favored their own continued existence (i.e., an optimal balance of altruism and selfishness).

Beyond these basic values, however, we must look to a more effi-cient mechanism of acquisition, namely learning. For the most part, those cognitive schemata that underlie the tremendous control which humans have over their environment have been acquired through the process of socialization. Some studies have, indeed shown that an individual's value orientation is related to his or her parent's child-rearing practices. In the study just discussed that deals with the prescriptive/proscriptive value dimension, we also looked at the university students' perceptions of their parents' child-rearing practices. Since parents reward positive action far more often than they do the absence of wrong-doing, and since parents punish wrong-doing more often than they do the absence of "doing good" (i.e., sins of omission), it would seem logical to assume that parents who are typically rewarding would have children with a prescriptive orientation, while the children of punitive parents could be expected to have a pro-scriptive value orientation.

This hypothetical relationship was supported in the McKinney study (1971) already discussed. The university students were also given a Par-ent-Child Relations Questionnaire (Roe & Siegelman, 1963). Respon-dents are asked to recall, via a great variety of items, how their parents would have responded to their behavior in a number of circumstances. Among the subscales which can be computed, four deal with reward ver-sus punishment. Using these subscales it was possible to compare prescriptively and proscriptively oriented students. Subjects with a prescriptive value orientation were significantly more likely to recall their parents as having been more rewarding and less punitive than proscriptively oriented subjects.

Another study (Olejnik & McKinney, 1973), dealt directly with behavioral and value orientations of both children and parents. On a simple behavioral measure of generosity (sharing candy), 78 four-year-old children were identified as givers (generous) or nongivers. It was found that giving children had a significantly higher prescriptive value orientation than nongiving children. Furthermore, the parents, both fathers and mothers, of giving children were more likely to use a prescriptive orientation in rewarding *and* punishing their children. That is, with the reward/punishment dimension held constant, a parental prescriptive regimen was related to generosity in the children—both boys and girls. When the value orientation was held constant, however, the effect of reward versus punishment on generosity was negligible. It was concluded that "emphasis on prescriptive values by parents teaches children what they ought to do, while emphasis on proscriptive values merely indicates to children what not to do without specific instructions on how they ought to behave" (Olejnik & McKinney, 1973, p. 311). Furthermore, since a behavioral measure was used, this study shows that there is a relationship between value orientation and the actual behavior of children.

Moreover, while the study demonstrates the relationship between a value orientation (or a general *process* of evaluating) and a specific behavior, other research has demonstrated convincingly the relationship between behavior and the adherence to specific values. For example, using measures of the terminal and instrumental values presented in Table 7-1, Rokeach (1973) has shown that:

> *Equality* is the value that is the most predictive of behavior involving interracial relations—joining NAACP, participating in a civil rights demonstration, eye contact between whites and blacks, and partisan political activity; *salvation* is the value that best predicts churchgoing; *a world of beauty* best discriminates between artists and other professional groups; the intellectual values—*imaginative, intellectual,* and *logical*—best predict whether one will become a professor, and so on. (Rokeach, 1973, p. 159)

Age and the Acquisition of Values

How early in a child's life are values acquired? Early investigators (Murphy & Murphy, 1931) doubted whether young children had the conceptual skills needed for the interiorization of societal values. Indeed, those few studies which have dealt with age trends in the expression of values suggest that values become more stable with age. Thompson (1946), for example, has demonstrated that in the area of aesthetic preferences, values are acquired gradually. Thompson used the well-known adult preference for rectangles of "golden-section" proportions (i.e., those with a length-width ratio of approximately 2 to 1) to test this. He found that there is almost no consistent preference among preschool children and that the change to the adult preference represents a gradual acquisition.

While Thompson examined the median preference of groups of children at different ages, individual young children are also known to vary their choices of goal objects over short periods of time. For example, the choice of one's favorite friend increases in stability (over a two-week period) with age (Horrocks & Buker, 1951; Horrocks & Thompson, 1946; Skorepa, Horrocks, & Thompson, 1963; Thompson & Horrocks, 1947) from early childhood into late adolescence. McKinney (1968) has demonstrated the same age trends in the increasing stability of choice for a wide variety of objects and situations (e.g., favorite colors, games, animals, school subjects). Over a two-week period, young children are significantly more likely to report changes in such "favorite" choices than are older children or adolescents. To the extent that such choices are assumed to reflect value differences, it would be reasonable to assume that value acquisition, like all learning, is a gradual process.

HISTORICAL CHANGES IN VALUE ORIENTATION

Given the relationship between value orientation and parental child-rearing practices, one might wonder whether the well-known changes in discipline techniques in the United States during this century have a corollary in value changes. Professor Urie Bronfenbrenner (1958, 1961) has ably documented the changes in child-rearing practices from 1930–1955. Basically he observed an increase in the use of love-oriented socialization techniques by American parents and a decline in the use of punishment:

> . . . (a) greater permissiveness towards the child's spontaneous desires; (b) freer expression of affection; (c) increased reliance on indirect "psychological" techniques of discipline (such as physical punishment, scolding, or threats); (d) in consequence of the above shifts in the direction of what are predominantly middle-class values and techniques, a narrowing of the gap between social classes in their patterns of child-rearing. (Bronfenbrenner, 1961, p. 74).

Interestingly enough, some researchers gathered value data by means of a questionnaire given to college students in 1929, 1939, 1949, and 1958 (Crissman, 1942, 1950; Rettig & Pasamanik, 1959). These observers noted an increase during these years in the severity of moral judgment by college students. On a 50-item questionnaire, it was shown that students tended to perceive a greater variety of moral issues as wrong (on a 10-point scale) with each succeeding decade.

It was possible to reexamine those data and compare the increase in severity of judgment on the prescriptive items (i.e., "not giving to charity," "not supporting religion," etc.) with that of the proscriptive items, (i.e., "having sex relations while unmarried" "kidnapping and holding a child for ransom," etc.) (McKinney, Connolly & Clark, 1973). As can be observed in Figure 7-1 which is taken from that study, the great increase in severity of moral judgment over these years can be accounted for by the prescriptive items. Since there were only seven such items, compared with forty proscriptive items, these data should be treated with caution, however. Furthermore, the college-student population was not as selective a sample of the population at large in 1958 as it was in 1929. Despite these obvious limitations, the data provide some support for the idea that an affirmative or prescriptive morality was developing during those years. In fact, the authors had speculated that the affirmative action taken by college students in the 1960s on such issues as civil rights, foreign affairs, political corruption, etc. was a product of just such an historical development. Surely,

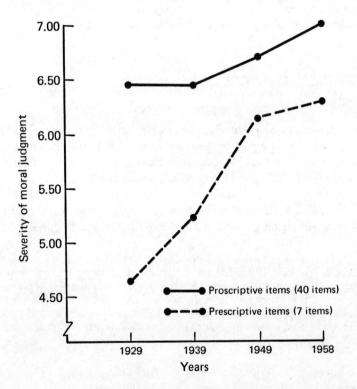

Figure 7-1. Changes in the severity of moral judgment by college students on prescriptive and proscriptive items between 1929 and 1958. (From "Development of a Prescriptive Morality: An Historical Observation" by J. P. McKinney, M. Connolly, & J. Clark, *Journal of Genetic Psychology*, 1973, *122*, 105-110.)

in any case, this was predictable from Bronfenbrenner's analysis of the changing child-rearing practices during those years.

A more recent analysis of value changes among college students (McKinney, Hotch, & Truhon, 1977) during the past decade was concerned with the decline in student activism after the early 1970s. Observers of college students had begun to witness a change of commitment from social issues to academic and personal, professional concerns. Gillespie and Allport (1955) had commented on the privateness of youths' values in the 1950s; it appeared to some that the same trend was about to be repeated twenty years later.

Students in 1975 were given the same sentence completion test which had been given in 1969 (and reported in McKinney, 1973) to study prescriptive and proscriptive values. As you'll recall, the two primary factors which emerged from a factor analysis of those data were an academic achievement factor and an ethical moral factor. (*See* page 207.) The achievement factor was composed of items which were entirely personal, while the items in the ethical-moral factor were all social in that they involved the respondents relations with others. The prediction was that on the sentence completion test, students in 1975 would produce more responses of the personal achievement sort and fewer of the social-moral type compared with students in 1969. The responses to two stems were analyzed to test this hypothesis: "I am proud of myself when . . . " and "I would be ashamed of myself if . . . ." The results clearly supported the hypothesis for the "proud" stem, while no differences emerged between the two groups on the "ashamed" stem.

One needs to be careful not to interpret these results to mean that the college students of 1975 were less socially conscious, or had less strong social-moral values than students in 1969. The data merely reflect the priority given to personal achievement versus social-moral concerns. The "versus" may be an artifact of the structure of the test. Indeed both sorts of values may be stronger. What has been demonstrated is a shift in the rank ordering of importance of these values. This caution, incidentally, must always be taken when one is dealing with rank ordering. For example, scales on which respondents are asked to list values in their order of importance (e.g., Rokeach, 1973) can be used to assess the *relative* importance of the values, but cannot yield information on their absolute strength for the subjects.

CONCLUSIONS AND APPLICATION

Since values appear to guide behavior of all sorts, both personal and social, the applications of the value concept are widespread. Authors have dealt with the importance of values in medicine (Goldstein, 1970), psychotherapy (Buhler, 1962), education (Jeffreys, 1962; Metcalf, 1971;

Raths, Harmin, & Simon, 1966; Simon, Howe, & Kirschenbaum, 1972),
and child-rearing (Lee, 1970; Olejnik & McKinney, 1975). I have chosen
two areas, education and childrearing, to illustrate such application.

Values in the classroom.   The area of value education has been fraught
with confusion and difficulty. Not long ago, some educators insisted on
value-free education and prided themselves on dealing only with facts,
and not values, which they contended were the province of the church
and home. The very act of teaching, however, presupposes its own set of
values, including, for example, achievement, nurturance, and the value of
education itself. To the extent that a teacher interacts with students, these
values are being modeled.

In the yearbook of the National Council for the Social Studies,
Lawrence Metcalf has provided needed clarification. He distinguishes between value objects, "the things people hold to be of worth," and value
judgments, "the standards by which people judge the worth of things"
(1971, p. 1-2). He notes that value judgments may contain positive,
negative, or neutral evaluations, and that value judgments can be made
according to several different points of view: aesthetic, moral, economic,
prudential, etc.

To teach students the process of evaluative reasoning and techniques
for resolving value conflicts is different from teaching which objects are to
be evaluated positively. Metcalf has suggested four possible objectives of
value analysis in education (1971, p. 4)·

1. To teach students that some value object is to be given a particular rating;
   to teach, for example, that the U.N. is a good thing or that premarital sex
   is wrong. This sort of objective is what people appear to have in mind
   when they advocate teaching values or teaching citizenship.
2. To help each student make the most rational, defensible value judgment
   he or she can make about the value object in question.
3. To equip students with the capacity and inclination to make rational
   defensible value judgments.
4. To teach students how to operate as members of a group attempting to
   come to a common value judgment about some value object.

If the community, itself, is to decide which of these objectives are legitimate
educational exercises, a value will be expressed. While the dogmatic aspects of the first objective will appear abhorrent to many communities, the
logic of, for example, the third objective may seem defensible, even urgent. Indeed, these two objectives appear almost antithetical in terms of
encouraging freedom, but that, itself, is a value statement.

The point to be made here is that there is a difference between teaching the content of values and the valuing process. Assuming that one
accepts the latter as a potentially useful goal, a number and variety of techniques are available. Teachers would be as ill-equipped to come to the task
without some prior training as they would be in any content area.

Teacher training might involve its own value analysis of the justification of value judgments as well as techniques for teaching evaluative reasoning. Current educational approaches to "problem-solving" involve similar objectives and techniques. The primary objective expressed by many writers in this area revolves around the student's increased capacity to *choose* freely. Raths, Harmin, and Simon (1966, pp. 28-29) describe the process of valuing under seven headings:

1. Choosing freely. . . .
2. Choosing from among alternatives. . . .
3. Choosing after thoughtful consideration of the consequences of each alternative.
4. Prizing and cherishing. . . .
5. Affirming. . . .
6. Acting upon choices. . . .
7. Repeating. . . .

While it is beyond the scope of this chapter to deal with specific value educational techniques, a number of references are available. Besides the Metcalf (1971) monograph and the Raths, Harmin, and Simon (1966) book, Simon, Howe, and Kirschenbaum (1972) have provided a handbook of strategies which may prove useful to teachers and students.

Child-rearing and the development of values. From the foregoing theoretical analyses of values, it is obvious that parents play a major role in a child's acquisition of dominant values. This is true whether one accepts a psychoanalytic view of parents as "significant others," a learning theory position of parents as "primary reinforcing agents," or a social learning theory view of parents as basic "models."

In an analysis of the acquisition of prosocial behavior, specifically generosity, Olejnik and McKinney (1973, 1975) discovered that the value orientation of the parents was a significant antecedent condition to sharing behavior in children. The kind of discipline emphasis, of reward or of punishment, was not a significant predictor by itself. In summary, children are more likely to adopt prosocial behavior when parents emphasize a "Thou shalt" orientation in their rewards and punishments, rather than a "Thou shalt not" orientation.

REFERENCES

Allport, G. W. Values and our youth. *Teachers College Record*, 1961, *63*, 211-219.

Allport, G. W., Vernon, P. E., & Lindzey, G. *A study of values.* Boston: Houghton Mifflin Company, 1960.

Aronfreed, J. *Conscience and conduct: The socialization of internalized control over behavior.* New York: Academic Press, Inc., 1968.

Bronfenbrenner, U. Socialization and social class through time and space. In E. E. Maccoby, T. M. Newcomb, & E. I. Hartley (Eds.), *Readings in social psychology*. New York: Holt, Rinehart and Winston, 1958.

Bronfenbrenner, U. The changing American child—a speculative analysis. *Merrill-Palmer Quarterly*, 1961, *7*, 73-84.

Buhler, C. *Values in psychotherapy*. New York: The Free Press of Glencoe, 1962.

Crissman, P. Temporal changes and sexual difference in moral judgments. *Journal of Social Psychology*, 1942, *16*, 29-38.

Crissman, P. Temporal change and sexual difference in moral judgments. *University of Wyoming Publications*, 1950, *15*, 57-68.

Dobzhansky, T. Human nature as a product of evolution. In A. H. Maslow (Ed.), *New knowledge in human values*. Chicago: Henry Regnery Co., 1970.

French, J. R. P., & Kahn, R. L. A programmatic approach to studying the industrial environment and mental health. *Journal of Social Issues*, 1962, *18*, 1-47.

Gillespie, J., & Allport, G. *Youth's outlook on the future*. New York: Random House, Inc., 1955.

Goldstein, K. Health as value. In A. H. Maslow (Ed.), *New knowledge in human values*. Chicago: Henry Regnery Co., 1970.

Hartshorne, H., & May, M. *Studies in the nature of character (Vol. 1): Studies in deceit*. New York: Macmillan, 1928.

Hoffman, M. Moral development. In P. H. Mussen (Ed.), *Carmichael's manual of child psychology* (3rd ed., Vol. II). New York: John Wiley & Sons, Inc., 1970.

Horrocks, J. E., & Buker, M. E. A study of friendship fluctuations of preadolescents. *Journal of Genetic Psychology*, 1951, *78*,131-144.

Horrocks, J. E., & Thompson, G. G. A study of the friendship fluctuations of rural boys and girls. *Journal of Genetic Psychology*, 1946, *69*, 189-198.

Jeffreys, M. V. C. *Personal values in the modern world*. Middlesex, England: Penguin Books, 1962.

Kluckhohn, C. Values and value-orientations in the theory of action: An exploration in definition and classification. In T. Parsons & E. A. Shils (Eds.), *Toward a general theory of action*. Cambridge, Mass.: Harvard University Press, 1951, pp. 388-433.

Kohlberg, L. Development in moral character and moral ideology. In M. L. Hoffman & L. W. Hoffman (Eds.), *Review of child development research* (Vol. 1). New York: Russell Sage Foundation, 1964.

Laszlo, E. A systems philosophy of human values. *Behavioral Science*, 1973, *18*, 250-259.

Lee, D. Culture and the experience of value. In A. H. Maslow (Ed.), *New knowledge in human values*. Chicago: Henry Regnery Co., 1970.

Maslow, A. H. *Religions, values, and peak-experiences*. Columbus, Ohio: Ohio State University Press, 1964.

Maslow, A. H. (Ed.). *New knowledge in human values*. Chicago: Henry Regnery Co., 1970. (Originally published, 1959.)

McKinney, J. P. The development of choice stability in children and adolescents. *Journal of Genetic Psychology*, 1968, *113*, 79-83.

McKinney, J. P. The development of values—prescriptive or proscriptive? *Human Development,* 1971, *14,* 71-80.

McKinney, J. P. The structure of behavioral values of college students. *The Journal of Psychology,* 1973, *85,* 235-244.

McKinney, J. P. The development of values: A perceptual interpretation. *Journal of Personality and Social Psychology,* 1975, *31,* 801-807.

McKinney, J. P., Connolly, M., & Clark, J. Development of a prescriptive morality: An historical observation. *Journal of Genetic Psychology,* 1973, *122,* 105-110.

McKinney, J. P., Hotch, D. F., & Truhon, S. A. The organization of behavior values during late adolescence: Change and stability across two eras. *Developmental Psychology,* 1977, *13,* 83-84.

Metcalf, L. E. (Ed.). *Values education: Rationale, strategies, and procedures* (Forty-first yearbook, National Council for the Social Studies). Washington: D.C.: National Council for the Social Studies, 1971.

Murphy, G., & Murphy, L. *Experimental social psychology.* New York: Harper & Brothers, 1931.

Murray, H. A. *Explorations in personality: A clinical and experimental study of fifty men of college age.* New York: Oxford University Press, 1938.

Olejnik, A., & McKinney, J. P. Parental value orientation and generosity in children. *Developmental Psychology,* 1973, *8,* 311. (Brief report.)

Olejnik, A., & McKinney, J. P. Parental value orientation and generosity in children. In H. C. Lindgren (Ed.), *Children's behavior.* Palo Alto: Mayfield Publishing Co., 1975.

Piaget, J. *The moral judgment of the child.* Glencoe Ill.: The Free Press, 1965.

Pugh, G. E. *The biological origin of human values.* New York: Basic Books, 1977.

Raths, L. E., Harmin, M., & Simon, S. B. *Values and teaching.* Columbus, Ohio: Charles E. Merrill Publishing Company, 1966.

Rescher, N. *Introduction to value theory.* Englewood Cliffs, N.J.: Prentice-Hall, Inc., 1969.

Rettig, S., & Pasamanik, B. Changes in moral values among college students: A factorial study. *American Sociological Review,* 1959, *24,* 856-863.

Roe, A. & Siegelman, M. A parent-child relations questionnaire. *Child Development,* 1963, *34,* 355-369.

Rokeach, M. *Beliefs, attitudes, and values.* San Francisco: Jossey-Bass, Inc., Publishers, 1968.

Rokeach, M. *The nature of human values.* New York: The Free Press, 1973.

Simon, S. B., Howe, L. W., & Kirschenbaum, H. *Values clarification: A handbook of practical strategies for teachers and students.* New York: Hart Publishing Co., Inc., 1972.

Skorepa, C. A., Horrocks, J. E., & Thompson, G. G. A study of friendship fluctuations of college students. *Journal of Genetic Psychology,* 1963, *102,* 151-157.

Smith, M. B. *Social psychology and human values.* Chicago: Aldine Publishing Company, 1969.

Thompson, G. G. The effect of chronological age on asthetic preferences for rectangles of different proportions. *Journal of Experimental Psychology,* 1946, *36,* 50-58.

Thompson, G. G. Do values belong in psychology? *The Catholic Psychological Record*, 1963, *1*, 11-16.

Thompson, G. G., & Horrocks, J. E. A study of friendship fluctuations of urban boys and girls. *Journal of Genetic Psychology*, 1947, *70*, 53-63.

White, R. K. *Value-analysis: Nature and use of the method.* Ann Arbor, Michigan: Society for the Psychological Study of Social Issues, 1951.

8

Can Values Be Taught?

EDMUND V. SULLIVAN

The title of this chapter has two meanings. It refers to a discussion of the *feasibility* and merit of some exemplary programs in value education and also to whether or not it is *desirable* to implement school programs that have as their objective the teaching of or reflecting on values. This chapter will concentrate on the topic of values and value teaching in the schools. It therefore deals with applied programs and the ideological issues raised when the question of value education presents itself in the context of schooling.

CURRENT INTEREST

Public interest in schooling changes from era to era. The last fifteen years in American education has witnessed some dramatic shifts in public opinion as to what the school is mandated to do in our society. The demands made on the educational sector after Sputnik forced a movement toward discipline-centered education (Hunt & Sullivan, 1974). Schools were criticized on the grounds that in their "child-centeredness" they had forgotten there was valuable subject matter to be learned. The rash of new subject-matter specialists led to the development of many new programs, especially in the sciences and mathematics. In many instances, these new programs were devised and developed with the help of expert scholars from these disciplines, such as mathematicians and physicists (Hunt & Sullivan, 1974). The period from 1960 to 1970 saw the initiation of special programs to deal with the problem of the so-called "culturally deprived." Here the schools were expected to respond to some of the moral problems that the society was concerned with during the civil rights era.

A change of climate has appeared in the 1970s. The optimism of the earlier reform movements is gone. It is a society which is post-Vietnam and post-Watergate. What went wrong? Regardless of what went wrong—education always seems to be saddled with the mandate to set things right. It strikes me that post-Watergate schools will be pushed to raise the conscience and morals of the nation—a task, as I will attempt to show, in which it is peculiarly ill-equipped to succeed. Why should the schools "rush in where angels fear to tread"? Heretofore, the American school was asked to steer clear of values-learning since it was the responsibility of the churches and the family. Why is the public now considering whether values should be part of the curriculum of the school? The answers to these questions are complex, if indeed, they are answerable at all. Nevertheless, these questions are now being posed in the public sector of education. Here is one educational policy-maker's view of it:

> As for the role of the churches, although they may not be on the decline in terms of membership or attendance, their impact on day-to-day secular conduct of most Americans is clearly small. Thus, if the schools decline to share in the task, the ethical upbringing of many young Americans will be grossly neglected. Moreover, while the role of parents and churches in the character formation of children is not a matter amenable to be strengthened through public policy making, the contribution of the schools—especially public schools—is. Schools are a more "movable" variable. (Etzioni, 1976, p. 9).

Muddled Mandate

Etzioni's quote seems to reflect a present consensus that today's society is in the thralls of a value crisis. As to how an institution or institutions are to respond to this crisis is an open question. Educational professionals agree that there is a need for improved moral education by some social agency, but they question whether the school should be that agency (Ryan & Thompson, 1975). If there is a mandate, it is a "muddled mandate" (Ryan & Thompson, 1975). There are several reasons why this is so and they revolve around the appropriateness of the school taking on a more active role (Purpel & Ryan, 1975).

First of all, the school's pluralistic character raises a problem area. Purpel and Ryan (1975) emphasize:

> Whatever the school's past and present failings in providing access to the children of all Americans, an open and pluralistic stance is fundamental to our public schools. Many religious, racial, ethnic, and even regional groups are distinguished by their values, the philosophical and theological bases for their morality, and their different standards of behavior. For this reason, many parents who believe in tax-supported education are loath to have the school take on a role they see as belonging primarily and sometimes exclusively to church and home. (Purpel & Ryan, 1975, p. 660).

Although this problem remains at present, the demand to separate the school from values has ended in the last five years.

The second reason centers on what is the primary task of the school in our society. When the school, as an institution, is concerned with the development of cognitive skills, one frequently finds proponents of this view arguing against the involvement of schools in value education. The argument against value education centers around the judgment that the school is currently failing to provide minimum intellectual education and, therefore, teachers should not go down some new avenue which will distract them from their essential task (Purpel & Ryan, 1975).

Third, teachers can be poor role-models or at least questionable ones. Here the question is put: What is the evidence that teachers are morally superior or have better values than the average citizen? Furthermore, what is there about the present teaching force which gives them any special knowledge or set of skills enabling them to improve the values and thinking of the young?

Finally, moral education in the schools raises the question of indoctrination. If the school formally enters the area of value education, will it be capable of preventing itself from indoctrinating the young (Purpel & Ryan, 1975)?

Despite these reservations, there persists a demand for value education, probably for some of the reasons mentioned in my introductory comments to this chapter. It is obvious that the question *Can values be taught?* will be interpreted differently depending on to whom the question is put. The rest of this chapter will attempt to clarify three ways to look at this question in the context of contemporary schooling. Although my choice of approaches can be considered arbitrary, I would nevertheless contend that a good attack on the question is made by *comparing* progressive, traditional, and post-critical approaches to value education in the schools.

PROGRESSIVE APPROACHES

How is the question *Can values be taught?* handled from the point of view of progressive education. Dewey (1959) addressed the issue of the relationship of values to schooling quite succinctly:

> We have associated the term ethical with certain special acts which are labelled virtues and are set off from the mass of other acts, and are still more divorced from the habitual images and motives of the children performing them. Moral instruction is thus associated with teaching about these particular virtues, or with instilling certain sentiments in regard to them. The moral has been concerned in too goody-goody a way. Ultimate moral motives and forces are nothing more or less than social intelligence—the power of observing and comprehending social situations—and social power—trained capaci-

ties of control—at work in the service of social interest and aims. There is no
fact which throws light upon the constitution of society, there is no power
whose training adds to social resourcefulness that is not moral. (Dewey,
1959, pp. 42-43).

From Dewey's progressive conception of the school, it is erroneous
to attempt to separate values from intellectual development. In *Democracy
and Education*, Dewey (1966) made note of a paradox that he saw when
values and schooling were discussed. On the one hand, morality is identified with rationality; reason is set up as the faculty for critical deliberation
in moral choices. On the other hand, morality and values are thought of
as an area in which ordinary knowledge and intellectual skills have no
place. Dewey saw this separation as having a special significance for value
education in the schools. If valid, it would render such an enterprise hope-
less by setting up the development of character as supreme, and at the
same time, treating the acquisition of knowledge and the development of
understanding as something separate from character development. Dewey
obviously saw the school as a moral and value laden enterprise. There is
therefore a rationale in Dewey's progressivism to have some reflection on
values in the school.

The work in "Values Clarification" advanced by Sidney Simon and
associates is one off-shoot of progressivism (Simon & de Sherbinin, 1975).
Values clarification is a term coined by Louis Raths. It is said to proceed
from Dewey's work in theory of valuation (Simon & de Sherbinin, 1975),
although it is not precisely clear how Dewey is the forefather of this
technology. Values clarification is a set of techniques to help teachers and
students clarify their values. Its specific aims are as follows:

1. It helps people to be more purposeful.
2. It helps people to become more productive.
3. It helps people sharpen their critical thinking.
4. It helps people have better relations with each other (Simon & de
   Sherbinin, 1975).

As a technology, values clarification has struck a favorable chord in teacher
education circles. Teachers gravitate to some of the techniques suggested
by this movement because they suggest some practical ways to deal with
values in the school.

In the context of progressive education and reform, Kohlberg's
cognitive-developmental approach to values and values education is more
explicitly allied to Deweyian progressivism than values clarification (Kohlberg, 1971b, 1975; Kohlberg & Mayer, 1972). Dewey was a "develop-
mentalist" in terms of educational aims:

The aim of education is growth or development, both intellectual and moral.
Ethical and psychological principles can aid the school in the greatest of all

constructions—the building of a free and powerful character. Only knowledge of the order and connections of the stages in psychological development can insure this. Education is the work of supplying the conditions which
will enable the psychological functions to mature in the freest and fullest
manner. (Dewey, 1964).

Kohlberg's stages of moral development are claimed to be psychological stages of moral development which add flesh to Dewey's developmental bones (Kohlberg, 1971b, 1975). Kohlberg (1971b) suggests that
his stages of moral development are a basis for developmental programs
in value education. Since they are formal stages (*see* Table 8-1), he claims
that they get around the problem of indoctrination.

Specifically, Kohlberg aligns himself with Dewey and reiterates, in
contemporary terms, the "progressive ethics"

1. That the aims of education may be identified with development, both intellectual and moral.

2. That education so conceived supplies the conditions for passing through
   an order of connected stages.

3. That such a developmental definition of educational aims and processes
   requires both the method of philosophy or ethics and the method of psychology or science. The justification of education as development requires a philosophical statement explaining why a higher stage is a better
   or a more adequate stage. In addition, before one can define a set of
   educational goals based on a philosophical statement of ethical, scientific,
   or logical principles, one must be able to translate it into a statement about
   psychological stages of development.

4. This, in turn, implies that the understanding of logical and ethical principles is a central aim of education. This understanding is the philosophical
   counterpart of the psychological statement that the aim of education is the
   development of the individual through cognitive and moral stages. It is
   characteristic of higher cognitive and moral stages that the child himself
   or herself constructs logical and ethical principles; these, in turn, are
   elaborated by science and philosophy.

5. A notion of education as the attainment of higher stages of development,
   involving an understanding of principles, is central to "aristocratic,"
   Platonic doctrines of liberal education. This conception is also central to
   Dewey's notion of a democratic education. The democratic educational
   end for all humans must be "the development of a free and powerful
   character." Nothing less than democratic education will prepare free
   people for factual and moral choices which they will inevitably confront in
   society. The democratic educator must be guided by a set of psychological and ethical principles which he or she openly presents to students,
   inviting criticism as well as understanding. The alternative is the "educa-
   tor-king," such as the behavior-modifier with an ideology of controlling
   behavior, or the teacher-psychiatrist with an ideology of "improving"
   students' mental health. Neither exposes his or her ideology to the students, allowing them to evaluate its merit for themselves.

6. A notion of education for development and education for principles is liberal, democratic, and nonindoctrinative. It relies on open methods of stimulation through a sequence of stages, in a direction of movement which is universal for all children. In this sense, it is natural.*

Table 8-1. Kohlberg's definition of moral stages.

Preconventional Level

At this level, the child is responsive to cultural rules and labels of good or bad, right or wrong, but interprets these labels either in terms of the physical or the hedonistic consequences of action (punishment, reward, exchange of favors) or in terms of the physical power of those who enunciate the rules and labels. The level is divided into the following two stages:

Stage 1: The punishment-and-obedience orientation. The physical consequences of action determine its goodness or badness, regardless of the human meaning or value of these consequences. Avoidance of punishment and unquestioning deference to power are valued in their own right, not in terms of respect for an underlying moral order supported by punishment and authority (the latter being Stage 4).

Stage 2: The instrumental-relativist orientation. Right action consists of that which instrumentally satisfies one's own needs and occasionally the needs of others. Human relations are viewed in terms like those of the marketplace. Elements of fairness, or reciprocity, and of equal sharing are present, but they are always interpreted in a physical, pragmatic way. Reciprocity is a matter of "you scratch my back and I'll scratch yours," not of loyalty, gratitude, or justice.

Conventional Level

At this level, maintaining the expectations of the individual's family, group, or nation is perceived as valuable in its own right, regardless of immediate and obvious consequences. The attitude is not one of *conformity* to personal expectations and social order, but of loyalty to it, to actively *maintaining*, supporting, and justifying the order, and of identifying with the persons or group involved in it. At this level, there are the following two stages:

Stage 3: The interpersonal concordance or good boy-nice girl orientation. Good behavior is that which pleases or helps others and is approved by them. There is much conformity to stereotypical images of what is majority or "natural" behavior. Behavior is frequently judged by intention—"he means well" becomes important for the first time. One earns approval by being "nice."

Stage 4: The "law and order" orientation. There is orientation toward authority, fixed rules, and the maintenance of the social order. Right behavior consists of doing one's duty, showing respect for authority, and maintaining the given social order for its own sake.

Postconventional, Autonomous, or Principled Level

At this level, there is a clear effort to define moral values and principles that have validity and application apart from the authority of the groups or persons holding these principles and apart from the individual's own identification with these groups. This level also has two stages:

(continued)

---

*Reprinted with permission from "Development as the Aim of Education" by L. Kohlberg & R. Mayer, *Harvard Educational Review*, 1972, *42*, pp. 493-494.

Table 8-1. continued

Stage 5: The social-contract, legalistic orientation. Generally this orientation has utilitarian overtones. Right action tends to be defined in terms of general individual rights and standards which have been critically examined and agreed upon by the whole society. There is a clear awareness of the relativism of personal values and opinions and a corresponding emphasis on procedural rules for reaching consensus. Aside from what is constitutionally and democratically agreed upon, the right is a matter of personal "values" and "opinion." The result is an emphasis on the "legal point of view," but with an additional emphasis on the possibility of changing law in terms of rational considerations of social utility (rather than freezing it in terms of Stage 4 "law and order"). Outside the legal realm, free agreement and contract is the binding element of obligation. This is the "official" morality of the American government and constitution.

Stage 6: The universal-ethical-principle orientation. Right is defined by the decision of conscience in accord with self-chosen *ethical principles* appealing to logical comprehensiveness, universality, and consistency. These principles are abstract and ethical (the Golden Rule, the categorical imperative); they are not concrete moral rules like the Ten Commandments. At heart, these are universal principles of *justice*, of the *reciprocity* and equality of human *rights*, and of respect for the dignity of human beings as *individual persons.*

SOURCE: Reprinted with permission from "From Is to Ought: How to Commit the Naturalistic Fallacy and Get Away with It in the Study of Moral Development" by L. Kohlberg. In T. Mischel (Ed.). *Cognitive Development and Epistemology.* New York: Academic Press. 1971a.

The research and development, both theoretical and applied, has been rather extensive on Kohlberg's stages (*see* the chapter by Turiel in this book, and Rest, 1974). In this chapter, I will give specific examples of my own work since it exemplifies a developmental approach to value education (Sullivan, Beck, Joy, & Pagliuso, 1975; Sullivan & Beck, 1975). In addition, since I will eventually adopt a critical attitude to the "progressive" approach, it seems more genteel to do it through a discussion of my own research.

An Example of a Moral Education Program

The discussions in this section are derived from personal involvement by myself and my research associates as teachers in pilot courses in value education in both elementary and secondary schools. A major motive in our efforts at the elementary level was our desire to understand children's thinking on value issues during the middle years of childhood. Initially, the work of Jean Piaget and Lawrence Kohlberg was most informative. Our work was restricted mostly to students in the later elementary school years.

A key notion in all of our work with students and teachers is "structure." The complexity of value questions and the uneasiness with which both teachers and students begin critical examination of value issues require, it seems to us, some ground rules and boundaries. Our approach has been to attempt to give students an initial sense of structure and order through what we call the " principled discussion" method. We outlined topics for fifth- and sixth-graders under the broad heading of *human relations*. For each of the topics, we offered guiding questions for the discussion. At first glance this structure seems rigid, but in fact it allows ideas to be examined within a broad framework. We labeled this framework a mini-course in human relations, with the following content topics, each of which might occupy about two 40-minute periods:

1. Rules people have given us
2. The place of rules in society
3. Exceptions to society's rules
4. The individual's need for other people
5. Helping other people
6. The self and others
7. The place of law, judges, and police
8. The place of governments and other authorities
9. Law-breaking and the place of punishment

In all, there are twenty topics suggested under this one unit. Children were given study notes on each of these topics to provide a structure and a sense of direction for the learning session or sessions.

Evaluation of our work in the elementary schools was both formal and informal. Of specific interest here is our formal evaluation procedure. Since we were interested in how children deliberate on moral issues, we found Kohlberg's work on moral reasoning directly relevant. In the fall of 1970, we interviewed 42 students who deliberated on Kohlberg's moral dilemmas. These students were divided into two groups: (1) those who would participate in our mini-course in ethics (the experimental group); and (2) those who, as a group, were matched on age, IQ, and social-class status with the experimental group, but who did not participate in the mini-course (the control group). We assessed these students, using Kohlberg's moral dilemmas, over a two-year period at three intervals. A pretest was given to all the students before the experimental group started to work with value issues. The first post-test was given at the end of the course. The second or follow-up was given to both groups one year after completion of the course. These interviews were scored in order to determine the stage of each child's moral reasoning.

On the pretests, all the students were assessed as being at the pre-conventional level, and the two groups were similar on this account. Both groups at the first post-test showed an advancement toward conventional stages, but there was some indication that the experimental group was somewhat more accelerated in this development. Finally, in a post-test follow-up done a year after the mini-course was completed, the experimental group showed significantly higher levels of conventional reasoning (i.e., Stage 4 thinking).

Looking at the results more descriptively—that is, from the difference between the control group which showed some development in moral reasoning without formal help and the experimental group which participated in the twice-weekly discussions—we would say that both groups show a general developmental trend from predominantly Stage 1 thinking on the pretest to predominantly Stage 3 thinking on the post-test. The differences between the two classes are seen in: (1) the emergence of Stage 4 reasoning in both the post-test and follow-up for the experimental class, while no Stage 4 thinking was apparent in the control group children; and (2) after the first year, the experimental children no longer responded at Stage 1 (external authority . . . avoid punishment), but began thinking more at Stages 2 and 3. On the other hand, the control group children did not drop Stage 1 thinking as readily. As with the control group, the experimental group began with the same reliance on external authority structures (preconventional), but by the end of the first year these students had definitely swung to an orientation in which they began to think more independently, using ideas of fairness, reciprocity, and equal sharing. At the same time, a few students began thinking in the larger context of society.

Our work with adolescents preceded our elementary school efforts. The major part was carried out in two different secondary schools over a period of about four years. In the first school, one of our staff took over a third-year class in the humanities two days per week to discuss moral issues. Students at this age level are normally in what Kohlberg calls the conventional morality stage. For the most part, the issues raised in class were designed to produce reflection on moral conventions and to consider alternative, sometimes novel, solutions. Thus we encouraged what Kohlberg calls postconventional morality. During the initial meetings with the students, we had a direct discussion of moral theories and principles. The teacher structured the class much more at the beginning, then increasingly relinquished control of topics as the class progressed. The discussions were always informal, however, in a relaxed atmosphere. This class lasted for only one semester and we were not sure what we could accomplish in so short a period.

The class consisted of 17 students who volunteered to participate in an "experimental" ethics course. A matched comparison group (control) was assessed on moral reasoning at various times but did not attend the "experimental" ethics course.

Members of the experimental ethics class were encouraged by the teacher to discuss a number of topics. Although the following sequence was not rigidly adhered to, and side topics were introduced occasionally, the topics were in general as follows:

1. Some distinctive features of moral goodness
2. Myself and other people
3. An individual's need for other people
4. Acting out of moral reasons
5. The place of mixed motivations
6. The importance of spontaneity and single-mindedness

 7. The place of moral principles and rules
 8. The value of the act versus the value of the rule
 9. Conscience
10. Justice, equality, and fairness
11. Developing mutually beneficial solutions
12. Moral diversity
13. The pursuit of happiness
14. An analysis of various virtues and vices

Our purpose as educators would be to draw out those ideas that embodied a more critical attitude toward moral issues through asking questions and helping students to sustain this kind of thinking in discussion. Since most of our students were reasoning at the conventional level (Stages 3 and 4), we attempted for the most part to delve into the reasoning behind conventional norms, an understanding which we would typify as postconventional reasoning. At least from the point of view of moral reasoning, the results of our efforts can be seen in Figure 8-1.

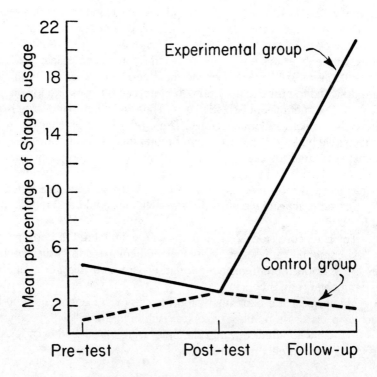

Figure 8-1. Mean percentage of Stage 5 usage for each group at each test time. (Reprinted with permission from "Stimulating Transition to Postconventional Morality: The Pickering High School Study" by Beck, Sullivan, & Taylor, *Interchange*, Winter 1972, 28–37.)

When the ethics class ended, there seemed to be no detectable difference between the experimental group and the control group. At first we attributed this to the fact that the class was too short in duration. More informal interviews with students, however, made us think that we had accomplished more than was indicated by the Kohlberg moral judgment questionnaire. The students in the ethics course seemed more reflective; their informal statements and evaluations of the course indicated a considerable amount of conflict which we felt was possibly growth-producing. In this light, the follow-up results were particularly intriguing. It would seem that the passage of time had tempered the feeling of conflict, and natural life experiences had produced opportunities for exercising some of the postconventional notions and skills gleaned from the classes. At any rate, the fact that the change that occurred was a Stage 5 change is reassuring, since it was in the direction of this kind of thinking that we had hoped to encourage our students.

After this initial effort in the secondary schools, we launched a full-scale effort for two semesters in another school. By this time we had devised an elementary ethics textbook for high school students and had identified other materials to bring to the classroom for discussion purposes. In our enthusiasm, both my associate, C. Beck, and I attended and conducted these classes; we also had some graduate students assisting us from time to time. At least from the point of view of Kohlberg's moral assessment, our efforts appeared to produce negligible results. The discrepancy between the results at this school and the one where we had previously been successful made us reflect on ways in which the two courses may have differed. First, the teaching format changed when we worked in the latter (unsuccessful) school, which we'll call School B. We used a structured textbook in School B that was not available when we worked at School A. Although the content was postconventional in orientation, it nevertheless reflected the initial interests of the teachers and not the students.

Notwithstanding some of our own mistakes, I have, after working with students in high schools for several years, come to the conclusion that the pervasive institutional life of the school as we know it impedes critical thinking. Our experience in the two high schools made us aware of the "hidden curriculum" discussed by critics of the school. We became much more sensitive to how the structure of a school can implicitly encourage a certain kind of morality—to be more specific, an authoritarian, conventional one. Many of the efforts of individual teachers to help students toward a post conventional (stages 5 and 6) level of moral development are frustrated by a school atmosphere and organization which constantly emphasizes lower-stage values and principles. Or, to put the point more positively, a school atmosphere and organization which exhibits postconventional features can greatly facilitate the development of students toward higher moral stages. Unfortunately, most school systems are run on broadly authoritarian lines. A relationship of mutual trust, respect, and co-operation between student and teacher is extremely difficult to cultivate in such an environment. I will return to this issue in the final section of this chapter since it relates to a critique of "liberal" experiments as exemplified in our own work.

The answer to the question *Can values be taught?* from a progressive view of education is *yes* with some serious reservations. Those reservations, however, bring into question whether the school is now, or ever has been, an institution amenable to progressive reforms.

TRADITIONAL APPROACHES

Taking Kohlberg's stages of moral judgment as the focus of a "liberal reform" conception of how values and value education should be handled, one can ask to what extent does this conception achieve a consensus among educators and also among other segments of the general populace interested in the school's role in the development of values. From my own personal experiences of presenting a conception of cognitive-developmental stages as a basis for moral education programs, I would judge that a substantial portion of the populace views this type of liberal-reform approach with considerable suspicion. Kohlberg acknowledges that the modal cultural, or most frequently occurring, level in his stage conception is the conventional level (Stages 3 and 4). Teachers are usually at this level when tested on Kohlberg's moral stages. In a 1975 survey by Ryan and Thompson, superintendents and principals, closely followed by classroom teachers, seemed to worry more about the lack of respect for authority on the part of young people than any other issue. Fifty-nine percent of the principals and superintendents rated it of great concern, while 47 percent of the elementary and secondary teachers did. As indicated by more recent Gallup surveys, the American people appear to be vitally concerned about school discipline. In that context they would not be interested in postconventional moral reasoning as a goal for secondary schools. School personnel and parents seem to identify moral stages beyond conventional as anarchic. Although there is a considerable amount of school disruption and dissension in our high schools, the usual solution for disruption and conflict focuses on manners, etiquette, dress, and hair-style (Alexander & Farrell, 1975). These are obviously not postconventional issues in Kohlberg's system. However, in the context of educational practice, Kohlberg may misjudge the importance of mores and custom (*see* Turiel's chapter), at least insofar as it is held to be very important in the eyes of the general populace.

If postconventionality could be considered a tolerable public objective for values education in the 1960s, it is clearly no longer the case. One of the more striking phenomena which appears to be emerging in North America today is a demand on the part of many parents, school boards, and educators for schools to get back to the basics (Morgan & Robinson, 1976). The demand for back-to-the-basics ranges over the areas of reading, writing, arithmetic, and standards of behavior which explicitly refer to school disciplinary standards. In order for the reader to get a feel for the pulse of this type of consensus, let me quote a manifesto of a group of people in Canada (Vancouver) as an example. This is a manifesto presented by a group called the Genuine Education Movement (GEM) to the Canadian Minister of Education:

> We of the Genuine Education Movement do not subscribe to any one political philosophy or to the policy of any one political party. We are united in wanting the children of British Columbia to have equal opportunity to the best education possible. We believe the following necessary to a good school system.
>
> 1. Teachers must be well qualified in the subjects they teach, and students should look to their teachers for instruction. High educational standards are indispensable and must never be sacrificed to experiment. On the basis of these guidelines, good teachers must be encouraged to remain in the system, and educators at all levels who prove unsuitable must be replaced or retired.
> 2. *Curriculum* should include as a *minimum basic* requirement:
>   a. A thorough grounding in English grammar and a competence in reading and writing and speaking the English language.
>   b. A thorough grounding in elementary mathematics
>   c. An understanding of the basic sciences that will enable a child to understand the physical world in which he lives
>   d. An understanding of world history and geography
>   e. An understanding of the public institutions and the political and economic foundations of Canadian life.
> 3. *Evaluation* is vital to the child and to the whole system. We shall institute a regular series of tests and examinations; these will where possible require answers in English sentences rather than selection from multiple choices. Periodic reports will be made to the parents so that the student's progress may be judged in terms of his own potential and the achievements of his peers.
> 4. *Discipline* should be firm but fair. While we do not advocate physical punishment, or any atmosphere demeaning to the human dignity of student or teacher, we believe that a child learns best where the teacher has authority to ensure an orderly atmosphere. We shall insist that the staff and school administration be given, and should excercise, the necessary authority to achieve this aim.
>
> *In summary* we believe that an educational system must encourage change where change is desirable, but changes must be gradual and carefully assessed for their immediate and long-range effects. We support thoughtful progress, building on what was effective in earlier systems and helping children to understand the past while preparing for the future.*

The ideology of GEM is a fair illustration of some of the concerns of the current back-to-the-basics movement. If you look carefully at the

*Reprinted with permission from "The 'Back to the Basics' Movement in Education" by M. Morgan & N. Robinson, *Canadian Journal of Education*, 1976, *1*, p. 7.

fourth item, you can clearly see a priority being given to discipline and authority. My own judgment is that the values propounded by this movement would demand alternative psychological technologies rather than the ones utilized in a conception of liberal reform. I would guess that behavior modification techniques, skill development technologies, and social learning theory and research with its emphasis on prosocial conventions would be some of the alternatives to liberal reform.

So the answer to the question *Can values be taught?* in the context of traditional ethics is yes, if the values encompass *discipline, respect for authority*, and *prosocial conventionality* that eliminate student disruptions. I will not elaborate further on the traditional perspective, although some of its concerns have some legitimacy. I will attempt to show that its concerns are ultimately short-sighted and misguided, since it does not attempt to face a value crisis such as can arise in a post-industrial society like our own. I will also point out how liberal, educational reform is, in a different manner, ill-equipped to deal with this value crisis.

A POSTCRITICAL APPROACH

A postcritical perspective proceeds on the assumption that values are already assimilated unconsciously and now must be made subject to a "critical awareness." This approach to values proceeds from a frame of reference quite different from the liberal and traditional conceptions of value education. A postcritical perspective starts with the assumption that our culture is in the thralls of a profound value crisis produced as a by-product of the development of advanced Western capitalism. Moreover, this crisis will not be alleviated to any appreciable extent by liberal reforms or by a return to the traditional virtues of a previous era (all the King's horses and all the King's men will not put Humpty-Dumpty together again). In fact, one can put the development of this problem at the door of liberal institutions and reforms.

It is not a question, from a postcritical perspective, of whether values can be taught. The school is now, and has always been, an institution immersed in values. In fact, it legitimates current societal values and consolidates and enculturates them for a new generation. If we are facing a value crisis, as I think we now are, it is a crisis of legitimacy of the values that our culture holds. It is a crisis of mass culture, embedded in the values of unending production and consumption—a set of values which is increasingly failing to merit the allegiance of the young, the poor, and the disenfranchised. If one considers the school a legitimizing institution, then it follows that the schools are currently involved in enculturating the virtues of consumer capitalism. One of the functions of education is to provide individual competencies necessary for the adequate performance of social roles; education therefore is fundamental to the social stability and functioning of any society.

Bowles and Gintis have a blunt, but I would say accurate, way of illustrating this enculturation process with reference to work roles.

> The way in which workers come to have a particular set of work-relevant personality characteristics or modes of self-presentation requires a more searching analysis.
>
> We find the answer to this question in two corresponding principles, which may be stated succinctly as follows: the social relations of schooling and of family life correspond to the social relations of production.
>
> We have suggested above that the social relations of schooling are structured similarly to the social relations of production in several essential respects. The school is a bureaucratic order with hierarchical authority, rule orientation, stratification by "ability" (tracking) as well as by age (grades), role differentiation by sex (physical education, home economics, shop), and a system of external incentives (marks, promise of promotion, and threat of failure) much like pay and status in the sphere of work. Thus schools are likely to develop in students traits corresponding to those required on the job. (1973, p. 78).

Moreover, this process is replicated throughout the educational bureaucracy. This may be seen from Ivan Illich's somewhat less than flattering view of schooling:

> School sells curriculum—a bundle of goods made according to the same process and having the same structure as other merchandise. Curriculum production for most schools begins with allegedly scientific research, on whose basis educational engineers predict future demand and tools for the assembly line within the limits set by budgets and taboos. The distributor-teacher delivers the finished product to the consumer-pupil, whose reactions are carefully studied and charted to provide research data for the preparation of the next model, which may be "ungraded," "student-designed," "team-taught," "visually-aided," or "issue-centered." (1972, p. 59).

It is not possible to develop this theme in elaborate detail for this chapter, but I hope the quotes present striking illustrations of what is potentially a powerful hidden curriculum whose values are more or less unconsciously appropriated. In the context of education, the question of whether values can be taught must be looked at from at least two perspectives. First, if education is a process whereby an individual acquires his or her world view from society, we must first look at the process itself (Bowers, 1974). Second, as to the process, we understand socialization from a theoretical perspective, but there is little actual knowledge of the particular cultural assimilation that is actually being transmitted from the teacher to the student (Bowers, 1974). There is a hidden curriculum of which we have little knowledge as to what assumptions and myths are being transmitted in classrooms and schools. I purposely used the quotes of Bowles and Gintes and Illich to provide for some readers a shock of awareness of the possible underside of a socialization procedure. Without this understanding of our own assumptions and myths, there is no way of assessing how they influence the psychic and social well-being of the individual who unquestionably internalizes them (Bowers, 1974). It is frankly difficult for educators to examine the mythical world they live in. (This reminds me of a statement attributed to Marshall McLuhan: I don't know who discovered water, but it certainly wasn't the fish.) The dominant assumptions about work, technology, consumption, success, progress, etc. are routinely transmitted in schools and classrooms without any concern about their validity or consequences (Bowers, 1974).

Consideration from a postcritical perspective of whether values can be taught demands a new process of reflection about schools. In a sense it is a reflection on the water that we are swimming in—the covert or hidden curriculum:

> The press of school routines shapes the student's sense of reality in a far more effective manner than the regular curriculum, but since this aspect of the school is seldom seen in political terms school boards and parents generally ignore it. Yet a case can be made that the school routines that make up the covert curriculum are regarded by teachers and school administrators as serving a more pedagogically important function than the academic curriculum. The strongest evidence supporting this generalization is that students are often dropped from school for exhibiting behaviour that challenges the routines of the school; they are seldom dropped, on the other hand, because they lack the intellectual ability to deal with academic curriculum. When viewed from this perspective, it becomes apparent that one of the chief functions of the academic curriculum is to serve as a vehicle for conditioning students to adopt the values of the school's covert curriculum. More importantly, when it is understood that traditional school subjects are used to teach values quite different from their officially stated purpose, there is no longer any reason to be mystified about why the school curriculum continues to be so uninteresting to students and irrelevant to what they need to learn. The irrelevance of the subject matter curriculum is necessary if the student is to learn the values and traits of docility upon which his academic survival and later his career as a worker depend. *

Let me now return to a criticism of my own work previously discussed in the section on progressive reforms. Recall specifically the difficulty we seemed to encounter in attempting to foster postconventional morality. The more one thinks about it, it becomes clear why it was difficult to encourage or stimulate postconventional morality. Such morality bucks a pervasive and hidden curriculum of schools which is embedded in fostering conventionality.

If anything, the high school consolidates conventional thinking if you consider the age range 15 through 18 years. We found (Sullivan, Beck, Joy, & Pagliuso, 1975) on a sample of over 200 students from three high schools, that there was a modal predominance of Kohlberg's Stage 3

*Reprinted with permission from *Cultural Literacy for Freedom: An Existential Perspective on Teaching, Curriculum, and School Policy* by C. A. Bowers. Eugene, Oregon: Elan Books, 1974, pp. 62-63.

thinking, with the beginning of Stage 4 and Stage 5 reasoning. It's easy to see why a course in value education simply will not work in encouraging reflective thought. The very structural life of the school is locked into a conventional set. In fact, even the discipline problems which "traditionalists" allude to are not at the level of postconventionality, but more likely are of a *preconventional* kind. That conventionality is precarious can partly be attributed to the arbitrary nature of school convention. In our discussions with students, they clearly indicated their cynicism for what they felt was implied mindless conformity to school officials' dictums. The possibility of joint decision-making about school conventions is hardly ever considered by school officials, and students appear not to expect any part in that decision-making. Moreover, the conventional consensus of our culture is breaking down as I have already suggested, and this is reflected in school disruptions. Nevertheless, it strikes me that our high schools succeed all too well in enculturating conformity in most students and fail completely in an experiment in democratic living. The problem as seen from a postcritical perspective is simply that the schools are not by their very nature in our society, programmed to enculturate a democratic process. Now however, the students do not appear to be wedded very stongly to the values implicit in the schools. This generation of students is coming into a post-industrial society and they are vaguely aware that the industrial model of the school and its hidden curriculum has precious little to offer them. *Can values be taught in the school?* can be answered yes, but it is becoming apparent that these values are dysfunctional.

There are no easy answers to our present problems. It is a cultural crisis. The types of resolution will not come from journeys "back to the basics" or by liberal, piecemeal, social engineering—which I would judge my previously quoted work to be. A postcritical perspective ultimately sees the situation as one needing transformation, which is in essence, radical change. As one distinguished educator puts it:

> My concerns are with autonomy and reflectiveness and justice, with the kind of knowing that penetrates and transforms. The problems of curriculum, as I see them, must be confronted in the contexts of the technetronic society and its multiple systems of channeling and control. The pressures on the individual must be taken into account, along with the inequities that persist throughout the culture, the erosion of standards, and the collapse of trust. The capacity of the individual to feel himself to be a subject is linked for me, to his ability to conceptualize effectively, yes, and competently—the structures and forces that dominate the situations of his life. For these reasons, I find it extraordinarily difficult to think in terms of either/ors, to believe that humanism excludes competencies, or that competencies are, by definition, inhumane. Nevertheless, like John Dewey at the beginning of *The Child and the Curriculum*, I would say that the apparent dichotomy confronting us grows " out of conflicting elements in a genuine problem—a problem which is genuine just because the elements, taken as they stand, are conflicting. Any significant problem involves conditions that for the moment contradict each other." (Greene, 1975, pp. 175-176).

This is "problem-posing" education, designed to raise consciousness. I would like to develop the concept of *problem posing* education which was first developed in the writings of the Brazilian educator, Paolo Freire.

PROBLEM-POSING EDUCATION AS CULTURAL ACTION FOR FREEDOM

Problem-posing education assumes that reality and, therefore, culture is conflictual in some essential features. Instead of assuming that the development of culture is simply a gradual development of institutional life, problem-posing education proceeds under the assumption that institutional development occurs as a dialectical process. For Paolo Freire, one of the fundamental conflictual themes of our epoch is freedom from dominating and oppressive social structures. The dialectical theme is therefore that of freedom/oppression. From this condition of domination Freire applies a conception of logical entailment and ventures a conception of dialectical logic when he claims that domination "implies its opposite, the theme of liberation, as the objective to be achieved" (Freire, 1974a, p. 93).

Freire's analysis of the South American experience is a creative attempt to establish a "pedagogy" for dealing with social and economic oppression. The situation of this pedagogy is in transcending alienating social relationships which he describes as oppressor-oppressed relationships. Cultural action is a solidified action of people who are in an oppressed condition, attempting to liberate themselves from this condition by modifying their relationship with the world and with other persons. Cultural action is an action which links theory with practice (praxis) in a movement from a "naive awareness," of social relationships within an oppressed condition, to a "critical awareness." *Naive awareness* does not deal with problems; it gives too much value to the past and its inevitability; it tends toward acceptance and mythical explanations. *Critical awareness* is a reflective cultural action (praxis); it poses problems about one's circumstances and is open to new ideas and new ways of looking at what was formerly considered an intractable state.

Linguistically, education for a critical consciousness involves a *dialogue* with one's world and events, such that the person involved in this dialogue is less prone to magical explanations for events in his or her world (i.e., mystification). Freire calls this process "conscientization," an equivalent in North American jargon to the term *consciousness raising*. *Conscientization* enables the oppressed person (or group) to reject the oppressive consciousness (naive awareness) he or she is submerged in and to become aware of the nature of his or her situation in the "naming of his [or her] world." *Naming of the world* constitutes an act of critical judgment couched in a language familiar to the person coming to critical awareness. Critical awareness is a process (praxis)—and not a final state representing a permanent effort for persons and groups—to engender a program of awareness (i.e., education) which is situated in a history (bounded by time and space) seeking to achieve a creative potential in assuming responsibility for the state of one's world. It is in this context that I would label Freire's problem-posing education, value education in its radical sense.

The critical awareness Freire advocates is relative to each historical stage of a people, and mankind in general. Freire's own particular analysis has been in the context of the historical experiences of South America. Specifically, his problem-posing education deals with a conscientization resulting from a literacy training program for Brazilian peasants. In content, he does not address the North American experience, except in a final section of his *Cultural Action for Freedom* (Freire, 1974b). There he links the general structure of problem-posing education to what he calls "Mass Society." What then is "oppression" in a North American context? It is a condition of a "submerged awareness" (naive) produced by oppressive conditions inherent in the development of large scale bureaucracies in the North American experience. *Submerged awareness* is a narcotic state produced by large scale institutions in an industrial society. These institutions, and their elite conception of what constitutes reality, rob people of their ability to critically analyze their experiences of oppression. Professional advertising, medicine, law, and schooling are just a few of these large scale bureaucratic enterprises. The development of "professionalization" produces an "elite" group (i.e., specialists or experts) who are seen as the superordinate definers of social reality in mass culture. A person in North American culture tends toward a state of dependency when he or she is confronted by the knowledge of the experts in the professions. Instead of "naming the world" (autonomy), there is a process of "having one's world named" (dependency) by depending almost totally on the judgment of experts. Therefore, school "experts" define learning; doctors define sickness and health; lawyers define legality and custom. This whole process tends to rob individuals of their own critical abilities in defining their world and experience.

From my own experience with schools in North America, I would say that it is clearly one of those institutions that detract from people's critical abilities. The school and its curriculum, as already pointed out, teach through a hidden agenda conformity and docility. Bowles and Gintis (1976) suggest that major aspects of the school structure can be understood as supporting the society's economic structure by producing skilled labor, legitimating the technocratic-meritocratic perspective, and molding youth to the social relationships of dominance and subordinance in the economic system. From this perspective, it is not surprising to learn that the school is found wanting in the area of radical social change. In this context, schooling supports societal equilibrium rather than societal transformation. Bearing in mind the functions of schooling as suggested by Bowles and Gintis, what can be expected from schooling as a transforma-

tive cultural process? Not much. Nevertheless, we should not underesti-
mate the ability of schooling to create conformity to a cultural world view.
My own suggestions on problem-posing education concede that schooling
in its present form will not alter dramatically in the near future. Consider
the following suggestions for education by Bowles and Gintis (1976).

Bowles and Gintis offer five broad guidelines which are consistent
with what I am calling a postcritical education. First of all, revolutionary
educators—teachers, students, and others involved in education—should
vigorously press for the democratization of schools and colleges by working toward a system of participatory power in which students, teachers,
parents, and other members of the community can pursue their common
interests and rationally resolve their conflicts. Under this heading, the recent work of Kohlberg and colleagues on the just community school is suggestive (Kohlberg, 1975). Their theory about a just community school postulates that discussing real life moral situations arising in the schools as
matters for democratic decision-making would stimulate a participatory
democracy providing more extensive opportunities for role-taking and a
higher level of perceived institutional justice. Kohlberg feels that the essential component of education must be a commitment to democratic decision-making in the schools.

> Democracy as moral education provides that commitment. Second, democ-
> racy in alternative schools often fails because it bores the students. Students
> prefer to let teachers make decisions about staff, courses, and schedules,
> rather than to attend lengthy, complicated meetings. Third, our theory told
> us that if larger democratic community meetings were preceded by small-
> group moral discussion, higher-stage thinking by students would win out in
> later decisions, avoiding the disasters of mob rule. (Kohlberg, 1975, p. 676).

Although this work is in its germinal stage, it nevertheless is a step, however minute, in a salutary direction.

The second guideline proposed by Bowles and Gintis (1976)
demands that the struggle for democratization be viewed as part of an
effort to undermine the correspondence between the social relations of
education and the social relations of production in capitalist economic life.
The development of critical reflection on the part of disenfranchised
groups is essential here, since groups that profit from the present social
order are not likely to tip the apple cart. A consciousness raising of how
schools are related to social stratification must be an essential part of a critical education for oppressed groups in our society (e.g., blacks, women,
and native peoples). This type of pedagogy must be suggested by "radical
educators" since it will come from nowhere else.

Third, postcritical education must reject simple antiauthoritarianism
and spontaneity as its guiding principles. Within a postcritical perspective,
it is not expected that every sort of free school movement is acceptable.

But we must develop and apply a dialectical educational philosophy of personal development, authority, and interpersonal relationships which incorporates important "critical reflective" processes which are suggested in a problem-posing education.

A fourth guideline suggests that educational reform must create a class consciousness for victims of oppression in our society:

> . . . teachers must not only demand control over their activities; we must also extend this control to students and to the broader community. We must also fight for a curriculum which is personally liberating and politically enlightening. We must reject our pretentions as professionals—pretentions which lead to a defeatist quietism and isolation . . . . (Bowles & Gintis, 1976, p. 287).

I would like to suggest two examples of educational reform to illustrate this guideline from a problem-posing perspective. Consider this first example. *Homer Price* is one of four novelettes offered to fourth grade students in British Columbian schools in Canada (Fridriksson, Jacobs, Lorimer, & Sanderson, 1975). The question these Canadian researchers are asking in this analysis is: Are these the types of values that we want Canadian students to be learning? *Homer Price*, the name of the work, also the name of the main character, is no random choice. The novel and character pay homage to U.S. "capitalism" and "progress" with all that that entails. Elements that are put forward as ideals are Yankee ingenuity, mass production, individual initiatives, and so forth. The researchers are not questioning that the benefits of these elements are given due positive regard in *Homer Price*. Rather, they question that the events are constructed in such a way that these elements are presented as "all right" and "the total answer."

The point I am trying to bring out here is the submerged values that are embedded in *content* areas as innocent as a reader for fourth graders. I don't think the example is atypical. In problem-posing education, it is important to explore the *content* as well as the *form* of the educational experience. The utilization of this example points to some of the problems with Kohlberg's earlier work where his conception of values placed a heavy stress of *form* over *content*. Its liberal bias left the content areas of the curriculum of the schools unchanged (Sullivan, 1977).

Now for a second example. Let's look at the language of decision-making in the schools in terms of hierarchy; let's look at one of the school experts, the counselor. Within the school context, counselors are considered experts in their understanding of students. This expertise is accepted in the area of the interpretation of psychological test results, learning theories, and other types of normative psychological data. The expert becomes, then, the focal point for decisions in the school structure. The belief that the expert "knows best" can eventually open the way to robbing people of their own moral judgment. Illich (1973) goes so far as to say that the ascendence of the expert is a cognitive disorder. He calls it a cognitive disorder because an illusion is created which makes people less critical in interpreting their own experiences. The "expert," the "professional," has the "objective" answers to problems, whereas the individual citizen does not.

Let me give a further illustration of how this expert mentality can distort the situation and ultimately become miseducation. Although I am using behavior modification as an example, the process should not be construed as confined to this particular approach. The specific example is a sequence cited by Burger (1972) which intended, as an objective, the teaching of language to six-year-old Navajo children. Burger attempted to show how the psychological "experts" in the school are, in some instances, insensitive to the social and cultural world of the people that they are trying to help. He observed with these Navajo children, that the psychologist directed the teacher to seat the children a few inches apart from her, with their backs close to the wall. At this, the children became uneasy. Apparently the Navajo is accustomed to open spaces. An anthropologist who was aware of this suggested that the children would be more at ease if they were allowed to have more space between them. The anthropologist further observed that the teacher might exchange positions with the children so that the pupils could back off into an open area. The behavior modifier ignored this suggestion and felt no need to accommodate this cultural information into his modification sequence. Here, as in several other examples cited, Burger (1972) developed the thesis that the expertise of operant behaviorism neglects the complexities of the culture. The expert, in his or her hubris, assumes means, goals, and rewards of the majority culture, hence imperializing his or her human subjects who tend to be in minorities.

Paulo Freire would label the above procedures "cultural invasion." He sees the expert's role in even a more negative light:

> Cultural invasion, which like divisive tactics and manipulation also serves the ends of conquest. In this phenomenon, the invaders penetrate the cultural context of another group, in disrespect of the latter's potentialities, they impose their own view of the world upon those they invade and inhibit the creativity of the invaded by curbing their expression . . . To this end, the invaders are making increasing use of the social sciences and technology, and to some extent the physical sciences as well, to improve their action. (1974a, pp. 150-151).

The example given is just one instance of a more pervasive phenomenon which puts psychologists in relationships with their clients in such a way that the paradigm for these relations is one of a monologue. The problem I find with liberal, progressive, educational reform is its unreflective belief that if the experts keep improving their theories and techniques (e.g., values clarification, cognitive-developmentalism), the schools will improve and cultural crisis will be ameliorated. The post-critical perspective sees the "experts" as part of the crisis and clearly part of the problem. Critique of expertise will be a necessary skill in the future from a post-critical perspective.

The institution of the school is also problematic from the perspective developed here. Some critics such as Illich (1972) point to the necessity of "de-schooling" society. Although many of Illich's criticisms of the schools have cogency, it strikes me that the schools as we know them will be with us for a much longer time than Illich anticipates. In 1968 I heard him say that they would dismantle themselves in five years. Illich is a perceptive critic, but a poor prophet. The question is: Can anything be done with the schools to transform their role in society? This is a moot question and I have no easy solutions to offer. The only suggestion I would like to make here is to encourage locally initiated experiments which attempt to move the schools in the direction of a more critical perspective of our lives and customs. This would mean that the school would not simply enculturate values, but also reflect on values already assumed in the society. I expect no astounding results from the schools as I know them, but it strikes me that this may be a step in a saner direction. I do not expect that schools should shoulder the "burden of democracy." All I am suggesting is concerted attempts, where possible, to veer schools away from autocracy and mindlessness. To do this, different curriculum formats will be needed from a post-critical approach.

> What is needed in schools is the development of new curriculum materials that provide the students with an opportunity to develop the awareness and skills necessary for deciding how their culture influences their existence. This would involve taking a systematic approach to the study of different facets of their cultural experience.
>
> Besides guiding students to pertinent historical sources, the teacher must also be prepared to think dialectically where a tension emerges between the student's activity of making explicit cultural definitions of space impinging on his life. This is essential if history is to help the student perceive his own cultural milieu differently and if his own cultural experiences are to lead him to ask new questions about the historical roots of his own culture. *

This proposal is what I have called problem-posing education. It has to be initiated in a cultural context (i.e., content saturated) and it cannot be value neutral. It can emerge in an infinite number of contexts, so I

*Reprinted with permission from *Cultural Literacy for Freedom: An Existential Perspective on Teaching, Curriculum, and School Policy* by C. A. Bowers. Eugene, Oregon: Elan Books, 1974, pp. 115 and 119.

would be foolish to spell out a program. Such a stance would be inconsistent with what I have been trying to say about "prepackaged" answers given by experts.

The position that I would like to see developed in circles where value education is discussed is to see it as cultural action for freedom. Cultural action is moral action when it is involved in the transformation of social structures which bind people to dependency relationships. Freedom is the activity and reflection (praxis) involved in liberation from oppressive structures.

The fifth and final suggestion for education by Bowles and Gintis takes seriously the need to combine long-range vision with winning victories here and now. A remark made to philosophers may be justly appropriate for the radical educator to consider:

> Let anyone disheartened by this procedure remember Neurath's remark that the philosopher's task may be compared to that of a mariner who must rebuild his raft on the open sea. How much more true this is in those periods of total criticism when the raft is caught in a storm and the repairs are as urgent as they are difficult and dangerous. (Unger, 1975, p. 119).

REFERENCES

Alexander, W., & Farrell, J. *The individualized system: Student participation in decision-making.* Toronto: The Ontario Institute for Studies in Education, 1975.

Bowers, C. A. *Cultural literacy for freedom: An existential perspective on teaching, curriculum, and school policy.* Eugene, Oregon: Elan Books, 1974.

Bowles, S., & Gintis, H. I.Q. in the U.S. Class Structure. *Social Policy,* January/February 1973.

Bowles, S., & Gintis, H. *Schooling in capitalist America.* New York: Basic Books, 1976.

Burger, H. G. Behavior modification in operant psychology: An anthropological critique. *American Educational Research Journal,* 1972, *9,* 343-360.

Dewey, J. *Moral principles in education.* New York: Philosophical Library, 1959.

Dewey, J. What psychology can do for the teacher. In R. Archambault (Ed.), *John Dewey on education: Selected Writings.* New York: Random House, Inc., 1964.

Dewey, J. *Democracy and education.* New York: The Free Press, 1966.

Etzioni, A. Public Affairs. *Human Behavior,* July 1976, 9-10.

Freire, P. *Pedagogy of the oppressed.* New York: Seabury Press, 1974. (a)

Freire, P. *Cultural action for freedom.* Harmondsworth, Middlesex, England: Penguin Books, 1974. (b)

Fridriksson, S., Jacobs, M., Lorimer, R., & Sanderson, P. *Beginning literature: An analysis of the content of some first novelettes for grade four.* Burnaby, B.C., Canada: Simon Fraser University, 1975.

Greene, M. Curriculum and cultural transformation: A humanistic view. *Cross-Currents*, Summer 1975.

Hunt, D. E. & Sullivan, E. V. *Between psychology and education.* Hillsdale, Ill.: Dryden Press, 1974.

Illich, I. *Deschooling society.* New York: Harrow Books, 1972.

Illich, I. *Tools for conviviality.* New York: Perennial Library, 1973.

Kohlberg, L. From is to ought: How to commit the naturalistic fallacy and get away with it in the study of moral development. In T. Mischel (Ed.), *Cognitive development and epistemology.* New York: Academic Press, Inc., 1971. (a)

Kohlberg, L. Stages of moral development as a basis for moral education. In C. Beck, E. Sullivan, & B. Crittenden (Eds.), *Moral education: Interdisciplinary approaches.* Paramus, N.J.: Paulist Press, 1971. (b)

Kohlberg, L. The cognitive-developmental approach to moral education. *Phi Delta Kappan,* 1975, *LVI,* 670-677.

Kohlberg, L., & Mayer, R. Development as the aim of education. *Harvard Educational Review,* 1972, *42,* 449-496.

Morgan, M., & Robinson, N. The "back to the basics" movement in education. *Canadian Journal of Education,* 1976, *1,* 1-11.

Purpel, D., & Ryan, R. Moral education: Where sages fear to tread. *Phi Delta Kappan,* 1975, *LVI,* 659-662.

Rest, J. Developmental psychology as a guide to value education: A review of "Kohlbergian" programs. *Review of Educational Research,* 1974, *44.*

Ryan, K., & Thompson, M. Moral education's muddled mandate: Comment on a survey of Phi Delta Kappans. *Phi Delta Kappan,* 1975, *LVI,* 663-666.

Simon, S., & de Sherbinin, P. Values clarification: It can start gently and grow deep. *Phi Delta Kappan,* 1975, *LVI,* 679-682.

Sullivan, E. V. *Kohlberg's structuralism: A critical appraisal,* (Monograph 15), Ontario Institute for Studies in Education, Toronto, Ontario, Canada, 1977.

Sullivan, E. V., & Beck, C. Moral education in a Canadian setting. *Phi Delta Kappan,* 1975, *LVI,* 697-701.

Sullivan, E. V., Beck, C., Joy, M., & Pagliuso, S. *Moral learning: Some findings, issues and questions,* Paramus, N.J.: Paulist Press, 1975.

Unger, R. *Knowledge and Politics.* New York: The Free Press, 1975.

9

Epilogue

NADINE M. LAMBERT

Now that the perspectives on moral development and moral behavior have been laid out before the reader, what generalizations can the educator and teacher take back to the school and the classroom? First of all, we cannot accept the proposition that formal instruction about rules of conduct, respect for the law, or drills in the principles of honesty, integrity, and responsibility will result in moral adults. Nor can we be assured that moral principles have been incorporated into the individual's behavior repertoire by relying on evidence of rules learned, or principles committed to memory. As we have seen, development of moral values and morality depends jointly on whether teachers understand the cognitive and affective complexity of the developing child and whether they provide learning experiences which capitalize on the everyday availability of value conflicts, moral dilemmas, and opinion differences.

The chapters in this book have constructed a frame of reference for considering aspects of classroom experiences involved in the promotion of moral development and, in turn, the capacity for moral reasoning and moral behavior. Therefore, instead of attempting a resolution of issues or a summation of all the work presented in this book, the epilogue will use this frame of reference to propose a set of linkages—some ways to prepare teachers to use this knowledge, to foster classroom discipline, and to consider alternative curriculum approaches, all to promote the development of children. In proposing these linkages, it is important to point out that the applications have not been tested and that they are developed from an outside perspective. I am a school psychologist who has not worked or conducted research on moral development. But, as school psychologists

245

are grounded in behavioral science theory and research and are trained to work collaboratively with educational personnel, their task often becomes one of finding the match between the theoretical and the practical. School psychologists use their knowledge to explain children's behavior to others, to assist teachers to consider individual behavior in the context of the classroom environment, and to help others become cognizant of differences among children and the relationship between individuality and educational planning. In finding the match between theory and practice in the area of moral development and moral behavior, this epilogue will draw selectively from the material presented in the previous chapters and propose a few applications of this knowledge in educational practice.

WHAT TEACHERS NEED TO KNOW ABOUT MORAL DEVELOPMENT

What knowledge is prerequisite for encouraging the development of the ability to reason about moral issues and to display moral behavior? Let's review some of the concepts from previous chapters that will help us to understand the course of development of principled adults and the acquisition of self-disciplined behavior.

We have learned from the structural-developmentalists that development of moral thinking progresses through ordered stages, and that the cognitive structures for reasoning about social events change from childhood through adolescence to adulthood. Children's development of concepts of justice and social convention follow a developmental sequence. The individual's processes of reasoning about justice and social conventions may parallel one another, but the reasoning processes may have different outcomes. While the structural-developmentalists can explain this orderly progression through moral stages, they do not attempt to explain the origins of self-control of behavior. The psychoanalysts and the social learning scientists provide indispensable perspectives for understanding the development of moral behavior. It is apparent that knowledge of more than one theoretical framework is necessary to understand moral development and moral behavior. The developmental approach helps us understand what is taking place in the child's reasoning. Social learning theories explain the importance of the environment on behavior. And the psychoanalytic theorists provide important insights about the role of adult-child interactions in development. The development of a principled adult results from an interactive process of individuals with others in their environments. Accordingly, the teacher's concepts of morality should include not only developmental and social learning principles, but an understanding of the necessity of adult-pupil interactions in daily classroom events.

An important derivative from stage theory is that the developmental level at which a child is functioning sets significant limits on what he or she can comprehend. Inferring developmental levels from mere obedience to classroom rules can lead to misinterpretation of the child's cognitive processes. An observant and knowledgeable teacher, on the other hand, can infer a child's developmental stage from the way he or she rejects explanations of social dilemmas. As Damon and Turiel have pointed out, children are more likely to reject explanations that are at a level lower than their stage of functioning, and they are more likely to accept, even though only tentatively, explanations at a level higher than their own.

Teachers can capitalize on classroom interactions and discussions to assess the child's developmental level. In so doing, it is important to also keep in mind that the stage at which a child is functioning limits not only what he or she can comprehend in social settings, but also the types of changes in understanding that can be stimulated. For example, if a teacher lectures a child who has violated classroom rules, a child of seven will understand and respond differently than a child of twelve. The seven year old might modify his or her behavior to avoid punishment, while the twelve year old might change because he or she considers the rule necessary for classroom order. The teacher of children younger than seven or eight should reject the notion that their moral judgments are based on respect for rules but realize that such a child's compliance reflects a desire to avoid punishment. Therefore, for these younger children, imposition of rules will lead to a higher probability of desired behavior. Later in the elementary and secondary school years, children's orientation to moral issues is based on their concepts of the importance of maintaining the rules of society. Thus, by age eighteen, while remnants of earlier stage reasoning may remain, pupils will begin to base their judgments on rules and principles such as the equality of human rights and respect for the dignity of human beings as individual persons.

We haved learned, as well, that the individuals's concepts of moral principles and justice are to be distinguished from principles derived from social conventions. Furthermore, children's conceptions of moral and social conventional issues are not stimulated by the same experiences. Moral reasoning is a consideration of situations involving physical or psychological harm, the sharing of goods or rewards, and matters of life and death. Social conventional reasoning, on the other hand, centers on experiences with neatness and order, regularities in fashion, sex-role conventions, forms of address, and other examples of socially routinized and ritualized behaviors.

As teachers understand moral development and social-conventional development and interact with children in ordinary classroom activities to appraise their reasoning level, a comprehension of the importance of teacher role is crucial. To appraise development, the teacher can observe the reasoning process, encourage discussion about moral and social behavior, and permit many different views and levels of reasoning to be exposed. The impact of the teacher on the pupils is related not only to the teacher's behavior, but to how he or she is perceived. The teacher as an authority figure might be observed by an outsider to behave similarly in primary, elementary, or secondary classrooms, but the pupils will perceive the teacher differently depending on the school grade and their developmental level. Teachers who promote development and at the same time encourage student respect are authoritative rather than laissez faire, consistent rather than capricious, and equitable rather than arbitrary.

SELF-IDENTITY AS A PREREQUISITE
FOR NORMAL DEVELOPMENT

As we contemplate the interrelationship of early life experience and moral and social development, it becomes apparent that we must consider more than cognitive structures. Psychoanalytic studies of early child development show the profound effect of the parenting process on personality, temperament, and affective attachment. The psychoanalytic perspective provides an important basis for understanding self-identity and identification with adults as prerequisites for moral development. The child's sense of trust in his or her parents and environment is shaped by early life experiences. Attachment, or the lack of it, and the rapport-building experiences of the young child's first years in turn shape his or her school behavior. The basic foundations for the sense of self and for one's relationship to others and the environment, and the prerequisites for cognitive and social development are firmly established by age three.

Resolution of the child's dependency and the development of attachments and identity with parents, and later teachers, provide the basic ingredients for the individual's expectations with regard to authority, responsibility, and privilege. These expectations underlie the child's notions of justice and social convention. The extent to which the parenting process facilitates trust, identification, attachment, independence, and self-worth will either promote or retard the child's progress through the developmental stages which have been proposed. Thus, the child who sets up a defense against all authority will have a diminished capacity to take another's point of view or to deliberate in socially conflicting situations. Similarly, parents who exploit the infant's dependency with excessively overprotective behavior will impair the development of autonomy, and likewise cripple the child's capacity to function and develop.

Attention to those aspects of a child's behavior that suggest deprived emotional experiences may be a first step toward conceptualizing interventions to facilitate the child's interactions with schooling. Teachers should take notice of the child who does not become attached to or identified with others. Failure to respond to the feelings or emotions of others is another sign of emotional problems. When a child manifests dependency behaviors that are appropriate for a much younger child, the knowledgeable teacher will interpret the behavior as a symptom of unfulfilled needs. While dependency and indifference to others often present troublesome behaviors in school, the teacher who comprehends that dependency and help-seeking continue only as long as they are needed for development of competence and independence is in a good position to develop strategies for assisting the child. By successfully integrating knowledge from the psychoanalytic and structuralist approaches, teachers can adapt the daily program to establish consistency of routine, to respond empathically to the child's needs and individuality, and to provide opportunities for the experience of psychological safety in the classroom.

ACQUISITION OF INTERNAL CONTROL

The psychoanalytic perspective shows how children's experiences with parents and other significant people in their lives shape morality and moral development. The structuralists and developmental psychologists help us center our attention on what is taking place within the child, and his or her ability to reason. But a knowledge only of cognitive and affective developmental processes and of their relationship to individual differences is not a sufficient knowledge base for the classroom teacher interested in promoting moral behavior. We must turn to social learning theory to provide a foundation for understanding how social controls work, and how children acquire self-regulatory behavior. The social learning perspective reinforces our notions of the importance of adults as models and as social control agents. The research from this field of inquiry helps us to understand the relationship between child-rearing practices and classroom behavior.

All of the theories presented in this book view the interaction of the child with his or her environment as crucial to developmental outcomes. But social learning theory leads to another important insight, that development may be facilitated by the imposition of social controls. Moreover, inferences from the field of social learning provide another element in our frame of reference, the means by which teachers can promote children's development through the process of achieving and maintaining classroom order.

In spite of the limitations of research contrasting level of moral reasoning and the quality of moral behavior, an appropriate operating assumption is that there is a relationship between children's reasoning about moral issues and their moral behavior. But what are the implications of the relationship between moral developmental level and the ability to conform to classroom behavior standards? One could argue that schools with rigidly enforced behavioral standards would serve to inhibit moral development beyond the conventional level, even though such schools might educate a greater proportion of the adult population to behave in socially approved ways.

How can schools respond to public demands for more disciplined classrooms and higher behavior standards, and still promote children's capacity for moral reasoning that will influence a later capacity for independent thinking about moral behavior? Are discipline, moral reasoning, and moral development mutually exclusive objectives? Based on the data presented in this book, they seem to be interdependent. The supposition that conventional reasoning is associated with the more rigidly organized schools that enforce codes for moral behavior should not be taken for granted.

The sheer number of adults who have attended schools with strict behavior standards as children and who have achieved postconventional reasoning as adults provides eloquent testimony that "disciplined" schools by themselves do not prevent the occurrence of moral development milestones. People who have accomplished postconventional reasoning did so because behavior codes provided a "naturalistic" set of moral dilemmas which they reasoned through. These naturally occurring moral dilemmas regularly confront children as they progress through the grade levels and provide "curriculum" material for moral education.

The teacher with established classroom behavior standards who accepts the requirement of conventional mores as necessary to an ordered social interaction can also encourage students to reason, to consider, and to confront the variety of moral issues that children experience everyday. In such an environment, the teacher becomes a model for judicious, nonjudgmental consideration of the behavioral alternatives and consequences associated with the problem under discussion. The rules for classroom behavior and the consequences for misbehavior provide content for reasoning and development. In a wide participation of the class members in the consideration of social and moral problems, children of diverse backgrounds may view the same dilemma differently. The teacher then simultaneously promotes development by offering opportunities for interaction and reasoning and widens children's understanding of social-conventional systems other than their own. Rather than search for the right answer, the teacher can manifest genuine acceptance of different points of view. But how does the teacher encourage the members of the class to observe the specific standards of the classroom and the school?

Social learning theory shows us how early socialization occurs through conditioning. Desired behavior in the child is reinforced by nurturance by the parent. Undesired behavior is suppressed by withdrawal of attention or more severe forms of punishment. The goal of the parent and of the teacher is for children to grow from the need for the imposition of external control of behavior through a variety of contingency management techniques, like concrete rewards and positive attention, to internalized controls where children assume for themselves the responsibility of maintaining behavior appropriate to the situation. Thus, social learning theory provides another element in our frame of reference, a perspective for understanding the factors that promote the development of internal controlling processes.

Internalization of controls is affected by early nurturance and strong emotional attachments to nurturing adults. Children imitate the adults they encounter. If the adults are nurturant, caring, and considerate of others, the nurturant adult caregiver provides a model of concern for others. In the interaction of caring and nurturing, the child develops the capacity for empathy. As the child grows older, he or she acquires an ever larger set of rules for behavior. When he or she experiences social and moral dilemmas, the rules the child has learned assist him or her to behave appropriately without the necessity for external control of behavior. The child becomes intrinsically motivated. In some instances, children experience competing rules for behavior and the child must set priorities and select the behavior from among his or her repertoire that is appropriate in a given situation. If the child's behavior is acceptable, or if he or she violates no rules, ordering of the control priorities is established for different situations. As we have seen, social learning theorists view moral development as the establishment and changing of priorities among internal controls for behavior.

For both the maintenance of classroom decorum and for the promotion of child development, external control of behavior may be required. External controls administered by a nurturant teacher assist the child not only to behave appropriately but to become identified with the teacher. One can define nurturant teachers as those who both are interested in and care about the welfare of their pupils and provide appropriate learning experiences for them, thereby offering a strong incentive for pupil interaction. Teacher-pupil interactions in such classrooms facilitate the empathy of the child for the teacher and mobilize internal control mechanisms.

To be nurturant does not necessarily mean teachers must "love" their pupils and become emotionally attached to them. Effective teachers maintain an appropriate level of emotional detachment, but manifest concern for children and their needs. Because children identify with such teachers, the likelihood of external control is minimized. This style of classroom discipline involves day to day verbal transmissions of values through reasoning, explanation, discourse, verbal disapproval of the child's behavior, inquiry into his or her motives, and suggestions for and reinforcements of corrective actions. The kinds of punishments that nurturant teachers use include withdrawal of attention, ignoring acting out behavior, and short-term isolation. They avoid verbal attacks on the children, such as "bawling them out," ridicule, or public shaming. Enlightened teachers reject such severe disciplinary actions because their own experience has taught them that the greater the level of emotionality in the disciplinary action, the less chance the child will reflect on his or her behavior, even though the disciplinary action causes the child to be obedient.

In classrooms where teachers are knowledgeable about developmental processes as well as the importance of the development of behavior controls, the child will have a variety of opportunities to observe and vicariously experience a wide range of external control measures as well as evidence of internal control mechanisms in their peers. Classroom discipline is effective because, as we have learned from the structural-developmentalists, the developing child reasons that he or she should abide by the rules to avoid being punished, and later reasons that rule-abiding behavior is in his or her best interest as well as in the best interest of others.

The consequences of laissez-faire classroom behavior standards are just as severe as the consequences of a punitive, authoritarian environment. Neither promotes desirable teacher-pupil interactions. Pupils with laissez-faire teachers have no systematic opportunity to react intellectually with rules and principles, and consequently they fail to have the stimulation necessary for modeling adult behavior and developing internal controls. We have learned that opportunities for reasoning about behavior and observing adults and others in the reasoning process are necessary for the development of new cognitive structures. The classroom that leaves all of the educational and behavioral choices to the pupils, permitting behavior without justification or challenge fails in two ways—by not reinforcing the social conventions necessary for an ordered society, and by not providing the interactive setting so necessary to the enlivening of new levels of moral reasoning.

The role of the teacher is paramount regardless of the tradition of the school, the type of classroom space, the differences among children, and the age of the class members. Besides being knowledgeable about factors that affect development of moral and social behavior, teachers must recognize and acknowledge their own value systems. Children should see adults and teachers as people with values, who often reason about behavior at a level different from their own. It is the nurturing behavior of the teacher, rather than the teacher's particular beliefs, that encourages the identification of the child with the adult. And it is the teacher's willingness to discuss the reasons for disciplinary actions, and to explore differences in reasoning about social conflicts that promotes the development of the individual child.

USE OF AVAILABLE CURRICULA TO PROMOTE DEVELOPMENT

In any consideration of the application of the principles we have explored, some will ask whether or not special curriculum materials would be desirable, or needed. Those interested in open education or individualized classroom approaches as well as those promoting competency-based education are likely to wonder what particular curriculum materials would be most influential in providing the educational experience necessary for the development of the child. The answer is that no particular type of school, or set of books, or learning aids will insure opportunities for development, but interactions among children and between children and adults will. Promotion of moral development can occur in any environment that offers opportunities for interchange and reasoning about regularly occurring human events and for examining the issues attending social-conventional behavior standards and cultural mores.

Are there no guidelines, then, for a moral development curriculum? Research on teaching has shown that the teaching-learning process is generally not interactive. In spite of what most of us likely believe, children learn reading, mathematics, and other knowledge and skills in the absence of much teacher-pupil interaction. Teachers instruct children about lessons, give directions for completing tasks, call upon pupils for answers to questions about an assignment, or explain a new concept. In a reading group, a pupil reads a paragraph and the teacher may correct or accept the performance, but there is rarely any discussion of what is taking place with the characters or the events in the reading material. In mathematics lessons, children take up their worksheets and complete assignments while teachers correct papers at the desk or move around the room helping pupils with their work. From naturalistic observations of classrooms, my research on teacher-pupil interactions has shown that only 15 to 20 percent of observable pupil behavior is accompanied by a teacher response of any sort. Moreover, teacher responses are associated most frequently with misbehavior. From social learning theory we can infer that the teacher's management behavior provides the external controls necessary for classroom decorum, but from a developmental perspective, the lack of interaction and failure to attend to pupil differences promote neither development nor intrinsic motivation. If the several hundred teachers who have been the subjects of these investigations are typical, then teachers generally view their primary role as one of manager of the curriculum delivery system rather than one of personal deliverer of an educational program for pupils. We have learned that teacher-pupil interactions are necessary for the development of empathy and for the internalization of controls as well as for the stimulation of moral and social reasoning. The absence of teacher-pupil interchange minimizes the creation of nurturant environment, inhibits identification with the teacher, and impedes development.

There are rich, daily opportunities for teacher-pupil interactions in discussions of children's literature or even the most traditional literary works for moral education. The *Bible*, the works of Shakespeare, *Pilgrim's Progress*, the writings of Jefferson and Paine, children's books, and current events have been curriculum content for moral development. The achievement of postconventional reasoning has not been attained only by those living in the last half of the twentieth century. An analysis of the writings of Jefferson and Paine would show that they achieved postconventional reasoning. What was their "moral education"? It must have stimulated reasoning and development.

As school children we learned that early Americans read or were tutored with both the *Bible* and *Pilgrim's Progress*, both traditional textbooks for moral education. The *Bible* provided a multitude of moral dilemmas for our ancestors. Next to the *Bible*, *Pilgrim's Progress* was perhaps the most widely read "moral education" curriculum. John Bunyan, a self-styled Protestant preacher, wrote it three hundred years ago when he was imprisoned because of his religious activities. It is instructive to review this book to show that while it could be taught as a religious tract, the allegory provides a rich source of moral dilemmas facing Christian as he abandoned his wife and children to search for a better life in the Celestial City. His hazardous route led him through the Slough of Despond, Vanity Fair, the Delectable Mountains, Doubting Castle, the Enchanted Ground, and finally to his destination. Bunyan's metaphors reveal a remarkable series of virtuous and venal characters such as Faithful, Hopeful, Prudence, Talkative, Ignorance, Save-All, Money Love, By Ends, Piety, Prudence, and Good Will.

Pilgrim's Progress was read to or read by generations of children and they identified with the moral dilemmas Christian confronted. In early years they no doubt explained his behavior as necessary to avoid punishment, and later as the observance of moral rules for behavior. But as the children grew up and became parents or teachers and again confronted Bunyan's allegorical tale, new understandings and meaning would be brought to bear upon the prose.

For centuries, the curriculum content for moral development has been available and postconventional levels of moral development have been reached. Individuals attained principled levels of moral reasoning in earlier times in less complex societies. Although societies may define appropriate social-conventional behavior, only the quality of opportunities for interaction with the environment, vicariously in interpretations of literature, or personally in social settings with families, friends, teachers, and classmates, seem to place limits on the development of moral reasoning. For as Bunyan concludes his tale:

> Now reader, I have told my dream to thee;
> See if thou canst interpret it to me,
> Or to thyself, or neighbor, But take heed
> Of misinterpreting; for then, instead
> Of doing good, will but thyself abuse,
> By misinterpreting evil issues.
>
> Take heed, also, that thou be not extreme,
> In playing with the outside of my dream,
> Nor let my figure, or similitude,

Put thee into a laughter or a feud;
Leave this for boys and fools, but as for thee,
Do thou the substance of my matter see.
    Put by the curtains; look within my veil;
Turn up my metaphors and do not fail.
There, if thou seekest them, such things to find,
As will be helpful to an honest mind.
    What of my dross thou findest there, be bold
To throw away, but yet preserve the gold.
What if my gold be wrapped up in ore?
None throws away the apple for the core.
But if thou shalt cast all away as vain,
I know not but 'twil make me dream again.

Moral development can succeed with even the most traditional curriculum, in schools that maintain strict behavioral codes. Since we know that pupils are progressing through orderly developmental stages—cognitive, social, emotional, and physical—their own developmental structures provide the dynamic force for growth. Our society needs schools with a population of educators who can capitalize on naturally occurring "moral dilemmas" as opportunities for introducing higher-level reasoning concepts and alternatives. As the child assimilates new ways of reasoning, his or her behavior changes from blind acceptance of authority, to conventional behavior for selfish motivations, to higher levels of moral judgments in which are manifest the applications of those principles which aim to protect the interests of society as a whole.

Index